STheCRET SIERRA

The Alpine World Above The Trees

The SECRET SIERRA

The Alpine World Above The Trees

By David Gilligan

Spotted Dog Press, Inc. • Bishop, California

The Secret Sierra: The Alpine World Above The Trees
By David Gilligan

© 2000 by David Gilligan
All rights reserved.
Published exclusively by Spotted Dog Press, Inc.
Bishop, California

For updates on this and other Spotted Dog Press books, please visit our website:
www.SpottedDogPress.com
If you have comments about this or any other Spotted Dog Press book,
please write to us at: POB 1721, Bishop, CA 93515

First edition 2000
Cover photograph:
Into the alpine zone on Blacksmith Peak (11,680') by Pete Yamagata
Back cover: Rock fringe *(Epilabium obcordatum)* by Martha McCord
Background photograph: The Minarets by Wynne Benti
The publisher would like to thank Edmund Benti for manuscript review
Printed by Central Plains Book Manufacturing in Winfield, Kansas

ISBN 1-893343-01-4

Library of Congress Cataloging-in-Publication Data
Gilligan, David, 1972-
The Secret Sierra: the alpine world above the trees/by David Gilligan--1st ed.
    p. cm.
Includes bibliographical references (p.) and index.
ISBN 1-893343-01-4 (sc)
1. Natural history--Sierra Nevada (Calif. and Nev.) 2. Mountain ecology--Sierra Nevada (Calif. and Nev.) 3. Cold regions. I. Title.

QH104.5.S54 G56 2000
508.794'4--dc21

00-027998

Printed in the United States of America

Acknowledgements

My deepest gratitude goes out to Skye Leone for showing me the way, Tom Fleischner for guidance support on this project, and Walt Anderson, Lon Abbot, and David Lovejoy for the eyes of scrutiny and delight.

Table of Contents

Magic in the World

It had been storming every afternoon in Humphreys Basin for the past four days. They were strange storms, blowing in from the east instead of the west where summer thunderstorms typically come from in the High Sierra. These suggested something bigger happening down south, perhaps off the coast of Baja. Every day I watched as the clouds brewed up, huge and magnificent, over the crest of the range. They might drop hints of a storm by early afternoon, but their true power was always revealed by sunset. The clouds blazed peach, scarlet, then crimson with the fading light. Opposite the setting sun, smoke had been smudging the evening sky for three days against the outline of the White Mountains. A fire burned below the mountain crest, somewhere down in the Owens Valley, seven thousand feet below. The smoke played with the evening light, turning it from pallid yellow-brown to brilliant tangerine. By nightfall, only a few cloud wisps remained in the indigo sky. Eventually, these too would dissipate, leaving the crystalline stars to sparkle through until dawn.

The fifth evening began just as the others had, but the air had an unusual quality. The darkening clouds enshrouded Mounts Humphreys and Emerson. As the entire eastern sky grew a deeper, darker charcoal hue, the steel gray of the Sierran granite was illuminated, washed over in the clear golden light of the setting sun. Then the clouds burst. The rain fell in wide streaks, like gold dust sprinkling down from a great trove enshrouded by the billowing thunderheads. In four separate places the rain came down like this, each shower equal in such tremendous quality. Then, as if a long-forgotten god had returned to prove his omniscience, a rainbow appeared. As the fullness of its arc came into view, it seemed a bridge, spanning the ineffable distance between darkness and light. I felt as if I were sitting at the center point around which different worlds revolved, touching each other in a kind of transient embrace. I was in the middle. If there was magic in the world, this was it.

It rained into the night. Thunder and lightning joined the ensemble periodically, as an extended aftermath of the evening. I lay awake, realizing my love for this place. I have been lucky, for I have never doubted this love. Something about these mountains draws me to them. The Sierra Nevada has bestowed upon me some of the greatest gifts of my life. Not all have been joyous and beautiful. At times I have been terrified, emptied, afraid for my life. Other lessons have been quiet in their telling, and soft in their teaching. Such nights serve as reminders that amidst a world that sometimes seems impossibly confusing, somewhere on earth the sun is sending rich, golden light across landscapes stark with primeval antiquity. I was seeking to experience such a land in that light, and if possible, to tell about it.

Sleep came without my noticing. I couldn't remember any dreams, and don't think they would have been possible after such an experience.

The clouds broke away in the morning to reveal the sun. I awoke to the rosy fingers of dawn and looked out across the wide glacial basin. The first sound was that of water trickling out from beneath a late-lying snowbank. September, and still the snows of El Niño's winter lingered at 11,000 feet. I looked for the Mountain Bbluebirds. They came every morning with the sun, perching on huge erratic boulders to view the land before them, flitting out to catch insects for breakfast. It was only minutes before they arrived. Yesterday a female blackbird had joined their company. Today she did not return. I sat quietly and watched the birds, their blue matching that of the sky, shining in the long light of morning. And a thought came to mind how much I cherished this place, and the life I've made here. For me, no other life is imaginable.

As a naturalist, I am a practitioner of natural history. One of the ways I see the land is as a story. Learn the language, and we can read the story. Human civilization may also be seen as a story, but as Henry David Thoreau stated over a century ago, there have been enough champions of civilization, and my interest lies elsewhere. Human history indicates with reasonable certainty that such civilizations will at least be around tomorrow and the next day. No rush to tell those tales. Wild land, however, is in grave, immediate danger the world wide. We need to tell the stories of these places before they are gone. Perhaps, if we are lucky, we can even stay the danger for awhile.

The work that follows is a story of the nature of a place, a history, of the Alpine Sierra Nevada. To tell such a story, we must first ask questions about it. What defines this place? How did it get here? When did it happen? Who lives here? Where did they come from? Why is this place important? Seeking the answers to these questions, we begin to probe deeper into the mysteries of land. This work attempts to provide the beginnings of answers to all of these questions. After a brief discussion of the history and philosophy of natural history, I set out to explore landscape geography of the Alpine Sierra. I begin with definitions: a geographic orientation to the Sierran alpine zone. This sets the stage for the next two questions, concerning origins. To answer these questions, I look into the geologic history of the Sierra Nevada, the story of the macro-evolution of the landscape over time, and the geomorphology, or present-day shape of the land. Also, I investigate the weather and climate of the mountains, and the interplay between climate and geology that determines the character of a place. Next comes life: an exploration of the alpine ecology, the plants and animals of the Alpine Sierra, where they live, where they came from, how they got there, how they relate to one another. The last question I have my own ideas about, but I invite the readers to determine the answer for themselves. Why is the Alpine Sierra Nevada important?

This work will be a unique contribution to the literature on the Sierra Nevada in three ways. First, it will assert the validity of natural history in modern times, and the increasingly important role of the naturalist as an interpreter in this age of ever-increasing information. I will do this in two ways, by defining natural history and naturalist, and by integrating personal narrative with the best knowledge that modern science has to offer. Second, the focus of this work is specifically on the alpine zone. I seek to synthesize what is known of the Sierran alpine zone in such a way that it is made accessible to a wider audience than the scientific literature allows for, integrating the all-too-often disparate disciplines of landscape geography and ecology. Third, I will incorporate and interpret recent findings on the geologic history of the range, which has gone largely unpublished in such an accessible form.

This work is an expression of my deepest gratitude to the land. When all else fails in life, friends, relationships, jobs, family, intellect, religion, the land always remains.

Introduction

A History and Philosophy of Natural History

Driving into the Owens Valley from the south, the mountains, that for so long seemed widely spaced, begin to converge into what appears to be a roofless hallway, walled in on the west by the Sierra Nevada, on the east by the White-Inyo Range. A deceptively timeless feel permeates this place, a seemingly eternal, immutable landscape. But this is only a deception. While the titanic platform block of crust that makes up the valley between is sinking like an elevator bound for the underworld, the mountains are alive, moving, relentlessly grinding their way upward.

As if this dynamic isn't mind-bending enough, the floor of the valley is actually thousands of feet below the surface. The entire valley is filled in like a ditch, with sediments washed down from the surrounding mountains over millions of years.

Zooming north on Highway 395, bound for the snowy Alpine Sierra of early May, it occurred to me that the landscape of the southern Owens Valley had the austere appearance of having been scoured by a giant wire brush. I reached into my shirt pocket to find that my three-by-five notepad was not there. Scanning the dashboard with no success, I checked the glove compartment, also with no luck. Swerving across the pavement, I reached down and felt along the floor of the passenger seat, fumbling between water bottles and sandals, but found nothing. Finally, I looked backwards into the wagon and began throwing my belongings from side to side in search of the pad. The wire brush thought was still on my brain when the gravel on the side of the road roared against my tires, reminding me that I was about to commune with sagebrush. I had to pull over.

I ripped the back of the car apart. Nothing. Other thoughts unexpectedly began to anemone onto the wire brush thought as I scanned the landscape in awe of the mountains being buried alive by the same sediments that were once such a part of them. As they become inundated in a rising sea of soil, like Tantalus the unforgiven, every time the mountains rose higher to the sky, the same gravitational forces that indirectly caused them to uplift were directly tearing them down. That is what the story of landforms is really all about. With the macro-philosophy of gravity in mind, I could begin to visualize the evolution of the land. Gravity was at both the beginning and the end.

The note pad was gone. I accepted that it was gone, and psychologically moved on to other options. I remembered my address book, the last page of which had never been used, the X-Y-Z section. I found a runaway pen and begin scrawling: O. Valley–wire brush–Tantalus–gravity.

The three-by-five notepad is perhaps the most indispensable tool of the trade for the field naturalist. Things come and go like breath. Thoughts, birds, storms, flowers, even patient rocks move in and out of our experience with kaleidoscopic repercussions. One learns with time that without some sort of artificial memory bank, much of this experience slips out of our conscious world view. In any case, new warblers inevitably come flitting by to capture our attention, and whatever happened last is abruptly pushed out of the forefront of our minds. The three-by-five notepad is the most compact, affordable, simple artificial brain I know of. One also, of course, needs a pencil.

In the town of Lone Pine I pulled over once again. This time I watched oval-shaped clouds form like flying saucers on the leeward side of the Sierra Nevada. At first there was just one, then a second, then three stacked atop one another, fattened discs of pale gray against the blue of the early afternoon sky. Within the hour the third had dissipated and the second was drifting east. Somewhere in it all was a story longing to be told.

Telling the stories of the land is like weaving an intricate tapestry, one whose fibers integrate science and a genuine love for land. In this tapestry, science provides the strength and substance for the weave, while love is the color, giving beauty and vitality. For the weave to have integrity, both science and love must remain undaunted by the other's often intimidating presence. They must complement rather than consume one another, support rather than subvert each other. The honing of this art is the pursuit of the naturalist. The tapestry as a whole reflects the genius of natural history.

Natural history predates all of the sciences, including biology, geology, and ecology, among others. It is the age-old foundation upon which these sciences sit, and indeed all of the modern sciences must claim natural history as their genesis. As such a foundation, it is what grounds the towers of science in the earth. Throughout history, the sciences have become increasingly specialized, their towers rising, threatening to overshadow natural history. Coming into the twenty first century, people are increasingly confused about what natural history really is. At the same time, the role of the naturalist, as an interpreter for the scientific community, has become more important than ever before. How has natural history evolved throughout time to bring us to our current situation? What is natural history today and what does the future hold for it? To answer these questions, we must look into the very history of the science itself.

Our ancestors have been studying the ways of the natural world for thousands, if not millions of years. The first four-million years of hominid/human existence are distinguished from subsequent periods by the fact that humans subsisted by hunting and gathering. The glory days of the Paleolithic Age (Old Stone-Age) required that our ancestors be expert naturalists. Survival depended upon a thorough knowledge of weather and climate, geography, animal behavior, and botany. Our speculations as to the ethical implications of such a lifestyle are based largely on fossil evidence left by extinct cultures, and what few Paleolithic cultures remain on the planet today. J. Baird Callicott explores the ethics and philosophies of these cultures extensively. It suffices to say that subsequent cultures derived from those of the Paleolithic. Every person on the planet finds his or her ancestral roots back in the Old Stone Age. Accordingly, so does natural history.

About 10,000 years ago, there was an explosion of agricultural and pastoral societies, one that would eventually cover the globe. With the upshot of these Neolithic (New Stone-Age) cultures, human populations became increasingly sedentary, produced surplus foodstuffs, and populations boomed. The agriculturalists prayed to the goddess of fertility and she delivered. Soon human populations spread across the earth. Study of the natural world was utilitarian, leading the way to new and better technologies. The wheel, the plow, irrigation, and other innovations saw their first dawn in the Neolithic.

As the Stone Age evolved into the Bronze Age, the first societies called "civilizations" by the history books emerged and became increasingly stratified. A recorded study of the natural world became reserved for those with ample leisure time: the upper class. The early ancient civilizations, Egypt in particular, provide the first clues that knowledge of the natural world was being pursued for its own sake, rather than for strictly utilitarian purposes. Interestingly, the roots of human dominion over the natural world and the subduction of the wild can also be traced to this time, as is suggested in the *Epic of Gilgamish*, the earliest surviving piece of literature from the Fertile Crescent of Mesopotamia. In the epic, Enkidu, the man of the wild, is tamed by the temptations of women. Enkidu then befriends Gilgamish, the civilized man, and together the two slay the wild protector of the forest. The subsequent human relationship to nature is reflected in both Eastern and Western culture. In their book, *Nature in Asian Traditions of Thought,* Callicott and Ames explore the East. Our focus is the West.

While it could be well argued that natural history is as old as the genus *Homo,* Western culture can trace its roots back to Hellenistic Greek civilization. Aristotle was the first to write voluminously on natural history, though he himself came from a lineage of philosophers including Plato, Socrates, Pythagoras, and the Ionians, among whom there was no distinction between natural science and philosophy. In a 1977 article in *Bioscience,* Lester Coonen referred to Aristotle as "the red-eyed seeker, the director and discerner of multifarious programs of investigation," writing on such varied topics as ethics, physics, metaphysics, astronomy, economy, political science, and mathematics, in addition to the botany and zoology for which he is best known in scientific circles. He was a herculean generalist, living in an age before disciplinary boundaries had been hammered out by the divergent vocabularies of specialization. Though much is lost, such as his work on botany, Aristotle's volumes on animals survived the tumults of history. Most noted of these is his "History of Animals" *(De Historia Animalium).* Others included "On the Parts of Animals" *(De Partibus Animalium),* "On the Generation of Animals" *(De Generatione Animalium),* "On the Progression of Animals" *(De Incessu Animalium),* and "On the Movement of Animals" *(De Motu Animalium).* Central to all of Aristotle's scientific writings was the importance of observation, which he believed to be the foundation of sound theory. He is further noted for his meticulous classification and descriptions of organisms. Thus he laid out the path for future naturalists for the next 2,000 years.

The Greek world view held that the world was an organism.

Like humans, the world had both a rational mind, a body, and a soul. All parts of the world participated in the processes of its mind, body, and soul, such that no distinction was made between living and non-living things. Accordingly, Aristotle believed that all things in the world had equal meaning, and similarly, that nothing was superfluous. This teleological reasoning implied that all things had an ultimate purpose, and that beauty was in the fulfillment of such purpose. His integration of what have today become completely separate academic disciplines is reflective of this world view. In particular, he laid the foundation for the integration of philosophy and science, key to the genius of natural history.

While Aristotle is hailed as the grandfather of natural history and the biological sciences, other figures of this time also made landmark contributions. Theophrastus, a pupil of Aristotle, has been called the father of botany. His true genius, however, may have been in his keen observations on the relationships between plants and their habitats, a foreshadowing of the science of ecology to come. Plato, teacher of Aristotle, observed the state of degradation of land around Athens with remarkable accuracy, bringing to light the negative effects deforestation and over-grazing inflicted upon the environment. The Greeks were remarkable in their pursuit of knowledge for its own sake, but as history turned the page on Greek civilization, the nature of natural history was to see some changes.

The imperialism of the Roman Empire put greater emphasis on utility as the basis on which people valued the natural world. Between mines, aqueducts, urban planning, and the upkeep of the world's largest army, there was little time for interest in natural history as an end in itself. Interestingly, it was a Roman writer, Pliny the Elder, who first coined the term "natural history" in 77 A.D., by making it the title of his greatest work, *Historia Naturalis*. This mammoth body of work covered nearly as broad a range of topics as did Aristotle, and between these two the pavement was laid down upon the road on which future naturalists were to tread. As Rome fell, Medieval society picked up its broken pieces and put them back together with the new mortar of Christianity. The Greco-Roman view of the world as a great organism persisted, though the focus of human attention shifted from worldly things to the divine. As the focus of human attention was bent increasingly towards God, it was accordingly distracted from the stuff of the earth. Thus, the practice of natural history was squelched by the hammer-hand of the church. Not until after Martin Luther's Protestant Reformation of the early sixteenth century was Europe to fully reclaim its human right to free thinking.

As natural history emerged from the darkness into a new world, science came to a crossroads. One road led to certainty, and the other led to uncertainty. The physicists of the sixteenth and seventeenth centuries employed experimental and mathematical methods, relying on quantitative data and the control of manipulative laboratory experiments, as well as the theories they could extrapolate from them. Meanwhile, aboard the ships of explorers and geographers on worldly exploration, naturalists continued with the comparative methods more suited to its field-based setting, relying on more qualitative information and the unpredictability of nature as the experiment. The former focused on the question of how, while the latter asked who, what, when, where and eventually, why. As philosopher of science Ernst Mayr points out, the biological sciences experienced a similar split, the functional biologists employed the methods of the physicists, while the evolutionary biologists (many of whom were also involved with geographic explorations) employed those of the naturalist, unwilling to go "indoors." The naturalists passed on their lineage to many of the evolutionary biologists, ecologists, conservation biologists, and geographers of today.

The Scientific Revolution of the sixteenth and seventeenth

centuries made a permanent mark on the collective consciousness of the Western world. Copernicus' heliocentric universe,
Gilbert and Kepler's gravity, as well as landmark work by Bacon,
Galileo, and ultimately Newton, necessitated a new world view.
Copernicus' contribution has often been misunderstood. The
position of the earth in relation to the sun that he proposed was
not a new idea. The Greeks had come to the same conclusion two
thousand years before. Copernicus expanded on the concept by
concluding that the matter of the universe was the same as that
of the earth, and therefore was subject to the same laws of physics
that applied at home. Thus the door to the universe was opened
to the physicists. Gilbert's work on magnetism, refined and
expanded upon by Kepler, gave us a mechanical model for our
solar system. Galileo, in opposition to the still-powerful church,
used the findings of the earlier physicists to determine laws of
motion. Finally, Newton, after securing the support of the church,
synthesized and publicized the work of the physicists, refining
and redesigning in accordance with the best knowledge of the
times. The subsequent Industrial Revolution, spawned in part
by the findings of the physicists, traded hand tools and manual
labor for power-driven machines, thus infusing the mechanical
paradigm of the Scientific Revolution into western culture.

Even before the Industrial Revolution, simple machines
abounded. As the Renaissance man looked around him, he was
surrounded by the new inventions of his time. The printing press,
the pulley, the clock, and the pump all confirmed the notion that
the world, rather than an organism, was a machine. As such, it
was a finished product, and any inkling of teleology was stamped
out. The new science seemed to offer a viable alternative to God.
The world according to human perception became "disenchanted,"
stripped of the mystery essential for humans to maintain a healthy
relationship with it. Perhaps it was not so much the discoveries
of the physicists that resulted in such disenchantment, however,

but the utilitarian purposes for which they were put to use. For many, the realizations of the Scientific Revolution instilled the world with greater mystery than it ever had before. While the sixteenth and seventeenth centuries saw great discoveries in the realm of physics, the following two centuries brought equally profound realizations in the field of natural history. In the early eighteenth century, naturalist John Ray first used the dead languages of Greek and Latin to avoid national and regional differences in the organization and classification of organisms. In the mid-eighteenth century, Carl Von Linne, a Swedish naturalist also known as Linnaeus, published his master work, *Systema Naturae*, which underwent twelve revisions in his lifetime. His tenth edition, published in 1758, became the cornerstone of biological taxonomy, using the simple binomial system of genus and species to classify every kind of organism then known to exist. As was Aristotle, Linnaeus was astounding in his efforts. In addition to his classifications, he also included a brief description of each organism's characteristics, as well as page references to the hundreds of natural history books he consulted.

For the next hundred years, naturalist such as John Bartram, his son William Bartram, Alexander Wilson, Meriwether Lewis, William Clark, John James Audubon, John Torrey, Louis Agassiz, Alexander von Humboldt, David Douglas, and Alfred Russel Wallace, explored the globe. Throughout the seventeenth to nineteenth centuries, vast cabinets of specimens, as well as detailed accounts of voyages, were contributed to the great vault of natural history. Even more importantly, naturalists were beginning to realize that there was more to understanding the natural world than discovering and describing new species. Observation could not help but lead one to recognize greater patterns and concepts at work. Relationships between organisms and their habitats began to be seen as worthy of further inquiry. Meanwhile, the scientific traditions of botany and anatomy also saw advancements, though these were primarily associated with medicine. As a result, physics was not the only field which blossomed during the European Enlightenment and the Age of Exploration.

In 1859, Charles Darwin published his master work, *Origin of Species.* This revolutionary work was reflective of the paradigm shift in world view that was occurring. The world was no longer a machine, a finished product with God as the divine maker. The world became a changing, evolving, developing process, a history, so to speak. The naturalist, once content with the discovery and description of fixed natural phenomenon, was now faced with the ultimate question of "why" posed by evolution and ecology. With the evolutionary perspective of the world, the finite became infinite, and it was understood that the processes of the world worked towards a purpose yet unfulfilled. Thus, teleology was reintroduced to western science.

Following the Darwinian revolution, natural history burst at the seams, exploding into a multiplicity of sciences, including biology, ecology, zoology, and others. Prior to the nineteenth century, none of these terms even existed, and the study of such subjects was encompassed by natural history. With the new vogue of the "ologies," the naturalist became somewhat of a threatened species. Those that survived the times came to be viewed with condescension, considered old-fashioned by the more "modern" scientists of the specialized disciplines. Meanwhile, naturalist writers such as Henry David Thoreau, John Muir, and John Burroughs were making names for themselves, speaking of nature on a more personalized level. While the new sciences developed exclusive vocabularies and spoke to increasingly specialized audiences, the naturalist writers used inclusive language, infusing the ideas of wilderness and the necessity of its protection into the consciousness of the world.

Well over a century later, further division has occurred. While scientific disciplines continue to specialize, many naturalist writers have drifted from their grounding in good science. As the disciplines of science build already lofty towers still higher to the sky, who will reinforce the foundation of natural history? Who will bring the discoveries of modern science down to earth? Aldo Leopold was among the first to lament the overshadowing of natural history when he asked, "What is our educational system doing to encourage personal amateur scholarship in the natural history field?" Since then, others have joined in the cry to save this tradition of such great antiquity. Reed Noss points out that college-level course offerings in ichthyology, herpetology, mammalogy, ornithology, taxonomy, entomology, and other areas of natural history are fewer and fewer. In addition to this, field courses and field trips are on the decline. He admits that "in private conversation virtually every biologist I speak with is seriously concerned about the death of natural history," and asks, "who will be the field-wise mentors for another generation of ecologists and conservation biologists?" Thomas Fleischner echoes similar sentiments in his inquiries into the history of natural history, calling for its revitalization among professional scientists and amateurs alike.

With their niches threatened, it is no wonder that naturalists have developed reputations for being eccentric. In his book *Pioneer Naturalists,* Howard Evans says, "Naturalists are individualists, preferring the wondrous products of organic evolution to the artificial world that humans have built at nature's expense. Sometimes they are cranky, a bit unworldly, even a bit mad." Thomas Lyon, as editor of an anthology of American nature writers, said, "naturalists and nature writers make up a distinctly nonconforming, even heretical minority."

Is natural history really dying, or is it being redefined? Evans, in the section of his book entitled *Naturalists Then and Now,* asserts that the role of the naturalist is "to speak of the unity of nature, the interrelationships of all its parts." In an age of ever-divergent scientific disciplines, natural history is the mainstay, the common thread weaving its way through all of these disciplines. The importance of the naturalist grows as further divergence occurs, but at the same time, the role gets increasingly difficult to play.

In modern times, the naturalist must be prepared to confront the reality that society bestows little economic reward on the science of natural history. Today's naturalist must value the days and nights outdoors above all else, and be willing to pay the price for such a lifestyle. Further, as science continues to decipher the endless riddles of the world, the naturalist must have command of a larger amount of knowledge than ever before. In an age of increasing specialization, the naturalist must remain a generalist, able to interpret the findings of such diverse disciplines as botany, zoology, paleontology, geology, and meteorology, among others. Many of today's naturalists are regional specialists, preferring this kind of specialization to that of disciplines. This reflects the fact that the majority of natural history practice takes place in the field, not in the laboratory. The naturalist is required to directly experience the land.

Many of the greatest secrets of the land are kept, often unintentionally, by those who speak the increasingly specialized languages of modern science. The naturalist is a notable exception. It is one role of the naturalist to serve as a liaison between the scientific community and the rest of the world, making the realizations of science accessible to non-scientists. While modern science seeks objectivity for validity, the naturalist seeks a participatory relationship with land. While emotional ties are often scoffed at as leading to "bad science," the naturalist may seek out such ties that he or she may speak more passionately of a place. Good science is indeed good sense, but without such undaunted love for land, a naturalist's work begins and ends as facts. While such facts may be informative, it is our connection with real land that gives them life, fosters imagination, and allows us to share in the magic.

Aldo Leopold pointed out the change in natural history that must take place, and its relationship to the recently diverged science of ecology as well: "Modern natural history deals only incidentally with the identity of plants and animals, and only incidentally with their habits and behaviors. It deals principally with their relations to each other, their relation to the soil and water in which they grew, and their relations to the human beings who sing about "my country" but see little or nothing of its inner workings. This science of relationships is called ecology, but what we call it matters nothing." Marston Bates echoes similar sentiments when discussing natural history and ecology, saying "as far as I can see, both labels apply to just about the same package of goods." Things have changed since the middle of the twentieth century. While it may have seemed for a brief moment that natural history and ecology were one, the trend of separation among disciplines has prevailed. Now, coming into the twenty-first century, ecology is moving indoors. Allan Shoenherr, in a brief discussion of natural history and ecology, stated that, "In recent years...ecology has become a highly theoretical and technical science." As Reed Noss observed, "Ecology and conservation biology are being dominated by keyboard jocks–mathematical modelers and statisticians often with scant experience in the field." Noss himself, while lamenting the loss of natural history, suggests divergence from it when he says "...before I was a conservation biologist or a vertebrate ecologist...I was a naturalist." It could accordingly be said that before there was conservation biology or vertebrate biology, there was natural history. And somehow there still is. Every time we go out into the field and feel the sun burning our skin, the wind whipping across our face, the titles of conservation biologist, ecologist, biologist, and every other branch of science with its roots in natural history, fall away.

What we are left with is that we are naturalists. That is enough. Natural history, like all other things, is evolving. From the corpus of Aristotle to the catalogues of Linnaeus, from the observations of Darwin to the lamentations of Leopold, natural history has grown as our knowledge and understanding of the land has grown. Certain characteristics remain, and hopefully always will. Natural history has always been a field-based science which employs comparative methods for understanding and interpreting the natural world. It has always been general, or holistic, in that it looks at the unified picture of the world. Although it went through a period where the focus was more specifically on the discovery and description of plants and animals, it is much broader than that. It both encompasses aspects of and provides the foundation for geology, astronomy, meteorology, botany, zoology, anthropology, ecology and more. Most recently, natural history entails understanding land on a grand scale of time. It seeks to uncover the mysteries of evolution, not just of species, but of the earth itself. It uncovers the past and speculates on the future. It tells the story of nature, from its most ancient beginnings to this moment right now. And yet it is the only science that requires so little specialized training to begin. To begin, all you have to do is go outside, look around, ask questions, and seek out their answers.

To sum it up in one sentence: natural history is a holistic, non-manipulative, field-based science employing comparative methods for understanding and interpreting the biotic and abiotic components of the land, the relationships among them, and their evolution through time.

Enough. We have arrived here at the present and found ourselves on the doorstep of the future. The history of natural history is a subject best wrestled with indoors, where the vast libraries of history and philosophy may be stacked high within the shelter of walls and ceilings. Now it is time to go outside.

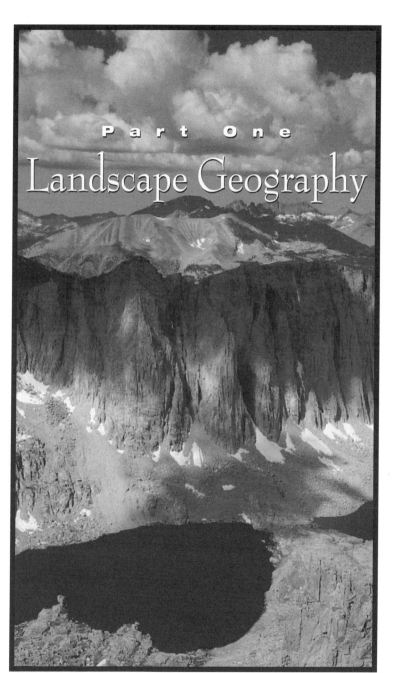

Part One

Landscape Geography

Una Gran Sierra Nevada
An Introduction to the Range of Light

"When I first enjoyed this superb view, one glowing April day, from the summit of Pacheco Pass, the Central Valley, but little trampled or plowed as yet, was one furred, rich sheet of golden compositae, and the luminous wall of the mountains shone in all its glory. Then it seemed to me the Sierra should be called not the Nevada, or Snowy Range, but the Range of Light. And after ten years spent in the heart of it, rejoicing and wondering, bathing in its glorious floods of light, seeing the sunbursts of morning among the icy peaks, the noonday radiance on the trees and rocks and snow, the flush of alpenglow, and a thousand dashing waterfalls with their marvelous abundance of irised spray, it still seems to me above all others the Range of Light, the most divinely beautiful of all the mountain-chains I have ever seen."

John Muir

Window of the World

One day at summer's end, I set out to discover the tilted summit of Mt. Humphreys for myself. I threw food, water, and clothes into my pack and set out across the wide girth of Humphreys Basin. Around shimmering lakes, across vast sheets of granite and ablating snowfields, I arrived at Humphreys Lake, nestled just at the base of the scree slopes fanning out from the broad southwestern flank of Mt. Humphreys. The mountain itself looked like an impenetrable wall, a fortress of high towers between which lay loose rock at the angle of repose, waiting for the slightest perturbation of a tiptoe to begin its trip downslope. Peering up for some time, I found what looked to be a long chute across the southwest face leading directly to the summit ridge. It began at the upper terminus of the scree fields and extended out of sight. I knew that somewhere up there the loose rock of the chute would give way to the stern stone of the summit block. I wiped the glowing beads of sweat off my forehead in restless anticipation. Then, I began my slog up the scree to reach the chute's bottom.

The earth slid out from beneath my feet with every step. Fist-sized and smaller chunks of metamorphic rock material were so heavily oxidized that they turned my fingertips orange-red at first touch. Occasional chunks of granite from up above

Landscape geography page: Mt. Hitchcock and the Kaweahs from Trail Crest on the Mt. Whitney Trail by Andy Zdon.

had made it down here, some with huge, oversized crystals, some buff in color, and even a few pieces of blackish gabbro. After creating countless miniature landslides, I reached the bottom of the chute.

The climbing didn't get any easier. In the chute, slightly larger pieces of rock were interspersed with patches of loose, sandy dirt. I clodded my way up, staying on solid stone surfaces as much as was possible, climbing a rubbly stairway to who knew what. I had received a premonition earlier in the day that I would not make the summit unless I found sky pilots along the way. Sky pilots, the quintessential flowers of the Alpine Sierra, were found only far above treeline in remote rock crevices. Their common name was in reference to those who lead others to heaven. Poking out from secret corners, these blue-purple delicacies lavished the pure mountain air with a fragrance like nothing else of this earth. One breath of this fresh aroma was enough to take your mind away from the immediacy of the crumbling surroundings. To encounter these flowers on a solitary climb was the greatest blessing I could hope for.

Just before reaching the northwest notch, I spotted them. Tucked deep in a rock cleft, those purple polemoniums seemed to look right into me like the jeweled eyes of a mountain princess. Its finger-sized, fern-like leaves sprung out of the bare granite like lacy adornment for the cluster of five-petaled trumpet flowers, rising ever so slightly above the soft foliage. I stopped and stared, overwhelmed by this omen of good fortune. Then I crouched down on my knees, moved my face into the cleft until my nose nearly brushed up against the flower petals, and inhaled. I breathed so deep I could feel it in my toes. It was a cleansing rush, opening me up and leaving me with a feeling of translucency.

East scarp of Mt. Humphreys (13,986') from the Buttermilks. Photo: Wynne Benti

I stood refreshed and looked upward, craning my neck towards the top of Mt. Humphreys. From my perspective, it appeared before me as a great regal throne. Serrated ridges of granite flanked all sides of this high seat, ornamenting its base. I could only imagine the summit, for it was obscured from my view. In my mind I pictured a single, upthrust chunk of pale rock, a block of stone twice as big as I, protruding from a jumbled heap of other such pieces of the mountain. Then I turned to look out upon the expanse of the basin. It was ringed on all sides by the high, ice-sculpted flanks of the High Sierran mountain peaks. I closed my eyes, imagining the basin filled with glacial ice, only the highest peaks rising above the flowing surface. I pictured the ice carrying the mountains away with it, sharpening the range like a grindstone on sawteeth, deepening valleys, serrating the ridges. I wished I could have been alive to see it all happen. Now, a mere twelve-thousand years later, the ice was all but gone. Only lingering suggestions of those once great glaciers remained. I opened my eyes, my softened inner gaze sharpening to the scene before me. The mountains seemed to go on forever. Of all the mountains in view, however, I could think of none so distinct, so carefully and characteristically carved, as that upon which I stood: Mt. Humphreys, the smasher of ego, the envoy of the neutrality of nature.

A few more steps and I made the notch, a narrow col affording a view to the east. I peered down into the steep, precipitous cirque of the mountain's northeast flank. It was just as I suspected: rock and ice. Wafts of smoke flew through the col, indicative of the fire burning off the eastern escarpment, somewhere near the Buttermilks of the Round Valley. From my camp in the basin, I had seen the beginnings of it days before, and watched the cumulus clouds condense around the fine dust particles within the smoke. They stacked up to gargantuan size, looming tall and ominous behind Humphreys' mass. In the evening, the dissipating clouds would reflect the red glowing light of the flames. I stood there in the col and bore witness that the fire still burned, growing over the days.

A tight chute led upward from the col, this time with a floor of solid granite. Narrow aretes, spine-like ridges of rock, bound the passage on either side. I scrambled upward, easy hand and foot action most of the way. I was far up now, on that final hump of the summit block. My heart pounded with dread and anticipation as the chute ended at a vertical wall extending upward one-hundred feet to the summit. A hint of color caught my eye, but it was no flower this time. A sling of nylon webbing had been carefully threaded onto the solid granite above. With rope and rack I could safely continue, sewing up a potentially treacherous line as I ascended. But I had no such gear on that day, and the climb called for less direct tactics. I had to go around.

I dropped my pack and edged out onto the arete to my right, then slowly, carefully, worked my way up its spine. It was not long until I came to a vertical crack. Completely exposed to falls that could result in serious injury or death, I stopped to breathe awhile, looked up, not down, and climbed on. The holds were excellent and the pitch short. Upon reaching a well-placed perch, I thanked the powers that be, inhaled, and scrambled across the summit ridge.

All the way up at nearly fourteen-thousand feet, I was impressed to find a second patch of sky pilot. I stopped once again to imbibe its rich perfume, certain now that the way was clear to the summit rocks. I craned my head around at the croak of a raven, to see a large black bird perched on a lofty pinnacle. This was the first living creature I had seen or heard since Humphreys Lake. It seemed simply to be saying hello, in a curious sort of way, continuing to croak in my general direction as I stood and watched. I gave it a nod and continued. It croaked once more and flew away.

Keeping my hands on the rock at all times, I picked my way across the summit ridge, unable to spot the summit block I had been imagining in my head. The ridge before me seemed always just high enough to obscure what lay beyond it, though I could be certain that the vertical climbing was over, for no stony mass loomed ahead. Then, quite suddenly, I was aware that the ridge was ending. The other side of the mountain came into view. Before it was a flat piece of pale stone, at least twice my size, slightly tilted, though not quite at the angle I had pictured. There was no doubt that it was the highest thing around. This was the summit block, the sill on the window of the world of the Alpine Sierra. I was on top.

The world dropped off on all sides to glacially excavated bowls and valleys. The ridge itself, sharpened by the same ice, was thrust upward like a gargantuan igneous hand, reaching to the sky. There I was, perched atop one of the fingertips, lying on my back for fear of dropping down, a speck in the sun across the endless Sierra.

I thought of people I loved and how I wished to have them there for this moment, and the tragedy of its impossibility, the potency of my journey alone. I felt the indifference of the land contrasted with the morality of myself. I felt painfully alone, the fear of death, and simultaneously, the exuberance of being alive. Here was wildness, the experience of primal sensation. If there is a reason for climbing mountains, this is it. Then, I knew it was time to go.

Climbing back down to my pack was only made easier by the fact that yes, I was indeed going down. Although down-climbing has a well-deserved reputation for being more dangerous than ascending, there is some consolation in knowing that you are intentionally going the same direction that you will go unintentionally if you take a fall. Upon landing, the satisfaction I felt from summiting Humphreys fell into my stomach, and without warning I threw up, surrendering my stomach contents to the granite. I kept going, feeling as if I had just made the due sacrifice for my elation. When my feet were safely on horizontal rock, I gave thanks deeply, ate, drank, and skipped, then wedged my way back down to the col.

The chute down was like a glissade at times. I found myself intentionally running downslope at full speed, completely present only because the activity required every ounce of my attention. Charging down the steep southeast slope of Mt. Humphreys, I was an evolutionary being, trimmed of excess

Mt. Humphreys and Humphreys Lake from the west. Photo: Martha McCord

and want, purely physical and pushing to the edge of my ability. I reached the upper Humphreys Lake breathless, dropped to the rocks, and rested.

Storms brewed over the mountain as I set out across the wide granite and dotted snowfields back towards my camp at Lake Muriel. My legs half running half the time, the wind pushed at my back, flecking it with drops of water from the quickening storm. As I passed Summit Lake and ascended the riser to Lake Muriel, the rains came down. I stopped to drink and put on more clothes, then rounded the lake to my camp near its outlet.

The storm did not last, though the rumble of thunder portended more to come. I stripped down and dove into the cold waters of Muriel, glad to be alive, glad to be home, and thankful for glimpsing through the window of the world, and returning to the living unscathed.

E v e r y w h e r e   Y o u   L o o k

A Geographic Orientation

Looking out from Mt. Humphreys, the center point along the north-south axis of the Alpine Sierra Nevada, you will bear witness to the extent of this matchless mountain landscape. In many places the mountains seem to go on forever, even past the distant horizon where the steel gray of Sierran rock meets the deep, royal blue of the alpine sky. There is snow, even in the deepest heat of the mountain summer, hugging flanks, filling recesses, taking cover from the light that will rid it of its solid form. Lakes, hundreds of them, are spread out across the land like sapphire jewels girdling the bosom of the earth. You will feel the wind blowing, perhaps beating on you, cooling and drying all surfaces with which it comes in contact. You will hear the breath of this wind, perhaps the squawk of a pika, and on a rare day, utter silence. You may see the pink tinges of the rosy finch flitting among the rocks, the sky-blue of mountain bluebirds catching insects, the bumbling bear-like form of the yellow-bellied marmot ambling its way to its favorite sunbathing spot. All around is stone, sharp, smooth, massive, crumbled, the body and bones of the mountains. This land is vast, grand, expansive.

To the south, the high peaks seem innumerable. This is the climax of the Sierra Nevada. The crest continues, undivided, rising ever higher in elevation, exceeding 14,000 feet for the first time at Thunderbolt Peak, at the northern end of the

Palisade Group. South, at Forester Pass, the boundary between Kings Canyon and Sequoia National Parks, the crest splits, severed by the deep fault of the north-south running Kern River. The western branch forms the Great Western Divide, culminating in Florence Peak, twenty miles south of the split, before descending into the trees. The eastern branch continues as the main crest, culminating in the Mt. Whitney group, rising to 14,496 feet, the highest point in the contiguous United States. Ten miles south, near Cirque Peak, the unbroken swath of the alpine zone comes to an end, the crest dropping in elevation abruptly. South of this point, only Olancha Peak rises above treeline, marking the southern end of the Sierran alpine zone. The Sierra Nevada continues for another hundred miles, gradually taking on the character of the desert ranges to the south. The southern terminus of the range is found at the Garlock Fault, near Tehachapi Pass, where what is left of the Sierra Nevada bows down to the smaller Tehachapi Range. The Tehachapis, running northeast-southwest, link the north-south trending southern Sierra Nevada with the east-west trending transverse ranges of southern California.

As you look to the north, the mountains trend northwest-southeast, paralleling the line of the coast. The high peaks gradually become lower in height. The main crest, characteristic of the Southern Sierra, is accompanied by several notable parallel crests, all of which are of the same geologic unit. In the Yosemite region, these lie to the west of the main crest, including the spectacular Ritter, Clark, and Cathedral Ranges. Around the northern boundary of Yosemite National Park, the characteristic granite of the Sierra becomes covered with the beiges and browns of volcanic rock, laid down atop the Sierran granite millions of years ago. Continuing just north of Sonora Pass, the continuity of the alpine zone is broken. North of this point, alpine areas do occur, but become increasingly small and isolated. Moving towards the Tahoe region, the Carson Range splits off and parallels the main crest to the east, along the east shore of Lake Tahoe. The montane forests, slowly creeping up the flanks of the northern Sierra, completely overtake its summits north of the Tahoe region, thus sealing off the alpine zone to the north. The Sierra Nevada continue, however, for another hundred miles. Their northern terminus is found just north of the Feather River Gorge, near Lake Almanor. Here, the Sierran rock dives beneath the younger volcanic material of the Cascades.

Looking west on a clear day, you can see the Coast Ranges, and wonder if maybe that purple blur way out there is the Pacific Ocean. From this perspective, the Sierra Nevada seems a mammoth boundary, separating the realities of California to the west from those of the Basin and Range to the east. From the rocky shores of the Big Sur, one climbs the rugged patterned hills of the Coast Range country, beguiled at the contrast between cool, moist redwood canyons, and searing hot ridges. Dropping down the east slope of the Coast Ranges, you behold the vast, flat plain of California's Central Valley. On a good day, you can discern the green wall of the Sierra Nevada, crowned by snow-white peaks mingling with the vault of the sky.

The Central Valley parallels the Sierra Nevada, running the entire length of the western mountain front. It is a huge trough, over 400 miles long and sixty miles wide, filled in places with 50,000 feet of sediments washed down from the Sierra region over millions of years. If you were to dig deep enough, you would find the place where the roots of the Sierra and those of the Coast Ranges meet in an unfathomable subterranean embrace. With such deep, fertile soils, the valley was for thousands of years, one of the richest wildlife habitats in the country. Over the past two centuries, nearly all of this land has been given over to agriculture, and has become one of the most productive agricultural areas in the country, supplying an abundance of fruits, vegetables, nuts, and grains to the nation. Consequently, the extensive wetlands that once characterized the region have been drained and filled to increase arable land and provide water for irrigation. The migratory waterfowl that once darkened the skies are seldom seen. The golden grizzlies, wolves, tule elk, and pronghorn have all been pushed out or exterminated.

The farms of the valley are fed by the mountain streams of the Sierra Nevada. Seventeen major streams drain the west slope. The southern streams, including the Kern, Tule, Kaweah, and Kings Rivers, terminate in the Great Central Valley. Formerly feeding the shallow lakes and rich wetlands of the southwestern valley, these lakes have since been drained. Their waters now provide irrigation for the agribusinesses of the region, as well as water for the millions of inhabitants of Los Angeles. The central streams, also in the service of the state, flow into the San Joaquin. These include, from south to north, the San Joaquin, Fresno, Chowchilla, Merced, Tuolumne, Stanislaus, Calaveras, Mokelumne, and Consumnes Rivers. The northern streams, including the American, Bear, Yuba, and Feather, all flow into the Sacramento River. These two master streams, the San Joaquin flowing north and the Sacramento flowing south, both issue forth at the Golden Gate, where their fresh water mingles with the brine of the sea.

As you look toward the Sierra from the Central Valley, what appears as a mountain wall is actually a long, gentle slope. The west slope varies in grade from two to six degrees, spanning fifty to seventy miles from the flat valley floor to the jagged Sierran crest. Ascending this slope affords a tour, in part, of the diverse plant communities of the western Sierra Nevada, culminating in the high country of the alpine zone.

It does not take long to rise above the Central Valley. You find yourself in a wide savannah of grassland, dotted by widely spaced oaks. As you ascend into the softly-carved hills, the oaks begin to grow closer and closer together, creating an open woodland understoried by grasses, and interspersed with chaparral, a closed-canopied community of shrubs dominating the driest slopes. The summers here are scorchingly hot and bone dry, while winters are mildly cool and moist. Snow is a rarity here. These are the foothills of the Sierra Nevada, the lowest of the plant communities on the western slope.

At about 2,000 feet in the north and 5,000 feet in the south, the woodlands and chaparral of the foothills gradually give way to the lower montane forest. Snow reaches down to these elevations in winter, and the forest is more watered than the woodlands below. Moving upslope, the pine-oak assemblage gives way to a wider variety of conifers. Dramatic rock outcrops and wide meadows, interspersed with the forest, give the slopes a distinctly montane feel. The middle-montane forest, above 7,000 feet in the south and 4,000 feet in the north, is the land of roaring streams, leaping waterfalls, black bears and granite monoliths. Even further upslope, above 9,000 feet in the south and 7,000 feet in the north, is the upper montane forest, also referred to as the subalpine forest. This is the snow zone, decorated with lakes and meadows. At the highest reaches of the upper montane forest, around 11,000 feet in the south and 9,500 feet in the north, is the treeline: a transitional belt separating the upper montane forest below from the open land of the alpine country above.

The Alpine Sierra Nevada is an open land, its character distinctly different from that of the forested slopes below. It extends upward from treeline to the highest summits, spanning over 150 unbroken miles from just south of Mt. Whitney to Sonora Pass, continuing in isolated patches both north and south. In the contiguous United States, the Alpine Sierra is the only large, continuous alpine habitat outside of the Rockies.

The Alpine Sierra is a land of extremes. The surface of the land is over half bare rock, often polished to a hard sheen by glaciers long ago. Wide basins are bound by vertical walls, serrated ridges that suggest nothing of the soft roundness of the lowlands. Water, held in thousands of crystal lakes, seems colder than the ice from which it came. The air temperature drops thirty degrees within minutes as a cloud momentarily blots out the sun. Snow covers the ground over half the year. The summer season is measured in weeks, rather than months. Many spots never even feel the warmth of the summer sun, shaded north and east-facing slopes hidden beneath tiny glaciers and snowfields. Plants are dwarfed, finding some small refuge in staying close to the ground, away from the wind, incessant, gnawing, truly howling. Skin burns, lips crack, toes freeze, while you wonder what ever brought you to such a forbidding place.

The beauty found in this austere landscape is unquestionable. Those same ice-cold lakes will invigorate one's body and soul to the point of screaming. The sky, free of the thick translucency of the lowland air, is unveiled in all of its sharpness and glory, deeper than blue, deeper than azure, truly and uniquely alpine. The sunsets pink the mountains with alpenglow, flushing the landscape with subtle light, washing the slate clean of the day. The falling light brings innumerable stars, the unmistakable froth of the Milky Way, the silver moonlight casting shadows long and far, the crispness of the air you can almost break in half. Morning brings only slight frost. The air is dry here, cold, stripped of excess, stark naked for the breathing. The plants hold the secrets of the land, the questions and answers

Elevation	Community		Life Zone
12,000'+	Alpine		Arctic-Alpine
	Based on the location of the upper treeline, the elevation of the alpine zone changes throughout the Sierra.		
	Upper Treeline/ Subalpine Forest		Hudsonian
9,000'+	Lodgepole- Red Fir Forest		Canadian
	Yellow Pine Forest		Transition
			Upper Sonoran
	Pinyon Woodland/ Lower Treeline		
			Lower Sonoran
	Alkali Sink Creosote Bush Sagebrush Scrub		
3,000'			

Lone Pine Peak (12,944') from the Owens Valley.
Photo: Bill Fettkether, China Lake NAWS

of how and why this place is so different. The rock and ice
bespeaks the honesty of it all, a mind-bending vastness of bowls,
basins, horns, and knife-edges that are sharp, angular, and true.
The land does not lay hidden up here.

Turning to the interior, the view to the east of the Sierran
crest is strikingly different from that of the west. The mountains seem to drop out from underneath you. As one looks east
from the crest, the mountains are a high, vertical, and serrated
granite wall. There is no suggestion of wide meadows and
basins here, only a bold assemblage of rock and ice. It feels as
though the mountains are even presently in a state of convo-
lution. One can't help but wonder if the walls won't crumble
in the night, frost action popping the granite apart and sending
it plummeting downslope. Spatially, everything is compressed.
Streams rush downward too quickly and abruptly to join with
others; thus the larger streams of the west slope have no
rivals here. Snowbanks and glacierettes, hung up on walls like
blank tapestries, take full advantage of the extreme shade found
in such vertical topography. An impression that this was the
end of the world would not be so far from the truth. The mountain world of the alpine Sierra Nevada ends here quite abruptly,
plummeting down the precipitous east slope to the valleys
below. This is the eastern escarpment, a world apart from the
gentle slope of the west.

The eastern escarpment is most pronounced in the south,
where it drops over 10,000 vertical feet in just six to twelve miles,
resulting in an average slope angle of 25 degrees as the mountains plummet to the Owens Valley below. At its deepest point,
the bedrock of the valley lies 5,000 feet below sea-level, though
the surface of the valley lies around 4,000 feet. Thus the bedrock
is covered by nearly 9,000 feet of sediments washed down from
surrounding mountains. The total relief of the valley, from the

summit of Mt. Whitney (14,496′) to the buried bedrock, is just short of 20,000 feet. This astounding basin, a hundred miles in length and only ten miles wide, is bound by 14,000 foot mountains on *both* sides: the Sierra Nevada to the west, and the parallel-running White-Inyo Ranges to the east. The White-Inyo Ranges are desert mountains, and exhibit the more horizontal profile of the Basin Ranges.

The seemingly vertical wall of the eastern escarpment is first broken near the town of Big Pine, toward the northern end of the Owens Valley. Here, the east slope forms a convex bend called the Coyote Warp. This rounded section of the east slope extends twenty miles north to the Round Valley, near the town of Bishop. North of Bishop, the warp ends, but the escarpment is further broken up by several spur ranges, separate geologic units from the Sierra Nevada. From south to north these ranges include Glass Mountain and the Inyo and Mono Craters which separate the Owens River watershed from that of the Mono Basin to the north, the Bodie Hills and the Sweetwater Mountains which bind the high Bridgeport Valley, the Pine-Nut Range just south of the Tahoe region, and the Diamond and Bald Mountains to the north.

The Great Basin, so named because no water entering it ever reaches the sea, extends to the east further than the eye can see. It is a predictable landscape, dozens of smaller north-south trending ranges separated by wide, high basins. A few of these basins host terminal lakes, where fresh mountain water flows in but never flows out, evaporating into the desert sky and leaving each lake a unique salty inland sea. Even more of the basins host the remains of such lakes, wide salt playas largely devoid of vegetation. These echo a time when water was more plentiful in these parts, and glaciers capped the higher ranges all around. The Sierra Nevada may be considered the westernmost of these ranges, and the valleys of the east-side the westernmost of the basins. Though gargantuan in size compared to the Basin Ranges, and so seemingly separate from them, the Sierra Nevada share a long geological and ecological history with the desert mountains to the east.

Water falling east of the Sierran crest drains into the eastern basins via dozens of short, quick creeks and a few larger streams to the north. The thirty southern creeks, from Haiwee north to Deadman, all drain into the Owens River, which formerly terminated in Owens Lake to the south. The lake has long been drained by the Los Angeles Department of Water and Power, and water from the Owens River is currently diverted to the urban centers of the south. The central streams, including Rush, Lee Vining, Wilson, and Walker, drain into the brine of Mono Lake. This ancient terminal lake was recently saved from meeting the same fate as Owens Lake, largely due to the conservation efforts of the Mono Lake Committee. North of the Mono Basin, the Eastern Sierra are drained by larger streams, including the Walker, Carson, and Truckee Rivers. Beyond the Tahoe region, several smaller streams drain the east-side of the northern Sierra. None of the water draining the east-side ever reaches the ocean.

Plant communities of the east slope differ greatly from those of the west. Generally, the alpine zone does not extend down quite as far. Treeline on the east slope is an average of 500 feet higher than on the west slope. The eastern version of the montane forest is compressed, with many west slope species absent altogether. The lowest reaches of the forest, dominated by Jeffrey pines, extend down to 8,000 feet in the south and 6,000 feet in the north, continuing to lower elevations along cooler drainages. Beneath the Jeffries are the pinyons and junipers, creating an open woodland. Below this woodland are the sagebrush covered basins. Along watercourses, narrow bands of lush riparian woodland stand in stark contrast to the desert scrub, and provide a haven for birds and mammals alike.

The Alpine Sierra has often been praised by hikers for its ideal weather conditions. Many summer backcountry travelers forgo the need for a tent, quite certain of clear, starry skies every night. In contrast, winter snows make the Sierra Nevada second only to the Coastal Ranges of the Pacific Northwest as the snowiest range in the country. The Sierra experiences a Mediterranean climate of cool, moist winters and hot, dry summers. Summer precipitation is rare, falling most often as local afternoon thundershowers, accounting for a scant five percent of the annual precipitation. In contrast, ninety-five percent of annual precipitation falls from October to May. Of this ninety-five percent, ninety to ninety-five percent falls as snow, which lingers in patches throughout the higher elevations during the summer months. Weather systems typically move from west to east, rising up over the range and dropping all of their moisture. Thus the east-side is left in the rain-shadow of the mountains. The alpine zone experiences slightly higher summer temperatures than alpine communities in other mountain ranges, largely due to high levels of incoming solar radiation throughout the clear summer days. As John Muir once said, "The Sierra might better be called the Range of Light, where the light grays of the granitic rock and the stark white of snow reflect the sun's light in a dramatic display of celestial brilliance."

Faces   in   the   Wind

The Human Interface

Stepping into a lost recess of the alpine country, we cannot help but wonder if we might be the first to see a place. The answer lies with the secrets of the ground we walk upon, footprints on the bare rock and sandy soil, fleeting apparitions of those who may or may not have come before us. The Alpine Sierra shares long history with human beings, stretching back perhaps tens of thousands of years. While the trails have all been walked before, and most all of the mountains climbed, there are yet pieces of land untrodden by the feet of humans, hidden, untraceable, in the hard stone memory of the mountains.

American Indians were the first to venture forth into the Alpine Sierra Nevada. For thousands of years before Euro-American settlement, the passes of the high Sierra were used as important trade routes between the native communities of the east and west slopes. These early inhabitants, like the land, differed greatly on each side of the range. Those of the east side, which included the Washo and Paiute-Shoshone groups, were mobile, subsisting largely on pinyon pine nuts, alkali fly larvae, fish, and small game. The communities of the west side were more numerous, with larger populations, reflective of the abundance and variety of food sources available to them. They were generally more sedentary, subsisting primarily on acorn meal, supplemented with fish, berries, bulbs, and occasionally game. East side communities typically traded pine nuts, sinew-backed bows, paint, pumice, and obsidian, while those of the west brought skins of large game, baskets, berries, acorns, and shell beads. The main trade routes in use included, from south to north, Walker Pass, Kearsarge Pass, Taboose Pass, and both the southern and northern Mono Passes. In addition to trading, the high country served as a refuge during the summer months to escape the heat of the lowlands. Native communities on both the east and west sides knew the high country well, and had well-established summer camps throughout the High Sierra. Recent evidence suggests that Native Americans spent far more time at altitude in the mountains of California than has traditionally been thought.

It was 1542 when Juan Rodriguez Cabrillo first named the mountains "una gran sierra nevada," or great snowy range, upon spying snow-capped mountains from his ship offshore of the central coast. Although these were not the true Sierra Nevada of today, the name stuck, restated in descriptive terms by Pedro Font in 1776, who takes credit for the naming. The Spanish, however, were interested in missions, not mountains, and kept out of the high country for the most part. It was not until 1826 that Jedediah Smith and his band of fur trappers crossed the Sierra Nevada at Ebbetts Pass, and though they ducked below the alpine zone, at 8,700 feet they came quite close to it. Among the Euro-Americans, if not Smith, it was Joseph Walker's party of 1833 that first beheld the truly alpine Sierra, crossing the range quite tortuously by following a route that essentially parallels Highway 120. The earliest Euro-Americans in the High Sierra seemed to have had a knack for trying to cross the range in October, when early snowfall was a possibility, ultimately resulting in disaster.

In 1863, the California Geological Survey, under the direction of Josiah Dwight Whitney, began its systematic study of the

High Sierra. Throughout the eleven years before the survey was brought to its official end, the team included such well-known individuals as William Brewer, Charles Hoffman, Clarence King, James Gardner, and Richard Cotter. Many places in the Sierra would later be named after them. Whitney, Brewer, King, and Gardner were all graduates of the Scientific School of Yale College. Whitney and Brewer had traveled throughout Europe and the Alps, and many of their ideas about mountain landscapes came from such exploits. King studied glaciology under Louis Agassiz, North America's expert on glaciology. In addition to the task of surveying, many first ascents were made, most notably Mt. Hoffman, Mt. Tyndall, and Mt. Clark. All told, the survey covered a lot of ground, studying and mapping the High Sierra as they went.

Next came shepherds, and with them, tens of thousands of sheep. The desiccating heat of the Great Central Valley necessitated that the shepherds move their flocks upslope to cooler summer grazing grounds. Increased competition for good feed sent flocks higher and higher into the mountains, until every major meadow in the high country was teeming with sheep. The shoulder-high grasses of these alpine and montane meadows were chewed down to their roots, the early summer wet ground of snowmelt trampled by countless sharp hooves, to be dried with summer to dusty wallows. The High Sierra would suffer two decades of this before the shepherds were pushed out due to enforced governmental protection of public lands.

John Muir, whose name has become more synonymous with the Sierra Nevada than any other, first arrived there in 1868. It was he who, when viewing the range from the west, first dubbed it the Range of Light. Muir was a Scottish immigrant from Wisconsin who had engaged in a number of adventures, from the exploration of Alaska's Inside Passage to a thousand mile walk to the Gulf of Mexico. Muir had studied under Ezra Carr at the University of Wisconsin, and from Professor Carr, who himself was a student of Louis Agassiz, Muir first learned of glaciers and their importance in forming landscapes. Muir came to the Sierra as a shepherd, using this temporary occupation as a means to get him into the mountains. It did not take him long to realize that the sheep were ripping apart the high country, and in the years to come Muir made every effort to get the shepherds and their flocks out of the High Sierra. In following years, Muir did what he could to earn the daily bread that would keep him exploring the mountains he came to love. He was an outstanding observer, and his investigations led him to perceive unity and inter-relatedness among all aspects of the land. Most noted of these are Muir's studies of glaciers in the range, and the all-important role they played in the shaping of the Sierran landscape. Muir eventually went head-to-head with Whitney, who denied the importance of glaciers in the Sierra Nevada, especially in Yosemite Valley, which Whitney believed to be fault-formed. Muir's ideas, though praised by Louis Agassiz himself, would not be widely accepted until championed by Francois Matthes, another student of Agassiz, decades later. Most of Muir's observations, however, were on a smaller scale: the falling leaf, the banner clouds, the water ouzel. These observations reflected Muir's underlying belief an the order and purpose in nature. For Muir, the realms of science and spiritual belief were tightly braided. It may well have been this synthesis that allowed Muir to lead the country on the forward path toward conservation, asserting the value of nature as an end in itself rather than as a means to a utilitarian end. He was instrumental in the establishment of Yosemite National Park, and, less directly, Sequoia-Kings Canyon and Grand Canyon National Park, dedicating his life to the preservation of lands wild and free. Muir was a visionary, a sage; some even called him a mystic.

The following decades brought floods of visitors to the Sierra Nevada. Of these, it was the city-based mountaineers who ventured most often into the high country. Such individuals as Theodore Solomons, Ernest Bonner, Bolton Brown, Joseph "Little Joe" LeConte, and James Hutchinson, combed the range from top to bottom, crossing the divides, climbing the crags, and ascending numerous peaks.

Francois Matthes, a Harvard educated geologist, studied the range extensively during this time, publishing his *Geologic History of the Yosemite Valley* in 1930, followed by several other papers concerning the geologic evolution of the range. He further popularized his ideas by appealing to a more general audience in his *The Incomparable Valley*. Matthes' work became the staple for the Sierra Nevada, though in subsequent decades many of his hypotheses were proven false.

It was the legendary Norman Clyde who spent more time in the High Sierra than any before him. From 1920 to 1946, Clyde made well over a thousand summits, over a hundred of which were first ascents. Unlike other mountaineers, however, Clyde was not just a visitor. Though he held a bed in Big Pine, in the Owen's Valley, he lived in the mountains, making the Sierra Nevada his home and living long to reflect their awesome nature. Like most of the few men of this sort, Clyde was quirky. He read the classics in Greek by the fire, carried hundred-pound packs regularly, had inexhaustible physical stamina, and was known to be "a proud and sensitive man, unable to grasp modern thinking." He was said to be the last of his kind, a dying breed, and as such, he left no heirs.

Since the end of World War II, the number of visitors to the High Sierra has increased exponentially. Hikers, fishermen,

Norman Clyde (photographer unknown)

climbers, artists, and scientists alike have been awed by the grandeur of the alpine zone. More people than ever flock to the high country in search of refuge from the summer heat. As the daily grind of life gets ever coarser, more and more people find themselves seeking sanctuary from their everyday lives. Fortunately, the impacts of modern society have been less severe in the Alpine Sierra than in the slopes and lowlands surrounding the high country. Nearly every acre of the alpine zone is currently protected as either national park land or federally designated wilderness. Nevertheless, though the sheep days may be over, impacts due to human activity are still a concern.

Today, four major problems threaten the integrity of the Sierran alpine ecosystem. The first of these is direct human impact, including devegetation and erosion due to foot traffic, and garbage. The second of these is the impact of stock. Every year hundreds of horses pack thousands of visitors in and out of the high country, leaving behind thousands of tons of excrement and tens of thousands of gallons of urine, much of which inevitably finds its way into water sources. Stock also cause severe soil erosion along both trails and off-trail areas where they are permitted to roam. Grazing is always a problem, causing severe damage to fragile meadows if allowed too early in the season. The third major problem comes from indirect human impact, largely as air pollution from the lowlands. Even Yosemite Valley is covered with a veil of smog during the summer months, due to the thousands of vehicles coming and going every day. Smog, largely a lowland problem, has the potential to affect the alpine areas in negative ways, causing acid rain, reducing photosynthesis rates among plants, and raising air temperatures. The fourth problem is human-introduced species, which compete with native plants and animals for the already scarce resources of the alpine zone. An example of this is seen in high alpine lakes, where introduced trout have eliminated populations of native frogs by both direct predation and competition. Though the alpine zone may be perched high on the crown of the world, the arm of civilization grows with every passing moment, touching even the farthest corners of the earth. The Sierra Nevada is no exception.

Lone Pine Peak, eastern escarpment. Photo: Martha McCord

Foundations
A Geologic History

"If by some fiat I had to restrict all this writing to one sentence, this is the one I would choose:

The summit of Mt. Everest is marine limestone."

John McPhee

C h a n g i n g   P l a c e s

Time, Composition, and Changes of the Earth

At Horse Creek Pass, along the northern boundary of the Tuolumne River watershed, the granite of the Sierra Nevada reaches upward like the unstoppable fingers of change grasping at the very roots of ancient time. The gray speckled rock of the rising Sierra Nevada has literally injected itself into the overlaying rock, which is darker, smoother, almost slate-like. It is almost as if the rising range, in all of its youthful vigor, has grabbed onto the crust above and cast it aside in some effort to accommodate for still more crust, like a great earth mover working from within to excavate for new development. It is a colorful scene, where the bending of rock requires a bending of the mind. Here, the modern Sierra Nevada tickles the belly of an ancient arc of volcanoes that once stretched from Mexico to Alaska, a vast mountain chain that rose to its prime while Tyrannosaurus Rex tromped the primeval swamps of the Mesozoic era, over 200 million years ago. It is a place of contact, where the stories of two of the greatest mountain ranges the world has known meet and intermingle, and become one.

In most places across the planet, the tales of the land's past are hidden beneath the ground. With each shovelful of earth we dig deeper into the story. The rocks, the bones of the earth, are typically laid out in this way: deepest is eldest, and every subsequent layer is the veneer of the next great chapter of time. The Grand Canyon is spectacular in that, aside from its aesthetic qualities, it illustrates this concept vividly. In the Sierra Nevada, however, the history of the world is turned upside-down. To go back in time you must ascend the highest mountain peaks, and to understand the present you must often look over, across, or far, far down.

I have laid in my sleeping bag on countless nights thinking these thoughts. For most of the planet's life, this place has been a sort of figment of the earth's imagination. It has sat quietly beneath the ebbs and flows of oceans. It has been thrown up as an island spewing lava, cruised the wide seas from west to east, and crashed into an embryonic North America. It has been rained on, eroded away, and redeposited as sediments along a wide continental shelf, just under the warm lick of a shallow sea. It has been injected and invaded by incomprehensible volumes of liquid magma, rising from below and erupting as massive volcanoes comparable to the Andes of today. It has been low-lying uplands worn down by warmth and water, covered in lush subtropical vegetation. It has been ripped and torn, stretched, and heaved upward once again. It has been wrapped in ice repeatedly and carved meticulously. This land has been through more than I can possibly imagine, but still I try.

If one sits quietly on a summer's night in the Alpine Sierra, and listens to the land, the mountains can be heard breaking to pieces, falling apart, crumbling down. It may be in the sound of water freezing and expanding in minute cracks in the rocks, wedging the stones apart with loud pops as they fracture into pieces. It may be in the sound of a stream carrying away the tiny particles of sand, only to deposit them in the bottom of a lake, grain by grain, slowly filling it in. It may be in the splash of glacial ice calving off into a half-frozen tarn. All around the landscape is changing, evolving, being built up and torn down, rent open and squeezed together, continuing a story that has been going on for hundreds of millions of years.

Understanding the present landscape of the Alpine Sierra Nevada is quite literally just scratching the surface. If we wish to truly know the story of this place, we must dig deeper, beginning by asking questions about origins. Where did this place come from? How did it get here? When did it happen? The answers to all of these questions lie in the bones of the mountains, the rocks. The rocks tell the stories of creation, etched in the great stone tablet of time. Everywhere one looks in the Alpine Sierra, the land bespeaks its history. If we learn the language of the land, we can decipher the etchings, and understand this history. If we understand the land's history, we can tell its story.

Stepping across the wide polished granite of the alpine zone can instill one with a sense of timelessness. The rocks seem ancient, the mountains wise with years uncountable. Surely these mountains have stood since the dawn of time, bearing testimony today to the primordial mystique of ages long forgotten. But it is not so. This is a young range, full of the jagged vigor of youth, and still very much in the making. In fact, the Sierra Nevada may be the youngest non-volcanic mountain range in the world. The rise of the Sierra, however, is a part of a rich geologic history with profound occurrences, a story that finds its beginnings deep in the recesses of time. To uncover the genesis of the Sierra Nevada, we must look into the greater geologic history of western North America.

Where the Sierra Nevada end at the north and south, other mountains begin. Their span reaches from northern Alaska to the tip of South America. Together, these mountains form a distinct belt, a vast mountain system known as the Pacific Rim Cordillera. The part of this system in North America is called the North American Cordillera, and includes the Alaska Range, Rocky Mountains, Cascade Range, Coast Ranges, Sierra Nevada, and Sierra Madre of Mexico. On a smaller scale, the Cascade Range, Coast Ranges, and the Sierra Nevada may be considered a separate system called the Western North American Cordillera, distinguishing them from the Rockies of the interior of the continent. It becomes evident. The story of the Sierra Nevada is intimately linked to that of the surrounding mountains of the Cordillera. To understand these mountains, we must try to *think like them.*

In Aldo Leopold's *A Sand County Almanac*, he spoke of "thinking like a mountain," stressing the importance of developing a long-term sense of time. Into every cubic inch of the earth has gone billions of years of development, and to truly appreciate a landscape we must acknowledge this. Geologists have done so by developing a system that divides the earth's history of 4.6 billion years into eras, periods, and epochs based on the development of life on the planet. Appreciating the geologic time scale from the perspective of our human lives can be fascinating, humbling, and even ridiculous. If we transpose the 4.6 billion years of the earth's geologic history onto a 24-hour clock, the origin of the earth being the stroke of midnight of a new day, humans have only been around for a portion of the last second, and human ancestors a fraction of the last minute. On the face of such a clock, the sixty to eighty-year lifespan of the average human may not even be perceivable through the lens of a microscope. The Sierra Nevada has only arisen in the last two minutes, at most, and even the rocks that form them were only emplaced in the last hour and a quarter. Panagea, that famous supercontinent, was assembled and torn apart all in the last two hours. From this perspective, it becomes evident that most of the earth's history is enshrouded

Figure 1. The Geologic Time Scale (adapted from Hill 1975).

Era	Period	Epoch	Years
Cenozoic (Age of Mammals)	**Quaternary**	**Holocene**	
			10,000
		Pleistocene	
			2-3 million
	Tertiary	**Pliocene**	
			12 million
		Miocene	
			26 million
		Oligocene	
			37-38 million
		Eocene	
			53-54 million
		Paleocene	
			65 million
Mesozoic (Age of Reptiles)	**Cretaceous**		
			136 million
	Jurassic		
			190-195 million
	Triassic		
			225 million
Paleozoic (Age of Fishes)	**Permian**		
			280 million
	Pennsylvanian		
			320 million
	Mississippian		
			345 million
	Devonian		
			395 million
	Silurian		
			430-440 million
	Ordovician		
			500 million
	Cambrian		
			570 million
Precambrian			
	Origin of the Earth		**4.6 billion**

in a past we know precious little about.

The entire first four billion years of the earth's history, translating to over twenty hours, is called the Precambrian era, referring to the time before life was abundant. From 570 million years ago until 225 million years ago is the Paleozoic era, meaning *old life*, also referred to as the Age of Fishes. It lasted from about 9:00 pm until 10:40 pm. Within this era are seven periods: smaller divisions of time within the era. These include, from oldest to youngest, the Cambrian, Ordovician, Silurian, Devonian, Mississippian, Pennsylvanian, and Permian periods. Following the Paleozoic era is the Mesozoic era, meaning *middle life*, also referred to as the Age of Reptiles. The Mesozoic spans from 225 million years ago to around 65 million years ago, from about 10:40 pm until 11:40 pm, and includes the Triassic, Jurassic, and Cretaceous periods. Next is the Cenozoic era, meaning *new life*, also called the Age of Mammals. The Cenozoic era began around 65 million years ago, at 11:40 pm, and continues at present. It includes the Tertiary and Quaternary periods, each of which are further divided into even smaller intervals called epochs. The Tertiary period, beginning 65 million years ago and ending two to three million years ago includes the Paleocene, Eocene, Oligocene, Miocene, and Pliocene epochs. The Quaternary period, which we are currently in, includes the Pleistocene and the Holocene epochs.

Throughout the 4.6 billion year geologic history of the earth, the countenance of the planet has undergone some profound changes. From a bubbling ball of molten lava to the big blue marble we know today, entire continents have come and gone while oceans opened and closed. Mountains have risen and fallen even as valleys have risen to plateaus, then sunk to become inland seas. To understand the cause of such changes, we must first consider the composition of the earth.

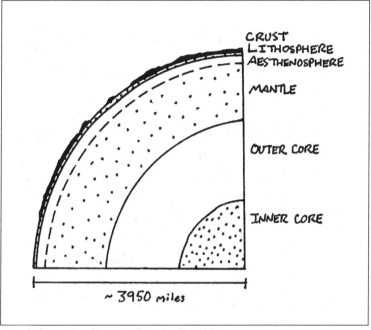

Figure 2. Composition of the earth. Illustration: David Gilligan

The present day composition of the earth is the result of the processes of gravitational differentiation. Imagine a huge bag filled with a mix of golf balls and ping-pong balls. If you shake the bag, the heavier, more dense golf balls will make their way to the bottom of the bag, while the lighter, more buoyant ping-pong balls will work their way to the top of the bag. Similarly, if you add oil to a pot of water, no matter how hard you stir, the oil will always end up on top. The stuff of the earth works in much the same way. Gravity's pull is greatest on those objects with the highest density, pulling them closer to the center of the earth (the bottom of the bag, or the pot), while less dense matter is displaced and moves away from the center (the top of the bag or pot). Gravitational differentiation began about

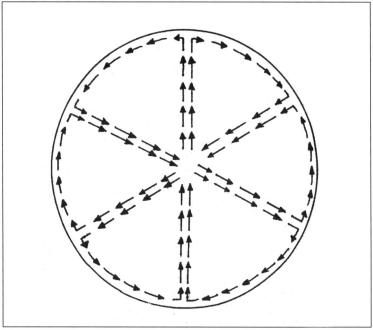

Figure 3. Convection cells. Illustration: David Gilligan

4.5 billion years ago, and is still going on today. This resulted in a series of concentric spheres within the earth, much like the layers of an onion or a jawbreaker candy, arranged on the basis of the density of the material comprised in each sphere (Figure 2). Both temperature and pressure increase the further inward you go, and the material found in each sphere is either liquid or solid, depending on the combination of pressure and heat. Liquification will occur if temperatures are hot enough to melt the particular material (all elements, of course, have different melting and boiling points). Solidification will occur if either pressure is greater than hot temperatures, or temperatures are not hot enough to cause liquification.

The innermost sphere of the earth is the core, consisting of incredibly dense nickel and iron. The inner core is completely solid due to the intense pressures of gravity pulling in the earth around it, while the outer core, made of the same stuff, is liquid due to slightly less pressure. As a whole, the core extends from the center of the earth at around 3,950 miles in depth, outward to around 1,800 miles depth. The second and largest sphere is the mantle, made of rocks rich in iron and magnesium. The majority of the mantle, also called the mesosphere, is solid, extending outward to around 220 miles in depth. The outer mantle gets a little complicated. From around 220 to sixty miles deep is the aesthenosphere, a relatively thin layer with temperatures just hot enough to result in semi-molten material with the equivalent viscosity of most malleable metals. From around sixty two miles depth to the surface of the earth is the lithosphere, where temperatures are cooler. The lithosphere is made up of solid rocks of the upper mantle and the crust. Atop the crust lies the hydrosphere, and beyond that, the atmosphere.

The earth's crust and the lithosphere and aesthenosphere beneath it are where all the tectonic, or building action takes place. The crust itself is made up of numerous plates, riding like rafts atop the semi-molten interior. There are generally two types of plates: continental and oceanic. The continental plates are composed of lighter material, varying in thickness from twelve to forty six miles. Because they are lighter, they ride on the mantle with greater buoyancy. The oceanic plates are made of denser volcanic material, typically four to five miles thick, and ride lower on the mantle. Heated matter in the mantle is constantly rising, displacing the cooler matter above, resulting in huge convection cells much like boiling water, which create numerous currents beneath the lithosphere (Figure 3). These currents cause the plates to be in constant motion, crashing, overriding, and sliding against each other, throwing up mountains and opening valleys, widening oceans and swallowing them whole.

Plates may converge together, causing a collision, or diverge apart, causing rifting. When continental plates collide with one another, large-scale mountain building occurs, resulting in such ranges as the Alps and the Himalayas. When continental and oceanic plates collide, the more dense oceanic plate dives, or subducts, beneath the less dense continental plate, resulting in mountain ranges such as the Andes and the Cascades. When oceanic plates collide with one another, one must subduct beneath the other, resulting in island-arcs such as Japan. When continental plates rift, certain blocks of crust drop down while others become tilted. If rifting continues, new molten material wells up from the mantle to fill in the gap, and ocean water eventually floods in to fill the trough, as is happening today in the Red Sea of Africa. As oceanic plates rift, molten material fills the gap continually, and the sea floor spreads ever wider, as exemplified by the Atlantic Ocean.

The geologic evolution of the Sierra Nevada may be considered in five stages, each with a central theme. The first I call *Westward Expansion*; this is the story of the origins and earliest days of Western North America. The second stage, *Setting the Stone*, tells the story of the ancestral Sierra Nevada mountain range, as well as the origins of today's Sierra. The third stage discusses the long period of time between the ancestral Sierra and the present day range, called *In Between Days*. The fourth stage, *The Mountains Rise*, is the story of the rise of today's Sierra Nevada. The fifth and final stage, *Fire and Ice*, brings us to the present, and tells of the volcanic activity and glaciation of the last three million years. All told, this tale spans some two billion years.

Stage 1: Westward Expansion

Prepaleozoic and Paleozoic Geologic Activity

The story of the geologic evolution of the Sierra Nevada begins far back in the shadowy past. Around two billion years ago, just past noon on the 24-hour geologic clock, the continents then in existence had been joined as a supercontinent called Rodinia, which was beginning to break apart. What was to become Western North America is believed to have been attached to Siberia or Antarctica. Around 1.2 billion to 750 million years ago, North America rifted away from the larger landmass, becoming for the first time an independent continent. As the new continent pulled away, the sea flooded into the widening rift, beginning the widening of an ancestral Pacific Ocean. At that time, the western border of the continent ran north-south through the middle of the Great Basin region, and lay beneath a wide, shallow sea. For 300 million years sediments washed down from the interior of the continent into this sea, eventually filling it with sediments over a mile deep. Over millions of years, these sediments hardened and cemented, or lithified, into layers of sedimentary rock, ever so slowly expanding the continent westward. This geologically inactive margin was considered passive, comparable to the present day eastern seaboard of North America. The land known today as California had not yet ben formed, and in its place was the widening ocean.

The western margin of the continent remained passive until 350 million years ago, during the Mississippian period, at around 10:00 pm on the 24-hour geologic clock. At this time, the Farallon oceanic plate moved in from the west and collided with the oceanic plate offshore of the continent, causing the latter to subduct. The friction from the subduction caused material from these plates to melt. As the melted material rose to the surface of the overriding Farallon Plate, it caused volcanic eruptions, resulting in the formation of island arcs along the plate's leading edge. As this plate consumed the other, it caused the island-arcs to smash up against the western edge of the continent, crumpling and contorting the deep sedimentary layers into low mountains. This began a series of accretions that would eventually build the western edge of the continent to its present day position.

During this same time, all of the earth's landmasses were converging to form the Panagean supercontinent. Eastern North America crashed into Europe and Africa, while South America collided with Southern North America, resulting in major mountain building in all of these areas. The western margin, though going through accretions of its own, remained free from such major continental collisions. All of this, however, was about to change.

Stage   II: Setting   the   Stone

Mesozoic Geologic Activity

It was 10:45 pm on the 24-hour geologic clock when the west was heaved upward and the foundations of the Sierra Nevada were finally laid down. Around 215 million years ago, during the Triassic period of the Mesozoic era, Panagea began breaking up, sending North America westward as the Atlantic Ocean opened and began to spread. This westward movement of the continent caused the Farallon oceanic plate, formerly offshore of the newly accreted western margin, to take a submissive dive beneath the overriding continental plate.

As the oceanic Farallon Plate subducted, it slid beneath the overriding continental plate (Figure 4). Friction between the underside of the continent and the top of the oceanic plate caused rock from both plates to melt. The low density molten material differentiated back toward the surface of the continent, rising like oil in water as teardrop-shaped blobs of magma. As the magma moved upward, it melted the even less dense continental material, adding this new material to the mix. Eventually, much of the magma reached the surface, cooking and bending the overlying sedimentary material wherever it came in contact with it. The magma itself erupted inland from the western margin as a huge arc of volcanoes spanning from Mexico to Alaska. This massive new mountain chain, referred to as the Sierran Arc, or the Ancestral Sierra, was comparable to the

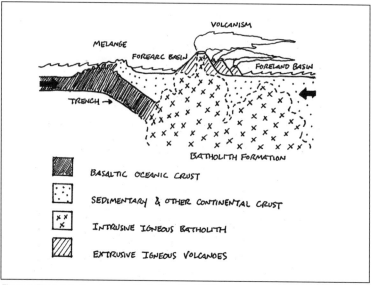

BASALTIC OCEANIC CRUST

SEDIMENTARY & OTHER CONTINENTAL CRUST

INTRUSIVE IGNEOUS BATHOLITH

EXTRUSIVE IGNEOUS VOLCANOES

Figure 4. The subduction dynamic. Illustration: David Gilligan

Andes of today, which were formed by similar geologic processes.

From 210 to 80 million years ago, from roughly 10:45 until 11:30 pm on the geologic clock, over a hundred magma pulses rose from underneath the continent. While many of these erupted, still more of them never made it to the surface, baking the solidified volcanic material above, and coalescing to form a vast reservoir of magma beneath the Sierran Arc. With time this magma cooled and solidified as plutons, forming the basement complex, or subjacent series, of the arc volcanoes. This basement is also called a batholith, meaning "deep rock." This batholith was later to rise as the great Sierra Nevada of today.

The rocks formed from these processes are all called igneous rocks, meaning that they are derived directly from magma. Igneous rocks that cool at or above the surface of the earth, such as those of the Sierran Arc volcanoes, are called extrusive igneous, or volcanic rocks. These rocks typically cool so fast that crystals have little or no time to develop, so volcanic rocks usually have a relatively smooth surface. Igneous rocks that cool below the surface of the earth, such as those of the batholith, are called intrusive igneous, granitic, or plutonic rocks. These rocks cool slowly, which allows time for crystals to form, giving granitic rocks a rough surface. The batholith formation that accompanied the Sierran Arc was one of the largest granite-forming events in the history of the planet, resulting in the emplacement of the Sierran and Klamath batholiths, as well as those of Eastern California, Nevada, and Idaho.

We can tell much about the magmatic material a rock was derived from by examining the color and density of the rock. Darker rocks are typically rich in heavy minerals such as olivines, pyroxines, and amphiboles, and thus formed from magma that originated from a greater depth. Such rocks are called mafic. Lighter rocks are rich in less dense minerals, such as mica, feldspar, and quartz, and are formed from magma closer to the surface. These rocks are called felsic, or silicious (referring to their high silicate content). A more felsic extrusive igneous rock is rhyolite, an intermediate is andesite, and the most mafic commonly found is basalt. Granite, diorite and gabbro are their intrusive igneous counterparts, having the same mineral composition but having been cooled below the surface. Dozens of other igneous rock types are recognized and classified according to their mineral composition, but these six are the most commonly referred to.

Among intrusive igneous rocks the darker minerals have the highest melting point, and thus are the first to crystallize out of the magmatic soup, typically forming smaller crystals. The lighter minerals have lower melting points, quartz being the last to crystallize and also forming the largest crystals. Accordingly, the darker, more mafic rocks such as gabbro typically have the smallest crystals, while the lighter felsic rocks such as true granite typically have the largest. Among extrusive igneous rocks, the most mafic, such as basalt, are the darkest and most dense (unless the rock contains air pockets), while the most felsic, such as rhyolite, are lighter in color and less dense.

The rising Sierran Arc put a tremendous amount of downward pressure on the surrounding area, causing the crust to sag beneath the weight of this huge mountain chain. This formed two basins on either side of the arc: a foreland basin to the east, and a forearc basin to the west. Even as they were forming, these basins began to fill with sediments as water and gravity worked together to erode the mountains. As the forearc basin to the west filled, the continent slowly grew westward. As the Farallon Plate continued to subduct, the leading edge of the continent scraped up material from the top of the oceanic plate, much like a bulldozer or a snowplow. This material became wedged between the diving ocean plate and the edge of the continent, compressing and deforming, gradually metamorphosing into a chaotic rock called melange. This particular melange is called the Franciscan melange, and became the foundation for most of today's Coast Ranges. Thus the forearc basin, presently beneath California's Central Valley, became bound by mountains both to the east and to the west. Melanges continued to accrete, that is, to develop and move, to the leading edge of the continent as long as subduction continued to occur. These accreted lands, called suspect terranes, formed the majority of Alaska, British Columbia, Washington, and Oregon, in addition to Western California. In this way, the continent grew westward by thirty percent, making the Sierran Arc further inland from the continental margin. The arc itself was not to last long.

S t a g e   I I I :   I n - B e t w e e n   D a y s

Early Cenozoic Geologic Activity

Around 70 million years ago, during the Late Cretaceous period of the Mesozoic Era (just past 11:30 pm on the geologic clock), North America rifted from Europe. This final breaking of the Panagean supercontinent caused the North American plate to accelerate its westward movement. As the continental plate sped up, the Farallon Plate subducted at an increasingly shallow angle. As a result of this shallow angle subduction, major mountain building moved east of the Sierra region, eventually to form the core of the present-day Rocky Mountains. As the mountain building ceased, the western margin of the continent became relatively quiet.

Then the rains came down, slowly washing the Sierran Arc volcanoes into the surrounding basins. The warm, moist climate of this time period only sped erosion rates up. Over the next 50 million years, these erosive forces reduced the 15,000-foot high ancestral Sierra to undulating highlands, gradually exposing the granitic batholith which had for so long underlain the arc. The coastline lay along what is now the western foothills of the Sierra Nevada, and was characterized by an elaborate system of swamps, lagoons, and bayous. The Central Valley lay beneath a shallow sea, bound to the west by a series of islands that would become the Coast Ranges.

Atop the freshly exposed granitic material were perched the highest remaining peaks of the Sierran Arc. These peaks, believed by some geologists to have seldom exceeded 5,000 feet, were made of the sedimentary and volcanic material that had been cooked and bent by the rising magma of the batholith (a body of granite). Heat and pressure, such as occurred here, alters the physical and/or chemical composition of rock, causing rocks to metamorphose from their original form. Accordingly, such rocks are called metamorphic rocks. Metamorphosed sedimentary rocks are called metasedimentary, while those of volcanic material are called metavolcanic. These meta-morphic peaks would eventually rise with the Sierra to become some of the highest peaks in the range, including Mts. Dana, Gibbs, Lewis, Parker, Wood, and Ritter, among others.

As the Sierran Arc quietly eroded away, all was not so calm in other parts of the range. Around 30 million years ago, during the Mid-Tertiary period of the Cenozoic era (around 11:50 pm on the geologic clock), violent rhyolitic volcanic explosions blasted their way across what is now the northern Sierra Nevada. Originating from vents near the present-day crest of the range, the erupted rhyolitic material blanketed the exposed basement rocks with an overlying layer up to a thousand feet thick. These explosions subsided around 20 million years ago, only to be succeeded by andesitic eruptions. The andesitic lava flowed forth from vents along the crest, often mixing with mud and water to form steaming, sticky, taffy-like flows called lahars. These andesitic flows covered the land with vast amounts of volcanic material, much of which has since eroded away. In the Alpine Sierra, these flows are best evidenced in the Sonora Pass area.

Stage IV: The Mountains Rise

Late Cenozoic Geologic Activity

Near 25 million years ago, during the Mid-Tertiary period of the Cenozoic era (around 11:54 pm on the geologic clock), the Atlantic Ocean far away to the east relaxed its spreading action sufficiently enough to slow down the westward movement of North America. Consequently, the Farallon Plate once again began to subduct at a greater angle, allowing it to dive deeper into the mantle and thus melt more. This brought the tectonic action away from the interior of the continent, where it had been for the last forty to fifty million years, and back to the western margin.

For millions of years, the southeast moving Farallon Plate had separated North America from the northwest-moving Pacific plate to the west. The junction of the Pacific Plate and the Farallon Plate formed a corner which pointed at South-Central California. As subduction of the Farallon Plate continued, the last slab of it between North America and the Pacific plate was devoured, bringing the corner of the Farallon-Pacific junction into direct contact with the continent. Remnants of the Farallon Plate continued to subduct to the north and the south, eventually forming the Cascades and the Mexican Volcanoes. In the middle, however, the tectonic regime shifted abruptly. Here, the northwest-moving Pacific Plate butted up against the continent, forming a huge system of lateral faults, or transform

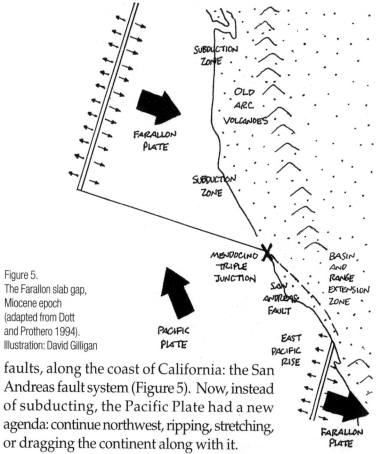

Figure 5.
The Farallon slab gap,
Miocene epoch
(adapted from Dott
and Prothero 1994).
Illustration: David Gilligan

faults, along the coast of California: the San Andreas fault system (Figure 5). Now, instead of subducting, the Pacific Plate had a new agenda: continue northwest, ripping, stretching, or dragging the continent along with it.

The Pacific Plate contacted the continent as a wide wedge coming more or less straight on. First only the tip of the corner touched, then gradually the contact area widened. In this way, the Pacific Plate replaced the subducting Farallon Plate, but did not itself subduct. This created an ever-widening slab gap beneath the continent, where the Farallon Plate, now completely devoured, no longer lay between the underside of the continent and the semi-molten aesthenosphere. As the remnants of

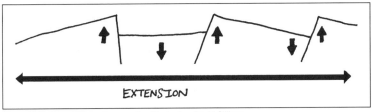

Figure 6. Basin and Range topography. Illustration: David Gilligan

the Farallon Plate continued to subduct, the slab gap grew both north and south, ending the subduction dynamic, shutting off arc volcanism, and putting more and more of the underside of the continent in direct contact with the mantle. This direct contact caused the continent to soften, losing much of its rigidity. As a result of this, when the Pacific Plate began to pull the continent northwest, the land was able to stretch far more than usual.

Stretching of the crust began in what is today southern Arizona, inland from the point where the Pacific Plate first contacted the continent, and spread north and south as the slab gap grew. The crust was stretched an additional ten to fifty percent its original width, shifting the Sierra region west up to 165 miles to accommodate expansion, and turning its southern tip toward the southwest. As the crust stretched, it thinned to twelve to nineteen miles, some of the thinnest crust in the world. As the crust thinned, the semi-molten material of the aesthenosphere was brought even closer to the surface, causing the thinned crust to bow upward. This broke the already thin crust into blocks, some of which sank, or down-dropped, others of which tilted as on a hinge, the opening end leaning upward (Figure 6). The down-dropped basins are called grabens, German for "sunken grave," while the tilted, uplifted blocks are called horsts. This action eventually resulted in the classic Basin and Range topography of today: widely spaced north-south trending mountain ranges or horsts separated by broad grabens.

The Basin and Range extension of the Mid-Tertiary period kicked off a series of events that eventually resulted in the uplift of the Sierra Nevada. To understand these events, however, we must first consider the principle of isostasy: how the thickness of the earth's crust relates to its flotation on the aesthenosphere.

The crust of the earth floats atop the semi-molten material of the aesthenosphere much like ice floats atop water. If you look at an ice cube in a bowl of water, a portion of the ice is above the water's surface, while a portion of it is below. The ratio of what is above to what is below remains the same, regardless of the size of the ice cube. Accordingly, if you were to cut away a portion of the ice above the surface of the water, the extra buoyancy pressure exerted from the subsurface portion, or root, would cause the ice cube to bob up to achieve equilibrium. On the same note, when cargo is removed from a barge it floats higher than when it is weighted. This principle, whether considering ice, boats, or the crust of the earth, is called isostasy. Mountains, for example, have deep crustal roots in proportion to their height, analogous to the subsurface portion of the ice cube. The ratio for ice is about ninety percent below the water's surface to ten percent above. The ratio for the stuff of the earth is around eighty to twenty.

The deep crustal root of the Sierran Arc lay for some time inactive, but intact, beneath the eroded surface of the mountains. As the mountains of old were worn down over time, the crust cooled and gained elastic strength. This elasticity was augmented by the mantle's contact with the thinning lithosphere. While the range had been in local isostatic equilibrium throughout the arc volcanism of the Mesozoic Era, as erosion occurred the root become overly deep, and the range failed to maintain such balance. The buoyancy pressure exerted

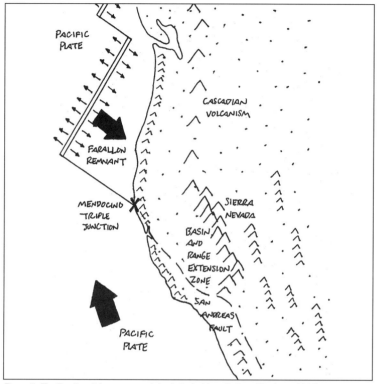

Figure 7. The Farallon slab gap, present day (adapted from Dott and Prothero, 1994).
Illustration: David Gilligan

from this deep crustal root was temporarily restrained by the
elasticity of the overlying crust, which acted like a thick, tough
rubber-band, preventing the root from bobbing up. The crust
stretched to a slight bulge throughout the region as the root
pushed upward from below. This was a time of great tension.
Something had to break.

When the extensional faulting reached the Sierra region, it
did not take long for the extra stress to cause the rubber-band
to snap. The crust broke along north-south trending faults in
two places: to the west, along the San Andreas fault system,

and to the east, along the Owen's Valley fault system. This extensional faulting caused two simultaneous events on either side of the range. The White-Inyo Range to the east was uplifted as a tilted block, while the Central Valley to the west was down-dropped. The Sierran root was freed from its restraints, and like an ice cube, finally bobbed upward.

The Sierra Nevada rose abruptly, uplifting two kilometers to nearly its present height. In the Northern and Central Sierra, the crustal root, laying beneath the eastern crest of the range, buoyed up the western foothills along with it. The crust did not break to the west, and the Central Valley acted like a sinker weight, or a hinge, from which the range uplifted as a tilted block. This oppressive weight caused less uplift in the foothill region than the root necessitated, and more uplift than the root dictated in the eastern part of the range. Faults along the eastern flank ripped at the seams, and the eastern blocks sank as grabens. This resulted in the long, gradual west slope and the steeper eastern escarpment that is characteristic of the region today. In the Southern Sierra, the range was faulted on both the east and the west sides. The southern part of the range therefore rose more uniformly, as the western flank was freed from the weight of the Central Valley. Faults also developed in the range itself, as is evidenced by the twin crests of the Mt. Whitney region and the Great Western Divide, separated by the Kern River Canyon.

Current wisdom holds that the Sierra Nevada rose from south to north, following the northward growth of the slab gap. As the Pacific Plate carried the continent northwest, the extensional zone opened like a fan, the hinge being the northward moving meeting place of the Farallon remnant, the Pacific Plate, and the North American Plate, known as the Mendocino Triple Junction (Figure 7). The junction, as the hinge, moved north at a rate of six centimeters per year, opening the fan to the south in its wake. Around ten million years ago, during the Late Tertiary Period (11:58 pm on the geologic clock), the junction was due west of the southern Sierra, with the subducting slab of the Farallon Plate to its north. As the junction continued north, it closed the page on subduction in the region and introduced the new plate dynamic of ripping and stretching. Accordingly, the repression of the Sierran root was broken first in the south, and moved north following the migration of the triple junction. While researchers still work to unravel the mysteries of precisely what happened where and when, most studies agree that the major uplift of the Sierra occurred nine to ten million years ago, in accordance with the related junction migration and introduction of crustal expansion to the region.

By the close of the Miocene epoch, five million years ago (11:59 pm on the geologic clock), the Sierra Nevada was a broad, plateau-like range with little vertical relief. The average elevation of the range was greater than that of today, although the maximum elevation was lower, and the range lacked its characteristic jagged peaks and deeply incised valleys. In physical appearance, the range must have looked much like the present day White-Inyo Range to the east.

Although raised, the uplift of the range was far from complete. The question remains: how did the Sierra Nevada take on its present day size and shape?

Stage V: Fire and Ice

Recent Geologic Activity

Three million years ago marked a great change for the still rising Sierra Nevada. It was then that glaciers first covered the range. The coming of the ice was itself linked to geologic phenomena all across the globe, which are further discussed below, in the context of climate change. In short, these changes brought on a cooling period that delivered the planet out of the warm-wet Cretaceous period and into the icebox of the Late Pliocene and Pleistocene epochs. The Sierra Nevada were repeatedly inundated with glaciers throughout this time.

Several major advances occurred during the Pleistocene epoch, separated by recessional stages during which the climate was markedly warmer. These advances included, from oldest to most recent, the Deadman Pass (during the Pliocene epoch), McGee, Sherwin, Casa Diablo, Mono Basin, Tahoe, Tenaya, Tioga, and Hilgard glaciations. Other sources assert that, while all nine of these stages may or may not be evidenced on the east-side of the Sierra, the west slope only shows reliable evidence for three stages: pre-Tahoe, Tahoe, and Tioga. The Hilgard stage is currently thought to be a recessional stage of the Tioga glaciation), the evidence for a Tenaya glaciation questionable, and the ambiguous Deadman Pass, McGee, Sherwin, Casa Diablo, and Mono Basin are skeptically lumped together as "pre-Tahoe." Other sources have asserted that the Mono Basin and Tahoe

glaciations are the same, based on similarities in soil development and weathering rates on both Mono Basin and Tahoe
deposits in the moraines of Bloody Canyon.

Despite controversy over the particulars of advances and
retreats, most sources agree that maximum glaciation occurred
from 60,000 to 20,000 years ago, during the Tahoe, Tenaya, and
Tioga glaciations. During this time the Sierra Nevada were
covered with an ice cap up to 4,000 feet thick, and a maximum
of 275 miles long, stretching from the Feather River in the north
to the upper Kern River in the south. The ice seldom reached
beyond the mountain front, except in the Bridgeport Valley
and Mono Basin to the east, which were glaciated during times
of heavy ice.

For over three million years, the glaciers plucked, scraped,
scoured, and carried away thousands of cubic kilometers of
material, working in conjunction with rockfalls and slides,
patiently sculpting the glacial landscape of today's Alpine Sierra.
As the glaciers cut up the mountains, transported glacially excavated and rockfall debris to the flanks of the range, and eventually themselves melted, the range bobbed up in isostatic
response to the dramatic decrease in above-surface material,
causing the most recent uplift of the Sierra Nevada. Although
the mean elevation of the range had been reduced by glacial
erosion, the maximum elevation increased through local isostatic
compensation. The topography of the range was dramatically
changed from a more even plateau-like landscape, to a jagged
expanse of high, vertical peaks and deep trough-like valleys.
The tilt to the west was amplified by these processes, as the
eastern crest experienced the most glacial erosion and thus
the most local isostatic compensation, while the west slope
received the additional weight of the glacial deposits and
no isostatic compensation. The Sierra Nevada continues to

seek isostatic equilibrium even today, rising at a rate of a hundred to 650 feet per million years.

In the shady recesses of the northeast-facing slopes of the Alpine Sierra Nevada are small glaciers. These glaciers, called glacierettes, are not remnants of the vast ice cap that once covered the range. They are more recent arrivals. Since the retreat of the last great glaciers 10,000 to 15,000 years ago, the climate has continued to fluctuate, though seemingly not as dramatically as during the Pleistocene, resulting in several advances and retreats. Following the Tioga and Hilgard glaciations, a climatic optimum of relatively warm average temperatures was reached worldwide, during which all the glaciers in the Sierra Nevada were completely melted. This period lasted from 7,000 to 2,600 years ago. Following the climatic optimum were alternating periods of cooling and warming, until around the year 1300 A.D., when things cooled sufficiently for new glaciers to form in the high mountain cirques left by the glaciers of the Pleistocene. This "Little Ice Age" lasted until around 1750 A.D., when the climate again warmed and the new glaciers receded. Since 1750 alternating periods of cooling and warming have occurred and the glacierettes of the Alpine Sierra have advanced and receded accordingly.

About the same time that glaciers began their work on the Sierra, volcanic activity resumed in the east-central part of the range. This activity, which continues to present day, has resulted in a stunning array of volcanic landforms east of the Sierran crest. Such extensive volcanism was the result of the thinner crust of the stretched and down-dropped eastern blocks, which allowed mantle heat to seep up, seeking structural weaknesses in the crust and extruding through faulted areas. This dynamic also resulted in the abundant hot springs along the east-side.

The eruptions of this new Basin and Range-type volcanism

began as basalt flows originating from vents at Cowtrack Mountain, to the east of the Sierra Nevada. The subsurface basaltic magma chamber melted the surrounding continental rock, thus adding it to the mix. Gradually the mix became less and less dense, turning to rhyolitic magma. Eruptions could not extrude the material as fast as it was building up, and the pressure increased. The eruptions culminated 700,000 years ago in a massive rhyolitic explosion from Glass Mountain, east of the crest. This eruption literally turned the region of today's Long Valley inside-out, emptying the magma chamber and collapsing the land into the new void. The explosion sent an incinerating cloud thirty miles southward toward Owens Valley, destroying everything in its path. Over 150 cubic miles of ash was blasted into the atmosphere and surrounding area with temperatures exceeding 2,300 degrees Fahrenheit. As the cloud settled, the superheated material within it fell to the earth and fused together, forming welded tuff. This tuff blanketed the Long Valley in 3,000 feet of ash. A surrounding area of 350 square miles was covered with a layer 600 feet thick, forming the wide tableland of the Bishop Tuff, extending south from Glass Mountain to just north of the town of Bishop. Other traces of ash from the explosion have been found as far away as Nebraska. Some sources suggest that the Long Valley eruption coincided with a pronounced period of subsidence of the eastern blocks, both the Owens Valley to the south and Mono Basin to the north.

Subsequent eruptions occurred around 600,000 years ago around the Mammoth Lakes area. Basalt flows, originating from vents along the San Joaquin River, blocked the river's eastward drainage and diverted it to the west. This basalt cooled fast and uniformly, resulting in the stunning columns of Devil's Postpile. Mammoth Mountain began to rise 400,000 years ago, a huge volcano perched atop older layers of volcanic material, constantly blowing up and covering the surrounding area with debris. Within the last 100,000 years, a new magma chamber, similar to that of Long Valley, has formed beneath the Mono Basin. Eruptions have occurred regularly since then, forming the Inyo and Mono Craters, among countless other geologic features east of the Sierra Nevada.

Since the retreat of the major glaciers around 10,000 to 15,000 years ago, the Sierra Nevada has continued its trend of frequent and extraordinary geologic activity. Glacierettes continue to advance and recede in the Alpine Sierra as climatic conditions continue to fluctuate. Mammoth Mountain sends wisps of steam curling from its flanks, evidence of the continuance of volcanic activity that was its genesis. Further east, Mono Lake bubbles as the magma beneath it seeks the surface. Hot springs well up from the grabens of Long and Owens Valleys. In 1872, an earthquake rocked the Owens Valley, uplifting the eastern mountain front thirteen feet and moving it twenty feet laterally. The quake woke up John Muir, hundreds of miles away in Yosemite, who reveled in such a grand shaking of the earth.

The Sierra Nevada is still in the making. From the slow accumulation of sediments in the Paleozoic to the Sierran Arc and batholith formation of the Mesozoic; from the stretching of the continent to the rise of the Sierra Nevada; all through time the land has been living and changing, growing, evolving. If we could live life at the pace of rocks, we might see the greater changes in action. For now, we must be content with the subtle evolution before us: the falling snow, the slow grind of ice, the rush of a May creek, the summer freezing and thawing, dust particles in an autumn wind.

Etchings on the Great Stone Tablet
Alpine Geomorphology

"And in the development of these [mountains, domes, canyons, ridges, etc.] nature chose for a tool not the earthquake or lightning to rent and split asunder, not the stormy torrent or eroding rain, but the tender snow-flowers noiselessly falling through innumerable centuries, the offspring of the sun and sea. Laboring harmoniously in united strength they crushed and ground and wore away the rocks in their march, making vast beds of soil, and at the same time developed and fashioned the landscapes into the delightful variety of hill and dale and lordly mountain that mortals call beauty."

John Muir

Inside the Lyell Glacier bergschrund. Photo: David Gilligan

The Lyell Glacier

Six-thirty in the morning, and the air temperature is just below freezing. I push my head out of the hood of my sleeping bag and look out across the upper Lyell Basin. It is September, and this place is like an undulating stage standing high above the forested canyon below. Devoid of trees, it bears the tough skin and bones of a landscape that has been ravaged and torn, reshaped, and reborn. Rounded boulders the size of Volkswagen beetles are scattered across the polished granitic floor like over-sized dinosaur eggs, conspicuously darker in color than rock of the basin. I breathe in the cold morning air, rolling over like a contented cat to have a look behind me. The glacier looms like the last forgotten king of ages long past. It is worn and diminished, yet noble beyond words. It is tired and overcome, yet tenacious and indomitable. It echoes a time when ice ruled this place like an immortal Caesar, only to wane for reasons not fully understood, leaving this place forever changed. Arms of dark metavolcanic rock cleave the glacier in two. I specu-late that these are the origins of the suspicious boulders below, tumbled and rounded by the once larger glacier that carried them downslope and dropped them off as the ice retreated. The boulders are erratics: irregular; random; eccentric; queer. How else could they be after a thousand-year ride inside a river of ice?

A look back to the east reveals mid-level clouds, pink against the pale sky. A storm will come today, and the ice will be awakened, reminded that again it may grow.

Eleven others lie around the camp, nested into their sleeping bags, most of them content to sleep until the first rays of the sun strike this place and warm them. Only one stirs, and upon seeing him I become aware of the familiar smell of coffee. It is David Lovejoy, my co-instructor. The rest are Prescott College students, here to study alpine ecology where it should be taught: in the alpine zone. We have been traveling in the mountains together for two weeks now, looking at this small but captivating glacier from afar. Now we are going to go inside of the Lyell Glacier.

An hour and a half later, we stretch and warm our hamstrings up a thousand vertical feet of steep, broken sheets of granite, the long riser between our camp and the snout of the ice. On top, we step off the solid slabs and onto piles of loose, unsorted material. Rocks twice as big as a person are precariously perched atop and mixed in with rocks ranging from fist-size to fine gravel. This does not resemble the neat, sorted nature of material that was deposited by water. This kind of mess can't keep its secrets from the inquisitive. The glacier brought this here. The rocks lack sharp corners but are still blocky, telling us that they had only been inside the glacier long enough to polish off the major irregularities, and had not traveled the longer distance of the boulders below. Way down in the lowland foothills of the range, the rocks were still more rounded, pushed into piles by the huge glaciers of the Pleistocene, encased in ice over four thousand feet thick for thousands of years, and ground across bedrock for up to a hundred miles. Here we are but a mile from the head of the glacier, standing on top of the most recent heap of bulldozed rock, probably deposited a mere few hundred years ago.

After sweating our way up the tipping rocks, we finally set foot onto the old crunchy snow that is the surface of the glacier. Beneath this relatively thin veneer is rock-hard glacial ice, made of that magical, enticing substance called water, one of the only substances on earth that can be found naturally occurring in all three states: liquid, solid, and vapor. The ice sends rills of meltwater downslope, gurgling against stone that is unlikely to melt so easily. The clouds billow in the western sky amidst an atmosphere of nitrogen and oxygen that alone can not achieve a solid state. I think of the places these grains of firnified snow have been, from oceans to clouds to quietly falling snow, and the places they may go. I hope that they will stay right here for a while, become a part of this reservoir of moving ice.

We kick steps up the hard morning snow, given dramatic surface relief by months of wind and meltoff. Suncups over a meter in depth are separated by hogbacked ridges of ice-crusted snow, like miniature mountain ranges turned on end. The texture makes for easier footing, as we trudge upward towards the Lyell-McClure col. Convection cells pump up dark clouds from the west, adding to whatever moisture some distant, dying tropical storm is throwing at us from the south. The clouds build quickly over the mountain crest, obscuring the deep blue with an ominous slate gray. Upon reaching the col, our facial expressions reveal the collective consciousness we are all sharing: the realization of the possibility of being snowed off the mountain.

The west side of the col drops off suddenly to sheer, precipitous cliffs plummeting down to the Hutchings Creek drainage below. Although the stone bears no living ice, every subtlety and nuance of the landscape bares testimony to a long history of heavy glaciation. Every mountain flank tells the tale of innumerable glaciers growing headwardly, eroding away at the resistant granitic rock, plucking off chunk after chunk of stone and replacing it with ice, undermining the side of the mountain until piece by piece the wall is wedged apart by water seeping into minute cracks, freezing, expanding, and popping off blocks of the mountain to be dropped onto or into the glacial ice and slowly carried away to some balmy distant valley. Slowly, the glaciers back into one another as both glaciers gnaw away at opposite sides of a ridge. The result is spectacular, deeply incised fangs of rock pointing skyward as gnashing sawtoothed ridges. Eventually, continued erosion allows the heads of the opposing glaciers to join, carving a low sag in the spiny ridge just like where we are standing, a col between high points. Once upon a time, the Lyell and Hutchings Creek glaciers met here for an icy kiss. Broken chunks of granite are all that stand here now.

The clouds continue to build, seemingly from all directions now. I imagine what it would be like if it just kept on falling, snow on the mountains for day after week after month after year. Three million years ago it did just that, until the entire Sierra Nevada, like so many other mountains of the middle latitudes, grew an ice cap that extended over a hundred miles in length and over fifty miles in width. For three million years the ice reigned supreme, covering the mountains and cutting them up, redistributing their broken pieces in the wide valleys below. Although these glacial advances occurred in pulses and were interspersed with warmer interglacial periods, for three million years the ice returned, dominating the landscape, dominating the times, spanning the Pleistocene epoch and leaving the signs of their presence across the land. The signs spell out quite clearly: "ICE AGE."

During those times the slate was wiped clean. Not only was

the landscape reshaped, but almost all life was pushed out. Thick soils were scraped up and carried away along with what ever plants grew there, and whatever animals lived there. It was close to total annihilation. The hardiest plants sought refuge on the high summits that stood above the ice as isolated islands. Only the fittest made it through such an evolutionary bottleneck. The rest got squeezed out, and left no trace of their coming.

Like the Alps of Chamonix or the Bugaboos of British Columbia, but with far, far more ice, the Sierra Nevada stood encased in the Pleistocene's best. Huge valley glaciers like those of Alaska or Greenland flowed out of the western front and into the foothills, terminating in spreading lobes among what are now rolling, grassy, oak-spattered hills. To the east, glaciers issuing forth into the Mono Basin terminated directly into the churning waters of the larger Pleistocene Mono Lake, calving off icebergs into what are now briny desert waters. The ice grew, extending at times to over 275 miles in length, from the Feather River Canyon in the north all the way into the Kern River Canyon to the south. Then, ten thousand years ago, it was gone.

Slowly the glaciers pulled back, revealing a new land. Twice, at least, they hesitated in their retreat as things got slightly cooler, but inevitably the warming trend continued. As the glaciers drew back, they melted off in an angry flood of outwash and sediment, reluctantly dropped erratic boulders out of their dying ice, filled in the slightest basin or depression with cold, icy water, and left. Eventually things got so warm that every last mountain glacier in the middle latitudes disappeared. The sun shone and melted ice, raising sea levels. People who had endured the ice as far back as they could remember figured out how to grow crops, and populations boomed. The formerly glaciated lands of the north began a slow, steady process of soil development. It was a time of plenty. Humans by foot,

Lyell Glacier. Photo: David Gilligan

beast, or boat set out to explore the world.

In the summer of 985 A.D., Eric the Red of Iceland set sail across the North Atlantic for the far shores of a rumored land to the west. After a harrowing journey across the Atlantic, he and a few hundred brave souls, along with livestock and provisions, set foot on the green, fertile soils of a northern land that resembled in so many ways their own homeland. Here, in the land now called Greenland, they settled into a simple but productive agrarian lifestyle, raising sheep and cattle and producing cheese, butter, and even grain. The settlers kept close ties with Iceland,

and trade with the motherland was a regular affair.

As the Greenland settlements prospered, the first reports of
ice floating on the ocean waters were made. The ice thickened.
Trade routes to the colonies were rearranged until eventually
the troublesome waters could no longer be negotiated. Cut off
from the rest of the world, the four thousand Greenlanders
watched their environment slowly turn to ice. Snow fell upon
the land as the air grew cold. Crops failed as permafrost
crept into the soil and spread like a disease. By the late 1400's,
most of the settlers had died and were encased in the frozen
earth, wrapped in their cloaks and shrouds. All over the world
new mountain glaciers were born and grew in the old cirques
of the Pleistocene. European farming villages in the Alps were
swallowed whole as the ice flowed downslope. The continental
ice sheets swelled, gained momentum, and advanced. In the
Sierra Nevada, the Lyell Glacier matured and went to work,
depositing new material at the base of the cirque. Since 1750
things have warmed up a bit, and no one knows for sure
what will happen next. I look down the broad white apron to
where I had stood an hour before, down to the unsorted mess
of rock and debris at the snout of the glacier. The Little Ice Age
did that. There will be more.

The sound of thunder echoes through the mountains. Once,
twice, and again the sky speaks. Then the snow begins to fall.
We opt to traverse the glacier below the bergschrund, the yawning
crevasse at its head, and try to work our way up and into the
ice. David and I kick steps in the hardened surface and get out
onto the white, looking for a spot where the ice is exceptionally
torn wide open. Ben Nanson, a student of experience, joins us
to offer the descender a belay. We chop away at the stiff snow
to hard glacial ice, where David works in a fine titanium screw,
twirling the hanger around his finger with ease. As the screw

twists its way in, ice emerges from the hollow of the screw like an anxious glacial caterpillar. Ben clips in the rope and ties on a munter hitch. David cuts a few steps in the steep surface and ascends fifteen feet before dropping over the lip of the bergschrund and into a shallow cave. "Great camp spot here," he yells, "but it doesn't go anywhere. I'm going to try it on the left." As he begins his traverse over, I step into the cave.

A hundred or more stalactites of ice hang from the ceiling like glacial tentacles reaching down for a bottom. As I crawl into the space, a dozen or so smaller icicles break off and clink against my helmet. One lodges itself between my shoulders and my jacket, a two foot spear of ice gently sliding against me. This place is beautiful. The ice walls are barely blue. With some slight modifications we could fit four inside, all sitting upright comfortably. I sit awhile, watching snowy crystals fall in through the open window.

Emerging back out into the white world, I traverse over to the larger opening, where I can walk right in. All twelve of us can fit in here without even going down into the dark ice cave. Precarious ice bridges and heavily-laden overhangs extend threateningly over the deeper recesses of the crevasse, which itself has ripped open a thirty-foot deep incision into the ice. It looks enticing, deep, blue, totally foreign to my everyday above-surface experience. In places, the ice has formed like hundreds of variously shaped incandescent light bulbs embedded in a wall of ice. No moisture licks my fingertips. Soon the others enter. I probe around for a good place to sit. All are amazed, inspired, awestruck.

In time, we continue working our way across the bergschrund, setting screws and lines once more to lip-in to yet another opening. Different than the last, this part of the crevasse tells still more ice tales. The head of the glacier can actually be seen tearing away from the rock wall of Mt. Lyell. I imagine the rock beneath being quarried away, the mountain thinning under the fattening glacier. The ice is starkly foliated. It tells a story of many years, which I have no time to count, of snow falling and metamorphosing into glacial ice. Like bands of gneiss or schist, or sedimentary strata being laid down over time, the foliations swirl through the ice, transfixing my attention. Above it is a thick, hard layer of snow, which I gather to be last year's gargantuan El Niño snowpack. The surface layer is much thinner, this year's snow now mostly ablated away. The falling graupel casts a thin veneer over the whole picture, glazing the past with the present.

Lightning to the west repeats itself several times, tempting us to stay, urging us to delve deeper. Not today. We make preparations for our descent. One by one, we move down the apron of the glacier. I linger, and am the last to leave this place. I do not want to go.

In the falling snow I traverse back towards the col, staying close to the bottom lip of the bergschrund, but not too close. I make my way down the snow. Descending, I step over a dozen narrow crevasses no more than two feet wide. In a few of these I can see no bottom. This ice is alive, a solid but flowing river, ever replenished by the falling snow. It is coming down all over the mountains, perhaps the first of many that will again encase the mountains in ice.

Perhaps.

A classic crevasse on the McClure Glacier. Photo: David Gilligan

Living   Ice
Glacial Dynamics

The present-day landscape of the Alpine Sierra is the result of countless millions of years of geomorphic (earth-forming) processes. Tectonic action in combination with erosion, weathering, and mass wasting has produced a wide variety of landforms, each of which tells a different part of the larger story of the mountains. All of these processes continue to occur, scratching the stories of today into the stone of tomorrow. Of all the forces at work in the continual reshaping of the Alpine Sierra, it is the work of glaciers that has been celebrated most.

Until John Muir's discovery of a living glacier on the east flank of the Clark Range, many believed that the small glaciers of the Sierra Nevada were all snowfields, called perennial because they were seen to remain intact year-round. Today, hundreds of perennial snowfields dot the Alpine Sierra, in addition to the seventy glaciers that tenaciously remain. These two consolidations of snow and ice are often confused with one another, and indeed may often become one another, and yet are considered distinctly different things. This brings up the question: what is a glacier?

A simple definition states that glaciers are "masses of ice and granular snow formed by compaction and recrystallization of snow, lying largely or wholly on land and showing evidence of past or present movement." This concise definition points out the structure of a glacier: snow and granular ice, the process by which it is formed; compaction and re-crystallization, and how it functions within the greater landscape; by movement. All of these criteria are met by snowfields except for movement. Movement, then, is the single factor that distinguishes a glacier from a snowfield. While the snow and ice of a snowfield may remain year-round, it is stagnant, or "non-living." The glacier, on the other hand, is a dynamic body of "living ice."

The process of forming a glacier is dependent on low temperatures and ample precipitation. Temperatures must be at or below the freezing point long enough each year to prohibit excess melting. Precipitation must be abundant enough to exceed meltoff. During the Pleistocene epoch, the Sierra Nevada were situated perfectly for heavy glaciation. Their proximity to the maritime influences of the coast, in combination with high elevation and the lower temperatures of the Ice Age, resulted in greater amounts of glacial ice in the Sierra Nevada than any other area of comparable latitude in the United States. The Coast Ranges, in comparison, held relatively few glaciers. While their proximity to the sea meant higher amounts of precipitation, the mild maritime winters, in combination with their lower elevations, resulted in air temperatures that were not low enough to prevent excess meltoff. The Basin Ranges to the east held relatively few glaciers as well. The continental temperatures were cold enough and the mountains high enough, but the rising ranges were cut off from the moist maritime air by the great wall of the Sierra Nevada, and precipitation was barely enough to form glaciers.

As snow accumulates in a given area, crystals develop in response to compaction and freeze-melt cycles. Snow crystals begin in a myriad of shapes and sizes, each individual crystal unique in its structure and form. As their transformation into glacial ice begins, crystals have their edges rounded off, shapes condensed and compacted, until eventually they become firn (German), or névé (French): hard, coarse grains of old snow found at the surface of glaciers. Technically speaking, true firn is snow that has survived and metamorphosed over one full snow season, measured from October first of a given year to October first of the next. Gradually, these grains of firn melt and refreeze to form ice crystals, which grow in size, filling the space between them. Eventually, as a light, fluffy snowflake transforms into hard, cold glacial ice, its density increases to nine times that of the original snow. The time of conversion varies greatly according to temperatures and precipitation rates, averaging five years from snowflake to glacial ice.

Ice crystals are minerals, and a glacier, being an aggregate of such minerals, is a rock. If a glacier is a rock, then what type of rock is it? Some would say it is all three types: sedimentary, igneous, and metamorphic, all at once. As snow falls on the glacier, it falls in layers, or strata, as shown in firn banding, which represent the total strata of annual snowfall. These strata are compressed and cemented together, or lithified, just as sedimentary rocks are, to form glacial ice. As firn melts and refreezes to form ice crystals, it behaves as igneous rock, which also crystallizes out of melted material, or magma. Pressure from the overlying glacier, as well as movement, causes ice crystals to bend, deform, and recrystallize, just like metamorphic rock. The topmost layers of the glacier may be seen as sedimentary, the middle portion igneous, and the flowing, or deepest portion metamorphic.

As mentioned before, the seventy glaciers presently found in the Sierra Nevada are all remnants of the Little Ice Age, and do not have any continuity with those huge sheets of ice that inundated the range during the Pleistocene epoch. They

The Geothe Glacier. Photo: Martha McCord

are considered alpine glaciers, meaning that they are restricted to mountain regions. Other glacier types not restricted to mountain environments include larger piedmont glaciers, which form when mountain valley glaciers meet flowing downslope, and the great masses of continental glaciers, such as those of Antarctica.

Alpine glaciers can be further divided into cirque glaciers and valley glaciers. Valley glaciers were common in the Sierra Nevada during the Pleistocene, though none remain in the range today. Originating from higher cirques, these huge glaciers flowed down all sides of the range, virtually covering the Sierra in ice. Though these rivers of ice have left their marks on the mountains, they have long since melted off. All of the glaciers currently found in the Sierra are of the cirque-type, meaning that they are confined to the high-angle slopes of half-bowls carved out by larger glaciers of the past. These cirque glaciers typically hang at angles up to forty degrees and higher,

The Conness Glacier. Photo: David Gilligan

too steep even for talus to hold on. They are found on lee slopes between 10,600 feet and 13,200 feet, where prevailing winds blow snow into recesses, sheltered from the sun by the high walls of the mountains. The largest Sierran glacier is the Palisade Glacier, which at thirty-seven degrees north is also the southernmost in the United States. Its total area is half a square mile. Second to the Palisade is the Lyell Glacier, wrapping up the northeast side of the highest peak in Yosemite National Park. The glaciers extend north to Northern Yosemite, at thirty-eight degrees north. They are found (from south to north) on the Palisades, Mt. Goddard, the Glacier Divide, Mt. Humphreys, Mt. Abbot, the Ritter Range, Mt. Lyell, the Kuna Crest, Mt. Dana, Mt. Conness, and the Sawtooth Ridge, among others. Other Californian glaciers can be found north of the Sierra Nevada on Mt. Shasta, as well as two tiny glaciers in the Salmon-Trinity Alps.

All glacial movement is governed by gravity. The rate of movement may vary greatly according to the slope angle, temperature of both the air and ice, the bedrock topography and structure of the underlying landscape. Typically, mountain glaciers flow at a rate varying from ten to a thousand feet per year, translating roughly from a fraction of an inch to several feet per day. Movement is typically slow and gradual, not something to be witnessed in an hour's sitting. Occasionally, however, larger valley glaciers will surge, flowing up to a hundred feet per day. Such surges occur most often in response to climatic fluctuations, and probably were somewhat frequent in the Sierra Nevada during the Pleistocene. They are best documented today among the glaciers of coastal Alaska and the European Alps. The small glaciers found in the Alpine Sierra, however, also reflect climatic fluctuations, and are more sensitive to minute changes due to their small size. They may advance in some years, while in others they may recede, or experience no movement either way. Much of their movement can be attributed to the steepness of the slopes they inhabit. Glaciers move in a variety of different ways, including slip, shearing, and plastic flowage. Slip occurs commonly among temperate glaciers, where pressure from the overlying glacial mass, and/or heat from within the earth, causes the base of the glacier to melt. A thin layer of water results between the glacier and the bedrock, facilitating slippage downslope. When slip occurs along the base of the glacier, it is called basal slip. When it occurs along the sides, it is called marginal slip. Polar glaciers, such as those of Antarctica, are cold enough so that their bases are permanently frozen to the bedrock; thus slip is less prominent.

Stress put on glacial ice will cause it to respond in one of three ways. Short and strong stresses, such as the frequent earthquakes of California, will fracture ice along planes, resulting in shearing. Shearing occurs when sheets of ice move across other ice along these fractured planes, much like a stack of loose paper placed on an incline. Long, mild stresses, such as the continuous pull of gravity, will cause ice to deform. Ice may stretch elastically to accommodate the additional stress, or it may flow plastically, in a solid state, when the internal stress exceeds the elastic limit of the ice. Flowage occurs by granular and intergranular shifting, and continuous recrystallizing. The ice crystals glide along their hexagonal planes by melting and refreezing in response to differential pressure, slowly moving in the direction of gravity's pull. This transfers the glacial material downslope like a creeping river. Such flowage will increase as ice thickness and slope angle increase. Plastic flowage is the primary mechanism of movement for most larger glaciers, though it also occurs in smaller ones, such as those of the Alpine Sierra.

Glacial movement occurs differentially throughout the glacier. In general, the middle part of the glacier tends to move faster than the sides. Velocity also changes with depth, and as a glacier moves over varied topography, different parts of the glacier move at different rates. To flow over a hummock, for example, the glacier must accelerate and thin, just as a river accelerates and becomes more shallow as it moves over a boulder. The deepest ice responds to this by either elastic or plastic deformation, but the upper ice has much less pressure on it, and so can not deform, or metamorphose. The brittle ice cracks, forming deep crevasses in the surface of the glacier. Crevasses may well exceed a hundred feet in depth, though those of the present day Sierran glaciers are rarely so deep. For much of the year their yawning openings are covered with snow, necessitating skilled probing techniques, technical mountaineering skills, and knowledge of glacial dynamics among backcountry travelers.

Foliations along the back wall of a crevasse. Photo: David Gilligan

The most predictable location of crevasses is along the top, or head of the glacier, where the ice separates from the headwall of the cirque. These crevasses, called bergschrunds, are typical of all mountain glaciers, and can be a good indicator of whether a suspect snowfield is indeed a glacier or not. Most Sierran glaciers exhibit bergschrunds, and some particularly good examples can be seen on the Palisade Glacier, Goethe Glacier, Lyell Glacier, and Dana Glacier. Other crevasses most commonly form diagonally on the sides of a glacier, more or less parallel to one another, pointing toward the center of the glacier in the direction of flow. Still other crevasses occur above areas where the underlying canyon topography changes. In general, glaciers on smooth, even-gradient slopes will have much fewer crevasses than those on irregular, uneven-gradient slopes.

For a glacier to remain living ice it must maintain a positive economy, meaning that the process of replenishment, or accumulation exceeds the process of loss, or ablation, over time. Sources of accumulation include precipitation, wind drifted snow, and avalanched snow. Moist climates, such as maritime regions, receive the highest amounts of accumulation, while more arid continental regions receive relatively little. Ablation may occur through melting, sublimation and evaporation, and calving of ice from the snout, or terminal downslope end, of the glacier. The key factor in determining amounts of ablation is, of course, temperature.

All glaciers have a zone of accumulation, found at the upper end of the glacier where accumulation exceeds ablation, and a zone of ablation, at the lower part of the glacier, where ablation exceeds accumulation. These two zones are separated by a zone of equilibrium, often (and inaccurately) called a line. It is the location of this equilibrium zone that determines the position of the terminus of the glacier. A glacier is considered balanced when accumulation equals ablation over time, and the terminus remains stationary. A positive economy occurs when accumulation exceeds ablation, and the terminus advances. Accordingly, a negative economy occurs when ablation exceeds accumulation, and the terminus retreats.

Seasonally, the economy of a Sierran glacier fluctuates tremendously. The small size of the Sierran glaciers renders them particularly vulnerable to fluctuations in temperature and precipitation levels. Summer drought can put the tiny cirque glaciers into a negative economy that only needs to last a few years before turning the living ice into a stagnant snowfield. In contrast, a few winters of heavy precipitation can trigger significant advances. We can only speculate on what the future holds for the glaciers of the Alpine Sierra. The past, however, is as clearly etched in stone as we are prepared to decipher.

E t c h i n g s

Glacial Landforms

Throughout the Pleistocene, mountain cirque and valley glaciers covered the Sierran high country. From the Tahoe area south to the Kern River, glaciers coalesced to form a continuous cap, varying in length and width in accordance with climatic fluctuations. The Northern Sierra was usually too low to support anything but cirque glaciers. During the maximum ice of the Wisconsin glaciation however, the ice cap extended 275 miles from the Feather River all the way down to the Kern. The highest peaks and plateaus stood above the glaciers as islands in a sea of ice, called nunataks, after their present-day Alaskan counterparts. The huge valley glaciers that helped carve the canyons of the west slope rivers looked much like those of coastal Alaska, except that those in the Sierra terminated in the foothills, rather than the ocean. From the foothills, the outwash from these masses of ice slurried its way through the Central Valley and issued forth at the Golden Gate, just as the streams of the west slope do today. The longest of these glaciers was the Tuolumne Glacier. This massive valley glacier extended over sixty miles, flowing from its sources in the high elevations of Yosemite, downslope to around 2,000 feet in the rolling foothills. Other canyons of the west slope hosted glaciers of comparable size, including the Merced Glacier of Yosemite Valley. Some of these glaciers exceeded 4,000 in depth, overflowing their canyons and spilling ice onto the flatter rims around them. When such overflowing ice from different valleys converged, it formed a Mer de Glace (French for "Sea of Ice"), as occurred between the San Joaquin, Dinkey Creek, and North Fork of the Kings River drainages.

To the east, the glaciers were truncated by the abrupt slope of the escarpment, averaging ten miles in length, and seldom reaching beyond the mountain front. In the Mono Basin however, glaciers emitting from Lee Vining, Gibbs, Bloody, and Parker Canyons calved chunks of ice directly into the waters of the Pleistocene Mono Lake. The lake level itself is believed to have been as high as 7,140 feet, 800 feet higher than its modern level. During these times Mono Lake was high enough to drain east and south, into what was then Lake Manning, now Death Valley. Such fluctuations coincided with the Ice Age Lake Lahonton, of which Pyramid and Walker Lakes and the Carson Sink are remnants, and Lake Bonneville, of which the Great Salt Lake is a remnant.

Only the land remains to tell us the story of these glaciers. It is written in two ways, each telling only a part of the whole story. First, we can look for what the glaciers took away from the land, leaving behind eroded landscapes such as topographic forms with grooved and polished rock surfaces. These erosional landforms are reflective of the nature and intensity of glaciation, the number of glacial epochs, and the nature of the bedrock. Secondly, we can look for where the glaciers put what they took, leaving behind depositional landscapes of ice-borne debris. In uncovering the glacial history of a region, it is the depositions that are looked at most closely. These are dated by Carbon-14 method, only effective on organic debris less than 40,000 years old, the degree of weathering on deposited rocks, soil development within depositions, and relationship with both younger and older strata. For example, if a glacial deposit overlays a lava flow dated at 3.2 million years, such as occurs near the town of Bishop, but another lava flow dated at 700,000 years overlays the glacial debris, then it can be concluded that the debris is between 3.2 million and 700,000 years old.

The glacial chronology of the Sierra Nevada begins around three million years ago, during the Late Pliocene epoch, and coincides closely with that of the continental ice sheets.

The Deadman Pass, McGee, and Sherwin glaciations coincide with the Nebraskan glaciation of the continent. The Casa Diablo coincides roughly with the Kansan, and the Mono Basin with the Illinoian. Considering the Sierra Nevada, these five separate glaciations are lumped together by some as simply "pre-Tahoe," on the basis of a lack of evidence showing their autonomy, or in some cases even their existence. The Tahoe, Tenaya (also questionable) and Tioga glaciations correspond with the Wisconsin, being the last glacial period of the Pleistocene epoch. Recent glaciations, including the Hilgard, Recess Peak, and Matthes advances, have all occurred during the Holocene epoch, which we are now in, and are collectively called neoglacial. Of these, the Hilgard and Recess Peak are questioned as being recessional stages of the Tioga advance. The Matthes advance corresponds to the Little Ice Age.

We arrive in the present landscape of the Alpine Sierra at an especially remarkable time. The big glaciers are gone, opening up the alpine country for inhabitation by countless manifestations of life, humans not the least of these. But the jagged topography, high relief, and thousands of crystalline lakes remain as post-glacial testimony to a rich heritage of ice. It is a precarious time, when the mystery remains as to when things will cool off once again and send the glaciers flowing down from their high cirques, or if the air will warm, the glaciers melt, and the trees begin to march up the sides of the mountains. Today, every point and curve of the Alpine Sierran landscape is tribute to the legacy of the glaciers, a legacy long in the making, and strong in the telling.

Most of the prominent landforms of the Alpine Sierra are the result, at least in part, of glacial erosion. Glaciers erode the land by abrasion, quarrying, and pushing. Abrasion is the result of rock material embedded in the glacial ice wearing away at the underlying surface. Fine particles in the ice tend to polish rock surfaces, while larger debris digs in more significantly. The particles themselves are also polished and striated in this process. Quarrying occurs when the base of the glacier plucks rocks loose from the underlying surface by thawing and refreezing water in joints and minute cracks of the rock. When the infiltrated water freezes it expands, bursting the rock apart. This process is called frost-riving, or frost-wedging, and is one of the main agents of weathering in high mountains. Quarried rocks are pushed along with the glacier or frozen into it. Pushing occurs when debris is pushed along the terminus, scouring as it moves along.

The very cirques that glaciers inhabit are formed in part by glacial erosion. As meltwater from snow and firn is released, freezing and thawing breaks the underlying rock apart. This quarrying eventually undermines the cirque's headwall, which itself falls or slides, usually onto the glacier, to be transported slowly downslope. In this way the cirque erodes in a headward direction, patiently carving away at the mountain. Many cirques have an icy-cold glacial lake, called a tarn, nestled in the bottom of their bowls, held in by the threshold at the down-valley edge of the cirque. Such tarns are often frozen well into the summer months, and in some years they are never free of ice. Cirques and tarns can be seen throughout the Alpine Sierra, along the flanks of nearly every mountain of the high country.

The varied types of erosional landforms found at the highest elevations of the alpine zone are the results of different degrees of erosion. Often cirques on either side of a mountain will experience headward erosion to the extent that they back into one another. This results in a serrated knife-edge that forms the top of both of the opposing headwalls, called an arete. Aretes vary greatly in size, ranging from feet to miles in length. Some exceptional examples of larger aretes in the Alpine Sierra include the Sawtooth Ridge of Northern Yosemite, Koip Crest, the Minarets of the Ritter Range, and the Kaweah Crest, among others. When cirques experience headward erosion to the extent that they destroy part of the arete, a gap, or sag, is formed in the ridge; and the resulting notch is called a col. Most passes in the Alpine Sierra are cols. Continued erosion of several glaciers can wear a ridge down to single peak, typically conical or pyramidal in shape, called a horn. Horns often will have aretes running down their flanks. A classic horn of the Alpine Sierra is Matterhorn Peak.

Moving downslope to where cirque glaciers once converged, the landforms become less angular and less vertical. What may have been a stepped topography prior to glaciation was accentuated by glacial scouring of the bedrock. It may be, however, that the glaciers themselves carved these giant staircases in response to differential resistance of the bedrock, resulting in an undulating topography. The staircases are made up of nearly horizontal sections, called treads, and more vertical sections, called risers. Treads indicate more resistant bedrock, too tough for the glacier to cut into. They may span anywhere from less than a hundred to several thousand feet. Risers indicate less resistant bedrock, which the glacier was able to cut into more readily. They may be anywhere from a few feet to several hundred in height. At the top of each riser along the downstream edge of each tread is a small hump, or knob of rock, called a riegal. Riegals often hold in lakes, one in each tread, strung together like beads by the thread of a gracefully cascading stream. For this reason, such lakes are called paternoster lakes, after the beads of a rosary. Glacial staircases with associated paternoster lakes are most common in the higher elevations of the Alpine Sierra, where temperatures are low and decomposition rates slow, allowing lakes to persist for tens of thousands of years. At lower elevations, lakes may have filled in, forming meadows with meandering streams along the treads, often with fantastic high volume waterfalls on the risers. Good examples of alpine glacial staircases can be seen by following most drainages from below treeline to the cirques of the highest peaks. Some great places to do this are French Canyon to Goethe Glacier, Woods Creek to Pinchot Pass, Evolution Valley to Muir Pass, or just about anywhere in the alpine country. The archetypal lower elevation staircase is that of the Merced River, from the floor of Yosemite Valley up to Merced Lake.

All along the glacial staircase is further evidence of glaciers at work. In some areas the granitic bedrock has been polished to a hard sheen by tiny particles within the glacier. A product of fine abrasion, such glacial polish can be a joy to the senses, smooth to the fingers as glass, almost shimmering in the late afternoon light. The bedrock may also exhibit chattermarks, crescent-shaped gouges in the rock, pointing in the direction of the glacier's flow. These are formed by the impact pressure imposed on the bedrock by rocks and boulders transported in the ice. Chattermarks may occur singly, or more often in sets, or lines, indicating forward movement of debris in accordance with glacial flow. Scratches and grooves are common in all glaciated areas, forming lines and indentations in bedrock, the result of abrasion. Polish, chattermarks, scratches, and grooves are widespread throughout the Alpine Sierra, and are especially evident in areas with abundant exposed granite, such as Evolution Basin. One doesn't have to look far for such areas because over half the Alpine Sierra is exposed rock!

Down below the trees you can find still more erosional landforms. Rocky outcrops along the glacial floor may become smoothed on their upstream side by abrasion, and irregular on their downstream side from quarrying. These are called roches moutonées, or rock sheep. Many believe Lembert Dome and Liberty Cap to be gigantic examples of such landforms. Lower still, where the mountain streams of today's Alpine Sierra converge with the main river channels of the greater Sierra Nevada, the glaciers of the Pleistocene converged to form the huge valley glaciers of the range. These valley glaciers scooped out the "V" shaped valleys of the unglaciated canyons, widening their bottoms and steepening their walls. Smaller side canyons that before glacial times flowed down the slopes of these "V" shaped canyons were truncated by the erosional forces of the valley glaciers, forming today's hanging valleys. Where once the glaciers of these tributary drainages flowed into the upper portions of the larger valley glaciers, today their streams free-fall down the steepened walls of the main canyons, forming leaping waterfalls which eventually feed their master streams. Yosemite Valley has long been hailed as the archetype of such glacial valleys, remarkably "U" shaped, with famously high waterfalls issuing forth from its many hanging valleys. Yosemite, however, is the exception and not the norm. Most glaciated valleys do not exhibit such flat floors and vertical walls, but rather have rounded "V" shaped profiles, modified by glaciers but not recreated by them. The degree to which the profile of a particular canyon has been modified depends, in part, on the volume of the glacier and the resistance of the underlying bedrock.

Thus far we have focused our attention on erosional landforms, as they are frequently the most obvious in alpine landscapes. Often less noticeable are those landforms that are the result of deposition. Glacial deposits occur in a variety of forms, from the smallest grain of rock-powder to boulders as big as a house. All material transported and deposited by glacial ice, meltwater streams, and floating ice is considered glacial drift. Material transported and deposited by glacial ice itself does not get stratified, organized according to its size and density, because it is suspended in a solid matrix, rather than liquid. This unstratified drift is called till, the most common form of deposition associated with glaciers. Till is typically a jumbled mess of boulders, sand, rocks, and clay. When it is deposited on the bottom of a glacier it is compacted and plastered over the underlying surface by the weight of the moving ice. When exposed, this lodgement till will often have rocks and pebbles that are aligned in the direction of the glacier's flow. Most till, however, is not deposited in this way, but is rather dropped out of the glacier when thinning or melting occurs, forming long hills of ablation till called moraines.

Moraines are the most common and obvious depositional landforms. There are several different types, based on when and where the till was deposited. Lateral moraines are deposited at the sides, or margins, of the glacier, often forming long even ridges. Lateral moraines only form downstream from a glacier's equilibrium zone, and so the upper limit of a lateral moraine may be used to determine the equilibrium zone at the time of deposition. Medial moraines are deposited in the middle of a glacier and indicate the convergence of two formerly separate glaciers. End moraines are deposited at the terminus of the glacier. As the glacier advances and recedes it will deposit several of these. The end moraine which marks the greatest advance of a glacier is called the terminal moraine. All end moraines upstream from this are called recessional moraines. Often lateral and end moraines are connected, forming horse-shoe-shaped outlines of the glacier's recessional stages, enclosing one another, indicating the shrinkage of the glacier.

The best examples of large moraines can be found well below the Alpine Sierra, where the glaciers of the Pleistocene epoch terminated at the foot of the mountains. These moraines are most visible on the arid east side, where trees do not obscure the lay of the land. All of the canyons of the east side, from the Bridgeport Valley south, exhibit lateral and end moraines, clearly indicating the recession of the glaciers over the ages. Some of the best examples are at the mouths of Parker, Bloody, Lee Vining, and Lundy Canyons, all of which drain into the Mono Basin, and McGee and Convict Creek Canyons to the south. Moraines found in the Alpine Sierra are mostly post-Pleistocene. Those found in the higher cirques of the range downstream from the modern Sierran glaciers indicate the maximum advance of the Little Ice Age, as well as more subtle recessional stages. Other moraines in the high country are scattered and hard to recognize, and may indicate recessional stages of the Tioga glacial period. End moraines will often dam up meltwater, forming large moraine-dammed lakes, such as Twin Lakes, June Lake, Convict Lake, and Walker Lake.

Glaciers move like bulldozers across landscapes, clearing away evidence of previous activity and dumping new evidence wherever they go. Patterns among moraines can tell us much about the glacial history of an area. End moraines upstream are always younger than those downstream. Moraines enclosed within others are always younger than the outer moraines.

Glacial polish with striations. Photo: David Gilligan

Overlaying moraines are younger than those they cut across.
All three of these topographic criteria are exhibited by moraines
in Bloody Canyon, where two sets cross in a perpendicular
fashion. The underlying lateral moraines run northwest-southeast, and have no terminal moraine that connects them. These
are believed to be deposited during the Mono Basin glaciation
of 130,000 years ago, when glaciers calved off directly into a
huge Pleistocene Mono Lake, which explains the lack of a
terminal moraine. The overlying moraines of Bloody Canyon
are more prominent. They run southwest-northeast, and have
only the edges of a terminal moraine. These were deposited

during the Tahoe Glaciation of 60,000 to 75,000 years ago, when the glaciers barely reached the lake. Within this moraine are at least two recessional end moraines, deposited during the more recent (and less extensive) Tenaya and Tioga glacial advances.

In addition to the above-mentioned criteria, older moraines will tend to be more degraded than younger ones, show more evidence of weathering, and have greater soil development, thus more vegetation. These last three factors rarely apply to moraines in the higher elevations of the Alpine Sierra, where processes contributing to soil development are incredibly slow relative to the lowlands. Little Ice Age moraines, even after 150 years, rarely show evidence of any soil development at all.

Other depositional landforms include erratics and perched boulders. Erratics are rocks, often huge boulders, that are dropped far away from their place of origin by receding glaciers. They are most noticeable when their color or type of rock differs from that upon which they sit. Not all erratics are deposited by glaciers, however. Every winter tons of rock material falls onto the Sierran snowpack, often rolling some distance downslope before coming to a halt. With the spring thaw these rocks are dropped to the ground, dotting meadows, perching on ledges, sometimes even coming to rest in the branches of dwarfed trees and shrubs. Erratics, large and small, litter the alpine landscape like herds of sheep. Almost any rock you see that is not attached to its surroundings probably came from elsewhere. If its edges are rounded, you can bet it spent some time inside a glacier. A particularly good spot to see erratics is Humphreys Basin, where the broad alpine basins are like huge platters covered with thousands of glacial treats. Large erratics, when more resistant to erosion than underlying rock, will serve as a hard cap, protecting the rock just beneath them from degradation while all around the local rock weathers away. This results in a perched boulder, or table rock, jutting out precariously from the surrounding stone.

Rock material may also be transported and deposited by water, and even wind. Such material can only remain suspended if the water or air continues to move fast enough to prevent gravity from drawing it back down to ground level. For example, an early summer alpine stream swollen with meltwater will move fast and have a high volume relative to other times of the year. In addition to this, the stream will move more swiftly over terrain with a high gradient, over or around obstacles, and through narrower sections of its stream channel. High volume and velocity will enable a stream to transport larger material, such as rocks and boulders. These will be the first to drop out if volume and/or velocity decrease, followed by rocks, pebbles, sand, and eventually clay, thus resulting in stratification. In this way, material transported by water and wind becomes stratified drift.

Fluvial sediments are deposited by meltwater streams, and may include rocks, gravel, sand, and even silt. They tend to be larger upstream, and increasingly finer as you move downstream. These are best seen in outwash plains extending in valleys beyond terminal moraines. They may also form eskers or kame terraces. Eskers are well stratified ridges of sand and gravel, deposited by streams flowing in tunnels actually within stagnant ice. Kame terraces are mounds of poorly sorted material which form ridges along the edges of glaciers, deposited by streams running at the edges of the ice. These are indicative of the girth of the glacial mass at the time of deposition.

Lacustrine sediments, deposited by lakes, are rarely seen except by those whose research brings them to lake-bottoms. These fine sediments are laid down every year as agitation of the lake water is quelled by surface freezing. The coarser sediments

A little ice age moraine at the snout of Kuna Glacier. The pea soup-colored tarn is due to tiny metavolcanic particles suspended in the water. Photo: David Gilligan

are deposited in summer, and the finer sediments in winter, resulting in a neat stratification of annual layers. Coring into these sediments gives researchers clues to past depositional rates and climate fluctuations. Pollen blown onto the surface of the lake settles with lacustrine sediments, also providing clues to the past floras of alpine regions. Aeolean sediments, such as the wind-blown silt called loess, are picked up by wind as they blow across outwash plains, and redeposited by the wind in other areas.

Other glacial landforms found in the Alpine Sierra, neither erosional or depositional in nature, are rock glaciers. Areas not presently cold or wet enough for true glaciers to form may host rock glaciers. These corrugated masses of ice and angular rock are shaped and move like true glaciers, but may be more rock than ice. A recent study investigated whether the ice in these rock glaciers is primarily glacial or post-glacial. All rock glaciers are actually part of a continuum of glacier types ranging from bare-ice glaciers to debris-covered, ice-cored glaciers, to ice-cemented rock glaciers. The main distinctions among these types are in the ratios of debris to ice. The study found that valley-floor rock glaciers are rather ice-cored, and the ice is glacial in origin, while valley-wall rock glaciers are ice-cemented, the ice being post-glacial in origin. Although common belief holds that the ice in rock glaciers has its origins in permafrost, the Sierra Nevada have none of the features indicative of modern permafrost. It appears that the ice originates from snow and ice that is buried in rockfall, as well as some input from refrozen precipitation. Many Little Ice Age moraines have been found with cores of ice, suggesting a transitional stage between moraines and active debris-covered glaciers. Such debris may actually insulate a glacier, allowing its ablation zone to extend to lower elevations than equivalent bare-ice glaciers, and may persist long after climatic changes have thinned or destroyed bare glacial ice. Good examples of rock glaciers can be seen on the South Fork of Big Pine Creek, Sherwin Canyon, and Mt. Tom.

Glaciers affect different landscapes in different ways. Thus far we have looked at the glaciers and the etchings they have left behind. We turn now to the tablets themselves, upon which the ice has wrought its stories. We will see how the nature of stone can vary greatly, and how two landscapes with similar histories may tell that tale in drastically different ways.

T a b l e t s

Rocks of the Alpine Sierra

Hiking north along the John Muir Trail, the gray-white splintered peaks, carved and sharpened into cirques, aretes, cols, and horns, seem the very essence of the Alpine Sierra. The glacial staircases, polish, and paternoster lakes become expected familiarities in this bright land. Surely without these, the High Sierra would not be what it is. But the Sierra Nevada is all this and more. Ascending Glenn Pass, the colorful stripes of the Painted Lady come into view. The next day you are baffled by the seemingly martian landscape of Pinchot Pass, and a week later, confused by the crunchy light-gray pebbles along the trail on the approach to Red's Meadow. Though it's difficult to be sure, massive Banner Peak seems too dark to be Sierran. At Tuolumne Meadows, you resupply and decide to continue on the Pacific Crest Trail to Sonora Pass. Things are getting better and better, and you don't want to miss what's up around the bend. For a few days it's back to the familiar granite. Then, the day you cross the northern border of Yosemite, the granite monoliths and countless lakes are overrun by deep brown and gray heaps of angular rock. Ascending Leavitt Ridge, it feels more like the Cascades. The high ridgeline drops to long, steady slopes of endless scree. You look hard, but can't find a single rock bigger than yourself. In the distance, are the Sweetwaters, looking unexpectedly pale bluish-gray, even pink in some places, as if blanketed in heaping layers of ash.

Granite, the common term used to refer to intrusive igneous, or granitic rocks, is undoubtedly the characteristic rock of the Sierra Nevada. True granite, a specific blend of minerals in specific proportions, is rare in the Sierra. All of the granitic rocks in the Sierra were emplaced during the Mesozoic era, during the Sierran Arc volcanism and related batholith formation. The main pulses of magma that rose and coalesced to form the Sierran Batholith are believed to have each lasted for 10 to 15 million years, separated by 30-million year intervals. Each of these pulses had its own particular mix of minerals, and solidified independent of other plutons around it, resulting in the wide variety of intrusive igneous rocks in the Sierra.

All throughout the Sierran Batholith are points of weakness in the rock called joints. Two master sets of joints are dominant. One runs southeast-northwest, following the grain of the range and running parallel to the abundant lateral faults to both the east and west of the range (Owens Valley, San Andreas, etc.). The other set runs perpendicular to the first, trending southwest to northeast. Both sets of joints are attributed to the extension of the continent under the influence of the northwest-bound Pacific Plate. Additionally, as the Ancestral Sierra eroded away the tremendous pressure put on the underlying batholith was released. This occurred again as the great mass of the Pleistocene glaciers was removed, as well as the material they took with them. The Sierra is heaving a sigh of relief, releasing the strain of millions of years. This process of releasing pressure is called unloading, and causes joints and fractures to develop. No one joint among the two master sets extends for more than several miles, though joints will frequently cut across plutonic boundaries. Although these two sets of joints extend all across the range, different areas will reflect them in different ways, according to the particular tendencies of the local rock.

The granite of the main crest, including that of the eastern escarpment, was emplaced around 90 million years ago, during the Cretaceous Period. It is characteristically fine-grained, resulting in an abundance of vertical joints. This close jointing makes this rock particularly susceptible to frost-riving, as water has plenty of cracks into which it can infiltrate; thus rockfall is common. This also makes the rock more vulnerable to glacial quarrying. Both of these factors work together, resulting in the jagged topography characteristic of the Alpine Sierra.

The granite of the west slope is of two different major pulses, both of which are older in origin than that of the east. These date back to 100 and 150 million years ago, during the Late Jurassic and Early Cretaceous Periods. The rocks of both pulses are relatively coarse grained, making their joints much more widely spaced than those of the crest. The older group, most common along the central west slope, exhibits these characteristics more dramatically than the younger, having such wide joints as to allow for the huge monoliths of Yosemite and Hetch-Hetchy. Such widely jointed rocks weather by a process called sheeting. In this case, sheets, or layers of rock, are exfoliated like layers of an onion. Sheeting causes angularities to be shrugged off of the rock, resulting in a rounded profile. This occurs due to several factors working in concert with one another. Repeated heating and cooling of the rock causes it to expand and contract ever so slightly throughout the 24-hour day. Periods of rainfall cause feldspar, a key mineral in granitic rocks, to turn to clay, making it swell when wet and crumble when dry. Frost-riving is always at work in the mountains, and also contributes. Slowly but surely, the layers wear away. Such sheeting is rare in the Alpine Sierra, and is best viewed at the middle elevations along the west slope.

Metavolcanic rock of the Twin Peaks ridge (12,323'). Photo: David Gilligan

Intrusive igneous rocks cool from the outside in as the margins of the pluton are exposed to cooler conditions. As the outer rock crystallizes, the inner material, still molten, exerts pressure on its hardening shell and eventually breaks it open into cracks. These cracks are almost instantly filled by rising lower density magma, which itself solidifies and recements the rock together (remember, this is all happening deep beneath the surface of the earth). These fillers, or intrusions, are called dikes, and are typically composed of highly siliceous rock, such as the light creamy colored aplite, or even pure quartz. They often appear as light-colored veins, or webs, lining the surface of the granite. The dike will often be more or less resistant to degradation than its surrounding rock, so that the dikes will form ridges (if more resistant) or incisions (if less resistant) in the parent rock.

Relative to other rock types all granitic rocks are especially resistant to erosion. Many of the glacial landforms of the Alpine Sierra reflect this attribute, and are only found in granitic areas. The undulating topography of the glacial staircase, along with its associated paternoster lakes, glacial polish, chattermarks, lines, and striations, are often completely absent from glaciated areas of other rock types. The steep precipitous walls and knife-edges also find their best expression in granite. Other rock types, however, have brilliancy of their own.

As the Sierran Batholith was emplaced throughout the Mesozoic it cooked and pressurized the overlying rock, metamorphosing whatever it contacted. Some of this was the volcanic material of the Sierran Arc. Other areas were sedimentary strata washed down from the interior of the continent during the Paleozoic era. These strata were slowly lithified, bent, folded, and contorted by island arc collisions. When the Sierra region entered into a long erosional phase, most of this metamorphic material was washed away, filling the troughs of the Central Valley and basins to the east with sediments thousands of feet deep. As the massive batholith was exposed the metamorphic material that remained stood perched atop the granite, forming the highest peaks of the weathered range. These metamorphic islands rose with the present day Sierra, forming some of the most prominent peaks in the range, including (from south to north) the Kaweahs, Painted Lady, the Silver Divide, the Ritter Range, Mts. Parker, Wood, Lewis, Gibbs, and Dana, among dozens of others.

Metamorphic rock exhibits different characteristics according to its original form, as well as the degree to which it was metamorphosed. In general, metavolcanic rock, such as that of the Ritter Range, tends to be relatively solid and darker in color, often gray, greenish, black, or brown. Metasedimentary rock is highly variable depending on its origin. Most found in the Sierra, including slate (from mudstone), quartzite (from sandstone), and marble (from limestone), is jumbled and lighter in color, usually light gray, orange, red, tan, or brown. Many of the peaks of Eastern Yosemite are classic metasedimentary summits: big rubble heaps with even-angled slopes (relative to granite), easy to walk up if you can stand the scree. Such rock usually has a poor resistance to glacial erosion, so it is rare to see much vertical relief or staircase-type landforms associated with it. The Ritter Range, being metavolcanic, is much more stable, though it too has a reputation for having loose rock. Accordingly, it may exhibit those glacial landforms most often associated with granitic rock.

The youngest rocks in the Alpine Sierra are the volcanics. During the rhyolitic explosions beginning 30 million years ago, millions of tons of volcanic material were blown into the air. This debris fell upon the mountains as a rain of fire, fusing together in places to form tuff, and covering other areas with rhyolite and pumice. The Sweetwaters, spurring off from the Sierra Nevada, are totally covered in this rhyolitic debris. In most other areas, however, subsequent volcanic activity covered up the evidence of the earlier rhyolitic explosions.

Around 20 million years ago the andesitic eruptions began, spewing sticky, steaming flows from vents. As these flows mixed with water they became oozing layers, crawling across the land and covering it with a thick brown layer of volcanic material. The Sierra Nevada north of the Yosemite border is covered with these flows and as a result, the Northern Sierra takes on an entirely different character than the south. In the Alpine Sierra, these Cenozoic volcanic landscapes are best seen between the northern border of Yosemite National Park and Sonora Pass. In some places the mudflows seem to have

Columnar basalt in the northern Sierra. Photo: David Gilligan

been frozen in action, forming pillow-like bulbs and beds, often with chunks of other rock material cemented in. Such conglomerations of volcanic rock matrix with foreign material embedded in it are called breccia. In other places, the high mountains rise above all else as heaps of small scree, ready to slide downward at the slightest disturbance. The slopes of these mountains, similar to those of the metasedimentary roof pendants, rarely exceed 35 degrees, the angle of repose. Such rock has a poor resistance to glacial erosion, and will not typically exhibit glacial landforms with the drama that granite does. A notable exception is Leavitt Ridge, which has a fine cirque on its northeast flank, complete with turquoise-blue Leavitt Lake nestled in its floor.

From the Mountains to the Sea

Weathering and Wasting

Rock types may differ, but they are all subject to the same processes that eventually crumble mountains into flat plains and wash them away into the sea. If you are standing on a metasedimentary summit, you are actually standing on what used to be at the bottom of the ocean. Even the granite of the Sierra was once well below the surface of the earth. Before that, it was magma, which was itself derived from material scraped off of the underside of the continent. Wherever you are, used to be someplace else, and with time will be someplace completely different. It is inspiring to think that a landscape such as the Alpine Sierra exists even for an instant, let alone a few million years.

In addition to glacial erosion, several other processes of weathering and wasting contribute to breaking the mountains down. Weathering refers to the degradation of rocks in place. Frost-riving, shearing (or exfoliation), and thermal expansion and contraction (also instrumental in shearing) are all types of weathering that change the rock's physical form. An additional kind of physical weathering occurs when plant roots extend along fractures in the rock, gradually prying the rock apart. Other types of weathering change the actual chemical composition of the rock. These processes are typically more important in warmer climates, though the transformation of

Frost-riven rock on Big Kaweah. Photo: David Gilligan

feldspar to clay is the result of chemical weathering, and is essential for the breakdown of granite into soil.

Wasting, also called mass movement, works with equal determination as glacial erosion at breaking the mountains down. The slowest type of mass movement is called creep, referring to imperceptible downward movement of rock material in response to gravity. This occurs among well weathered material close to the surface, where vegetation, and in some cases even rock beds, will appear bent in the direction of the creep. Frost may heave sections of land upward, and when it melts, will drop it slightly downslope. A different variety of frost phenomenon occurs when the ground freezes to a depth of at least a few feet. When the upper layer thaws, the under-lying frozen ground prevents the meltwater from soaking in. The upper layer becomes saturated and slides downslope, leaving the ground looking as if it were slowly oozing away. Terraces or downslope-trending lobes, called solifluction terraces, are indicative of this phenomenon.

The faster, more dramatic and conspicuous types of wasting include landslides, avalanches, and rockfall. Frequent earth-quakes in California are often the progenitors of such cata-strophic events, sending thousands of tons of rock crashing downslope in relatively short periods of time. Landslides, more appropriately called rockslides in the Alpine Sierra, involve large amounts of material that have somehow been detached from the bedrock and come careening downslope. As can be imagined, such slides often have disastrous results, or fantastic, depending on your point of view. Avalanches are much the same as rockslides, but involve snow, and have relatively little influence on the actual ground surface, though vegetation can take a huge loss. Rockfall, most often triggered by frost action, is perhaps the most underestimated agent of degradation in the Alpine Sierra. It occurs when individual blocks of rock are dislodged and plummet downslope, often taking with them significant amounts of other material. Rockfall is most common in spring and fall, when freeze-thaw cycles are most frequent and extreme. Recent studies have asserted the great impor-tance of rockfall in the shaping of the present day Sierran land-scape, asserting that it has had an even greater impact than glacial erosion. Much of the morainal material thought to have been eroded by the glaciers may in fact be rockfall which landed on the glacial mass and was thus transported and deposited in moraines. The task of quantifying the amount of rockfall that actually occurs in the Alpine Sierra is not an easy one, for few if any are willing to endure spring and fall conditions in the high country for long enough to get adequate data.

Fallen rock, whether it fell individually or as a slide, will continue moving downslope only so far, stratifying much as fluvial sediments do. Larger boulders will typically stop first, coming to rest at the upper ends of debris slopes. The boulders merge into talus (rocks smaller than a person and larger than a fist). Below the talus is often scree (rocks and pebbles smaller than a fist) spreading out like vast fans from the flanks of the mountains to the glacial basins below. Scree is notorious for creating difficult traveling conditions, as the slightest touch makes it slide out from beneath your feet. Smaller material (relatively rare in alpine areas) will settle out in the basins. During glacial periods, most fallen material was transported away by the moving ice and deposited at the mouths of canyons east and west. The glaciers essentially cleared the slate for a new age, and much of the material presently found in the Alpine Sierra has fallen since their retreat.

With so many agents of destruction working together to bring them down, it is indeed a wonder that the Sierra stand at all. It is of course these very same agents that give the mountains their distinct character. The granitic rock, the curious roof pendants, the blankets of lava, three million years of exceptionally intense glaciation, earthquakes, frost-riving, rockfall, all of these are integral parts of the recipe that makes the Sierra what they are today. The coincidences that have occurred seem almost uncanny, the timing perfect. For now we revel in such a gift, standing upon the stone that seems eternal as it slowly falls into the sea.

Rising Above the World Below
Mountain Weather and Climate

"Days when the hollows are steeped in a warm, winey flood the clouds come walking on the floor of heaven, flat and pearly gray beneath, rounded and pearly white above. They gather flock-wise, moving on the level currents that move about the peaks, lock hands and settle with the cooler air, drawing a veil about those places where they do their work. If their meeting or parting takes place at sunrise or sunset, as it often does, one gets the splendor of the apocalypse. There will be cloud pillars miles high, snow-capped, glorified, and preserving and orderly perspective before the unbarred door of the sun, or perhaps mere ghosts of clouds that dance to some pied piper of an unfelt wind. But be it day or night, once they have settled to their work, one sees from the valley only the blank wall of their tents stretched along the ranges. To get the real effect of a mountain storm you must be inside."

Jane Austen

The End of Indian Summer

I awoke to water dripping on my face. Opening my eyes, blinking, I waited for the gloomy light of dawn to come, but it did not. In the pitch darkness, I fumbled clumsily for my head-lamp, brushing my bare arm against cold, wet, sagging nylon, the saturated wall of the tent. Continuing my search, I felt my sleeping bag and could not tell if it was indeed as wet as it felt or if my hand was now wet from elsewhere, and I was spreading the whole mess around. Finally my anxious fingers found the familiar shape of my headlamp, and after a few good whacks with the palm of my hand, I managed to make contact between the two internal pieces of copper that meant light. It was a pale, yellow glow, the kind that is indicative of a failing battery. Nevertheless, it sufficed for me to have a look around.

The tent had become a dripping wet nylon cave. The walls, stretched by the water and the overlying weight of snow, sagged inward so that it was a wonder I had not ended up sucking on them in the night. My sleeping bag, though somewhat water-proof, was wet on the surface from head to toe. Water pooled between the floor and the groundsheet, and down by my feet were puddles within the tent itself. My hiking partner Tracy Wright slept soundly, oblivious to our soggy situation. I checked my watch: five am; two hours until light. Another drop hit my face, and several others landed with a "pat" on my sleeping bag. This was miserable, and I was exhausted. If I could just sleep for two more hours in this wet hole, then I could be free of it. I lay back down and closed my eyes. Then I got the all too familiar feeling that I needed to relieve myself. I waged the battle of brain versus bladder for a few minutes. Bladder won. I worked my way out of my sleeping bag and sat up, turning toward the vestibule of the tent. Then I unzipped the door and stood up.

No sooner than I had taken one step, I fell down to my knees in the snow. My head was whirling, spinning, careening through a dizziness that seemed inescapable. After what seemed like a night of this, it evolved into a dull throb. There I was, on my knees in well over a foot of snow, barefoot, with my head in my hands, trying to collect myself and understand just what was happening. The answer came as I slowly stood back up, turned around, and looked upon our tent. It was totally covered in white, sealed off from the world. Without any ventilation we were running out of air, our breath condensing on the inside of the tent and raining back down on us. We had risked asphyxiation, only to be saved by my need to fulfill one of the most basic of biological functions. I stooped down and pulled on my wet, icy shoes, then began the task of digging the tent out. It was October and we were not carrying a shovel, so I used my hands. Digging and batting all around the tent awoke Tracy, who seemed even more groggy and confused than I had been. When I was done, I reluctantly crawled back into my sleeping bag and fell back asleep.

We had begun our hike just over a month ago, on September seventh, at Horseshoe Meadow just south of Mt. Whitney. Our intent was to hike the backbone of the Alpine Sierra from end to end, which would bring us to Donner Pass by mid-October, hopefully before the first snows of winter forced us down

and out of the high country. It was a toss-up. I had seen some
bad storms in the Sierra in October, but in other years the mountains remained virtually snow-free through much of November.
Typically the Alpine Sierra Nevada are blessed with the most
beautiful Indian summer weather one could hope for: clear
warm days with temperatures into the sixties, crisp, cold, starry
nights, golden meadows, lengthening shadows, and best of all,
solitude. By September the heat of summer has passed, so local
thunderstorms are much less frequent. Winter has not yet come,
and neither have the week-long storms that accompany it.
October usually brings the first big snow, though local storms
may briefly cover the high country with snow throughout
summer and fall. In most years, the October storms wholly
or partially melt off, leaving the ground bare for yet another
four to six weeks before blanketing it for the winter. So far our
trip had followed the classic weather prescription for this time
of year. Being in the midst of an October snowstorm however,
I was less likely to make predictions about the future. From my
perspective winter had begun.

Hiking through Desolation Wilderness was like being back
in the southern Sierra in so many ways. Overlaying blankets
of andesite had been completely eroded away, revealing the
true Sierran granite beneath, carefully carved, scoured, and
polished by glacial activity throughout the Pleistocene. As we
climbed out of the wilderness, Dicks Pass marked the last of
the Alpine Sierra that we would experience close at hand. The
snow flurries that enamored us there once again gave way to
countless stars. In the morning, the sun had me convinced that
we would yet make Donner Pass before the ground was covered.
Even as we began our day's hike however, sheeted cloud cover
wove its way about the vault of the sky, hiding from us the blue
of certain delight. All that this sky promised was snow.

It began as afternoon flurries, not the first of the year, falling like feathers in the slight wind of autumn. By the time we reached Bear Lake Creek, the wind had grown in ferocity, sending the snowflakes into a wild dance, whirling and whipping as the wind seemed to draw ever more snow from the sky. The juncos that had braved the flurries now took cover. Only the mountain chickadees remained, seemingly crazed by the storm, performing flips and twirls on the outer branches of the conifers. My companion and I stood there beneath the whitening boughs of the firs, hemlocks, and lodgepole pines which stood straight and tall beside the creek, and weighed out our options. It was October the eighth. Five o'clock in the evening. Our destination of Donner Pass lay two or three days distant. The nearest road, Forest Service Road 3, was only three miles to the north. We were cold, wet, hungry, and tired after a fifteen-mile day. We decided to make camp, glad, but in truth, we were both melancholy. This was it, the storm that would close the season and end our hike, wrapping the Sierra Nevada in the frozen white of winter.

I slept little that night, fitfully maneuvering my body inside the cocoon of my sleeping bag, listening intently to the tinkling sounds of snow landing on the roof of the tent. All through the night the snow fell ceaselessly. I batted the roof and walls periodically while listening to the accumulated snow slide down the nylon, slowly piling up like an army laying siege to a fortress intent upon starving out its occupants. In anticipation of such a tactic, the occupants of the fortress stockpile as many provisions as possible. Our provision was air, and the falling snow was cutting us off from our supply. As we finally slept, we breathed what precious little the tent could hold as the snow gradually encased our shelter. As the walls of snow rose, they blocked the flow of air coming in from beneath the rain fly. Eventually the snow began to adhere to the steep sidewalls of the tent itself. As we breathed what could have been our last, the moisture of our breath condensed on the roof. Soon, it began to rain inside our tent.

As if an alarm had sounded, I awoke abruptly for the second time, relieved to find that the first light of morning had finally come. After lying there like a wet log for a few minutes, I came to my senses and burst out of the confines of the tent. Mystified by the changed face of the mountains, I stood there, knee-deep in snow, staring all around me. It was beautiful. In that moment it seemed that I was twice as far away from anything, living twice as many years before the beginning of time, and twice as alive as yesterday. Given enough time, these "snow flowers...the offspring of the sun and sea," as Muir said so long ago, might once again inundate these mountains in glacial ice, scraping the slate clean for the new days that would follow. "This changes everything," I thought, watching my breath form miniature ephemeral clouds in the cold air of morning.

As I walked out into the winter world I noticed how much of the snow had been caught and held by the boughs of the trees. Our tent was pitched in an open area, where the snow was knee-deep, but beneath the canopy of evergreen it was less than six inches. Our hike out would not be so bad, given that the majority of it would be beneath the trees. A short section of meadow might have us swimming chest-high in drifts, but the winds had not seemed so bad during the night, so deep drifts would not be likely. I leaned back, glancing up, half expecting a lump of snow to slough off and hit me square in the face. "Not yet," I thought. "Give it a couple of hours and about ten degrees." The juncos were out again. For now the snow had ceased, though the gray hue of the sky portended more to come. I wandered around for a time, eventually retrieving our bear hang and bringing our last three days of food back to camp.

Without questioning each other we packed up for our hike out to Forest Service Road 3. This was the end of the trail for now, though I knew I would be back in spring when the snow hardened up enough for travel. Not long after we left our campsite the wind picked up and began hurling freshly made batches of snow and sleet from out of the sky. Even with all of our layers on while walking, we were still cold, the wind seeming to gnaw through clothes and flesh alike to our very bones. I counted drainages to keep track of our progress, as the going was slow and visibility poor. By the time we reached the meadows we knew we were in the last third of our walk before the road, and resolved to push on before stopping to rest and eat. We did not know what to expect of Forest Service Road 3, other than it led downslope to Lake Tahoe, which seemed as fitting an end as any to our trip.

Once on the road, I spotted a small building. As I drew closer to it, I recognized it as a Forest Service trailhead bathroom. Freezing, we sought shelter inside. I stripped off my parka and sat down on the commode as if it were the most luxurious lazy boy ever made. Then I remembered a special treat we had picked up during our resupply at Tahoe: coffee! I quickly unpacked the stove and fired it up. I boiled water, added the coffee, some powdered milk, and a handful of chocolate chips from our gorp bag. As the wind raged across the mountains all around us, there we sat in a small stone building, a bathroom, safe and relatively warm, enjoying one of the best cups of coffee of our entire lives. We had opened the door to winter, and written across its threshold was the end of Indian summer.

W e r e   i n   t h e   W o r l d ?

Global Climate Patterns
and the Sierra Nevada

The Alpine Sierra Nevada experiences an extraordinary combination of weather conditions which result in a mountain climate like that of no other range in North America, if not the world. It is a virtual desert in summer, a scant five percent of the annual precipitation falling from June through September, usually as brief afternoon thundershowers. The remaining 95 percent falls from October to May, as huge cyclonic storms sweep over the region, dropping enough snow on the range to make it the second snowiest mountain range in the continent. Of all the alpine areas in North America, the Alpine Sierra Nevada is significantly more mild. Average July temperatures of fifty-five degrees Fahrenheit in the Alpine Sierra are five degrees warmer than those of alpine regions in the Rockies and the Appalachians. Sub-zero temperatures, common in other alpine regions, are uncommon in the Alpine Sierra. Such a combination of cool-dry summers, crisp-clear autumns, and mild-snowy winters is uniquely Sierran, as weather lays its best across the range of light.

Weather, simply stated, is the condition of the atmosphere at any particular time and place. Climate, in contrast, is the accumulation of daily and seasonal events over a long period of time. All of the mysteries of weather derive from a simple premise—heat rises—and the surface of the earth is heated

A winter orographic storm over Mt. Williamson. Photo: Martha McCord

differentially. Different masses of heated air are rising at different times, displacing cooler air, which sinks. This constant shifting around of air masses due to differential heating has some pretty fantastic effects, especially in mountain regions such as the Sierra Nevada, where the space these air masses have to shift around in is compressed by the elevated landscape.

Mountains, such as the Sierra Nevada, are characteristically colder, wetter, brighter, and windier than the lower regions surrounding them. Like islands in a sea of lowlands, the larger they are the more they can create their own climate; the smaller they are, the more their climate matches that of the surrounding lowlands. In many mountain regions, extreme weather conditions are the norm. The diverse topography of the mountainous terrain compacts contrasting environmental conditions into a

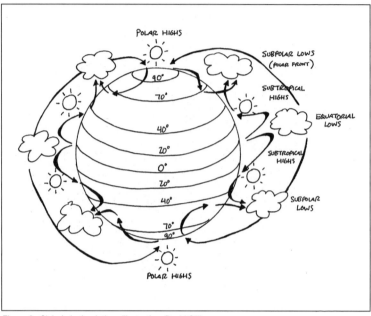

Figure 8. Global air circulation. Illustration: David Gilligan

relatively small space. For example, the Sierra Nevada, taken as a whole, cover less land area than the Central Valley. A ten-square mile section of the Sierra, however, contains slopes that face south, north, east, and west, and vary in slope angle and elevation. All of these variables affect the weather locally, resulting in a lot of variation within a relatively small space. A ten-square mile section of the Central Valley, in contrast, is more or less flat, showing little to no topographic variation, and thus little to no variation in weather conditions. Other factors contributing to the high diversity of weather in mountain regions are thinner air and the relatively high reflectivity of the land surface, both of which result in dramatic changes in weather on a daily basis. This combination of diverse land areas and high diurnal fluctuations does not, however, exempt mountain regions from being affected by the same factors that dictate the greater regional climate within which they are situated, no matter how large the mountain mass. These include latitude, continentality, altitude, incoming solar radiation (insolation), and winds.

The latitude of a region dictates much about its climate. As we know, the equatorial regions experience the most direct, consistent sunlight: twelve hours of daylight and twelve hours of darkness year-round. The tropics experience the warmest average annual temperatures, and the least extremes of heat and cold. The poles, in contrast, experience the least direct, most inconsistent sunlight: twenty-four hours of sun in summer, and twenty-four hours of darkness in winter. They experience the coldest average annual temperatures and the most extremes of heat and cold. Moving away from the equator, air cools at the rate of about one degree Fahrenheit per seventy miles. This means that at sea level, the air 2,000 miles north of the equator will theoretically be thirty degrees cooler. Other factors, most notably the tilt, revolution, and procession of the earth (collectively referred to as the Milankovitch cycles), complicate this, but on a global scale the simple truth prevails: it's always colder at the poles than at the tropics.

The climate of a given region is determined, in part, by global air circulation and its related pressure systems (Figure 8). Far to the south, the warmer air of the tropics is constantly rising, creating a low pressure zone over the equator. As this warm air rises it cools, releasing its moisture, and resulting in relatively high annual rainfall in the equatorial regions. Once the air masses cool, they are displaced by new air masses rising from below, and the cooler air moves away from the equator, either north or south, and sinks. These descending air masses, pushing down on the air beneath them, create a series of subtropical high

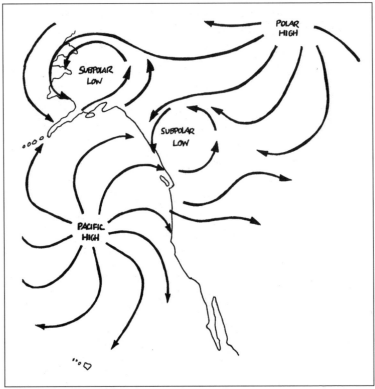

Figure 9. The Pacific high in summer (in winter the high moves south). Illustration: David Gilligan

pressure zones between twenty and forty degrees latitude, both north and south of the equator. These high pressure systems deliver characteristically cool, dry air to the region, bringing fair weather as they push storm systems away from their center. North of the subtropical highs, rising air once again results in a subpolar low pressure zone, between forty and seventy degrees north and south. These air masses find their way down over the poles, creating another set of high pressure zones between seventy and ninety degrees north and south.

The Alpine Sierra are situated between 36.5 and 39 degrees

north of the equator, at the northern end of the subtropical high. The center of the high pressure cell, called the North Pacific High, lies offshore over the waters of the ocean (Figure 9). The descending air creates winds blowing outward from the center of the high pressure cell in all directions. The Coriolis effect, governed by the rotation of the earth, illustrates how these winds bend to the right, or clockwise, forming a huge swirling system known as an anticyclone. The winds radiating northward of the high bend to the east, become the prevailing northwesterlies of the mid-latitude Pacific Coast. The winds radiating to the south bend to the west, creating the tropical trade winds. In the subpolar latitudes of forty to seventy degrees, the northwesterlies of the North Pacific High encounter easterly winds as they come down from the polar high, resulting in an erratic, stormy boundary known as the polar front. Here, conflicting winds send each other spinning opposite their original direction, called cyclones. Meanwhile, the sinking polar air dives under the warmer air of the North Pacific High, resulting in rising air masses, low pressure, and high amounts of precipitation throughout the subpolar low pressure zone.

Like most high pressure cells, the North Pacific High migrates seasonally, moving to its southernmost point in the winter and its northernmost point in the summer. Accordingly, the subpolar lows and polar highs migrate south and north as well. During the summer, the North Pacific High sits just off the coast of California, shielding the state from the storm systems of the polar front, sending them careening into the coastline of the Pacific Northwest. Meanwhile, the Alpine Sierra, along with the rest of California, enjoys fair weather all summer long. Other then an occasional local afternoon thundershower, only a rare dying tropical storm system sneaks in from the south, via the Gulf of Mexico or the Gulf of California, to wet the high country for a while. In autumn, the Pacific High begins moving south, and the first cyclonic storms to make it to land usually hit in October. Soon after, there is nothing to stand in their way, and the long storms of winter enshroud California and the Alpine Sierra until spring. Come April, the high is on its way back north, and system storms become a rarity in the month of May. This type of climate regime, typical of California as a whole, is called Mediterranean, after the Old World region which experiences similar conditions.

The Alpine Sierra's geographic proximity to the Pacific Ocean has further implications for its weather and climate. Because water heats and cools much more slowly than land, it moderates the climate of land regions in close proximity to it. Accordingly, maritime regions experience cooler summers and milder winters than adjacent inland regions. Maritime regions also tend to be wetter than adjacent inland regions. The degree to which a region is subject to these influences is called its continentality. The more continental a region, the more extreme temperatures it will experience, and the more arid the climate will tend to be. Accordingly, the Sierra Nevada, situated seventy to ninety miles inland from the coast, experiences cool summers and mild winters, temperatures rarely dipping below zero, with a tremendous amount of snowfall during the winter months. The White-Inyo Range, just east of the Sierra Nevada at the same latitude, experiences blazing-hot summer days, winter temperatures that regularly plummet well below zero, and markedly less snowfall than the Sierra to the west. Even within the Sierra Nevada, the more maritime west slope typically gets more snow, but has higher average temperatures then the more continental east side, which has lower average temperatures and receives relatively less snow.

The Sierra Nevada themselves act as a huge barrier between

the maritime regions to the west and the continental regions to the east. Not only do they block the moisture-laden ocean air from the interior, but they also block the cold, dry continental air from the maritime areas. Relative to the Coast Ranges, the Sierra may seem tempered by continental influences. The lower ranges of the coast, however, are not nearly as effective a barrier between the ocean and the interior as the Sierra are to those lands to the east. In contrast to the extreme desert mountains of the Basin Ranges, there is no doubt the Sierra Nevada has been moderated by maritime influences.

Working together, the geographic factors of latitude and continentality result in an Alpine Sierran climate that is milder than any other mid-latitude alpine area in the continent. The maritime influence and southerly mid-latitude situation of the Sierra Nevada allow them to enjoy the Mediterranean climate of California, making the Alpine Sierra the only alpine region with a Mediterranean climate in North America. The mountains create the eastern boundary of this climatic region, acting as a barrier between maritime California and the interior, thereby influencing the climate of the continent all the way to the Atlantic Coast.

Mountain Highs and Valley Lows

The Influence of Altitude

As one ascends into the high mountains, the air becomes crisper with every upward step, cooling skin in summer, biting in the winter. Puffy white clouds march like rows of cottonballs to the summits as the day waxes. Experiencing the ethereal brightness of the landscape seems divine grace, an apotheosis, though the sun spares no skin of its burning. Everything about this place is different; the air, the light, the land. All of this takes some getting used to.

Before even reaching treeline, respiration becomes labored as the mountain air thins with altitude gain. Each breath feels more invigorating than the last, ironically, even more precious, as one requires more of the thinning air to do the same work than down in the lowlands. The human body races to build new capillaries in order that what precious scant oxygen exists reaches the body's extremities. Lightheadedness, often mistaken for pure elation, settles into a dull throb.

Altitude is associated with mountain regions perhaps more than any other factor. As you go up in elevation, air temperatures drop, air density decreases, water vapor lessens, the carbon dioxide content lowers, and impurities in the air become a rarity. The prevailing westerlies bring moisture-laden air masses in from the Pacific. As they encounter the great wall of the Sierra Nevada, the air masses are forced to ascend over the mountain barrier. In the summer months, this is augmented by local rising air masses heated by the summer sun. The ascent of such air masses is called orographic lift.

At sea level, air is most dense because of the downward pressure of all the air above it. As it rises the air pressure decreases, and the air mass expands. As the air expands, it cools at a rate of about three degrees Fahrenheit per thousand feet of elevation gain, called the moist adiabatic because moisture will eventually condense out of the rising air mass. As the air cools, its ability to hold water vapor decreases by fifty percent for every twenty degree temperature decrease. Thus, rising air becomes saturated, unable to hold onto its water vapor, and the moisture condenses to liquid. Tiny water droplets form clouds, eventually coalescing to the point of precipitation. These processes are most easily witnessed during the summer, when local winds bring up warm air from the lowlands, forming lines of billowing cumulus clouds riding up the slopes of the range. These clouds are often flat-bottomed, indicating the condensation level. As cumulus clouds coalesce, they form cumulonimbus clouds: huge, flat-topped thunder heads ready to dump their loads on the high country. Thus, precipitation levels increase moving upslope, and the mountains become wetter (and greener) with altitude. In the Sierra Nevada, most of the moisture in the air is dropped at the middle elevations, between 6,000 feet and 10,000 feet, on the forested flanks of the west slope. Above 10,000 feet, the water vapor in the air has all condensed and dropped out, and the air is much drier. Water vapor is the main heat holding agent in air, and without it, the air will cool (or warm) at an even higher rate. As the air continues to rise over the crest of the range, it cools at 5.5 degrees per thousand feet, called the dry adiabatic rate. In the alpine zone, any water in the air is almost instantly condensed into

liquid form and dropped out. When it is not precipitating, it is
typically clear and dry.

What the mountains give in precipitation on the windward
side, they take away on the leeward side. By causing an air
mass to rise, the mountains draw the moisture out of it, and
accordingly, causing it to sink makes it drink the moisture back
from the surrounding region. Moving over the crest of the
Alpine Sierra, air begins its abrupt descent down the east slope.
Warming at the dry adiabatic rate of 5.5 degrees per thousand feet of descent, the thirsty airmass increases in its ability
to retain water vapor, rushing down the mountain slope as a
decimating breeze, sucking the moisture out of everything in
its path. Thus the Sierra Nevada casts a wide rainshadow spanning east all the way to the Rocky Mountains. The deserts
created by this rainshadow are comparably hotter than the
valleys of the west slope, also due to the adiabatic cooling
and warming of air due to orographic lift.

A typical summer air mass over the Central Valley, at sea
level, begins with an air temperature of around ninety degrees.
Moving upslope it cools at the moist adiabatic rate of three
degrees for every thousand feet of ascent. At 10,000 feet, the
air, now sixty degrees, has reached its saturation point. Huge
thunderheads billow and crackle with lightning, dumping a
mix of rain, snow, and everything in between, down on the
mountains. From 10,000 to 14,000 feet, the air continues to rise,
now cooling at the dry adiabatic rate of 5.5 degrees per thousand feet. Atop the crest of the range, the air temperature hits
its low at thirty-eight degrees, chilly even for the alpine zone
in summer. As it descends 10,000 feet to the Owens Valley below,
it warms at the dry adiabatic rate, absorbing any and all
moisture from the land and air it comes in contact with. The
air mass reaches a maximum of ninety-three degrees at the

valley floor, three degrees warmer and 4,000 feet higher than its starting point in the Central Valley. If we were to continue to track this same airmass to the floor of Death Valley, at 282 feet below sea level the airmass would achieve a temperature of approximately 116.5 degrees–scorching.

The dryness of the alpine air has several effects on the mountain environment. Most importantly, it results in high diurnal temperature fluctuations, as there is little water vapor in the air to keep heat from escaping at night. Even when a cloud blots out the sun for a minute, the mercury can sink thirty degrees or more. This is further augmented by the lack of dust and other particulates in the air, which aid in the insulating effect. The dry air has a desiccating effect on everything it comes into contact with, creating desert-like conditions in the summer throughout the alpine zone. Such conditions contrast sharply with the cold, trickling waters of snowmelt sliding through a soggy meadow in August. But nevertheless, ten feet away the ground may lie parched, dried to a crispy golden hay beneath the chapping winds.

Grand   Illumination

Mountain Light

There is no quality of light quite like that of the Alpine Sierra. The blue of the sky, the white of the snow, and the glow of golden, peach, then rose light of the waning sun on the granite have no match in the lowlands. On a full moon, the landscape reflects silver light with such clarity that you could track marmots through fell fields by night. The flush of pink as the first rays of the morning sun strike the highest splintered peaks allows for no further slumber. The light beckons you to awaken and bear witness to its pervasive effects on the land.

In addition to latitude, continentality, and altitude, insolation is another primary climatic factor in alpine environments. In the Alpine Sierra, insolation levels are high relative to other alpine areas in the continent. This is due to their mid-latitude geographic location, clear summers, warmer temperatures, and high altitude. In all mountain regions, the amount of insolation is greater than in the lowlands, where much of the short-wave radiation is filtered out by the higher concentrations of water vapor, carbon dioxide, and particulates in the air. With less of a filter, the alpine sky scatters light, rather than reflecting it. While reflection affects all wavelengths, scattering primarily affects the blue, resulting in the rich, deep hues of the alpine heavens. On clear sunny days, alpine areas receive up to fifty percent more ultraviolet light during the summer than areas of similar latitude at sea level. During winter this increases to up to one hundred and twenty percent. Slopes also affect the amount and quality of insolation. The angle and aspect of a slope determine the length of its exposure, as well as how direct the insolation is. In the northern hemisphere, south and southwest-facing slopes get the most exposure to insolation, and thus have higher temperatures, higher treelines, and often higher levels of biological diversity.

Reflectivity also plays a major role in insolation levels. Lighter land surfaces, such as snow, water, and lighter rock, reflect much of the insolation back into the atmosphere, while darker surfaces, such as forests and darker rock, absorb more insolation. A surface's level of reflectivity is called its albedo. The Alpine Sierra has a higher albedo than most other alpine regions because of its abundant snow, light-colored granitic rock, and surface water. These three factors work in combination to allow for the kind of grand illumination of the Alpine Sierra that prompted John Muir to dub it the "Range of Light." High albedo also contributes to high diurnal temperature fluctuations. When the sun sets, what little insolation has been absorbed by the surface is quickly given back to the dry, particle-free alpine air, and the heat is radiated back out into space. Accordingly, the clearest nights are the coldest, as no cloud cover insulates the land to prevent heat from radiating back out into space.

Breathing   In   and   Out

Winds

On any given day in the Alpine Sierra Nevada, the stillness is more apparent than the wind. Wind is the norm here, and the lack of it is a notable exception. Besides, it takes such a moment of stillness for one's words to be heard by others in the same party. Poorly prepared backcountry travelers curse the wind and the damage done to their ailing tents, with flies torn and poles broken. Sleepless hikers pack the remains of their shelters back down to the lowlands. On some days, when "maddening" seems more fit to describe the wind than "howling," you may tighten your hood around your face, only to find that this technique merely changes the frequency of the relentless roar in your head. Windy days are rarely lonely ones, as it often seems the mountains have been howling at you all day long. At night, duct tape on your tent zippers keeps them from ceaselessly clinking together; plugs in the ears help ease you into sleep. This is the breath of the mountains, heaving in and out.

Mountain regions are among the windiest places on earth. They act as barriers which winds must funnel over and/or around, increasing wind speeds by constricting the area air has to move through. Mountains also project higher into the atmosphere than surrounding lowlands, acting to intercept fast-moving winds that only occur up high. In the mid-latitudes, these high altitude winds eventually culminate in jet streams.

In general, wind speeds tend to be greater in the mid-latitudes than at the tropics or the poles. Winds also tend to be greater during the day than at night, greater during winter than summer, greater in maritime than continental regions, greater on windward sides of mountains than leeward sides, greater on valleys parallel to the prevailing winds or ranges perpendicular to prevailing winds, and greater on isolated peaks than large mountain masses. The Sierra Nevada, situated in a maritime region of the mid-latitudes, oriented perpendicular to the prevailing westerlies, makes it a prime target for ripping winds. The alpine zone is particularly ravaged, as there are little to no obstructions blocking the wind's path. Within the range, as the above criteria suggest, winds vary greatly due to local topography and orientation.

Winds may be conveniently divided into two categories: local and non-local. Local winds originate within the mountain system itself and reflect the character of the local topography. Like all weather phenomena, they are driven by differential heating of the land surface. Unlike most weather phenomena, they tend to follow a highly predictable daily routine. Every morning the sun begins its task of heating up the air, especially in lower elevation areas such as the lowlands surrounding the mountain region, where the air can get much hotter. As the air heats up it rises, flowing up the slopes and valleys of the mountains, cooling adiabatically as it ascends. Larger scale winds of this sort, called valley breezes, move through the main valleys of the mountains. Smaller scale winds of the same type are called upslope winds, and are not confined to the valleys. Both types typically begin a few hours after sunrise, reach their top speeds in early to mid-afternoon, and begin calming with dusk. After sunset there is no more heat pumping the air upslope, and the colder air of the mountains begins to sink, creating downslope winds, which usually begin around midnight. Larger scale winds of this type are called mountain winds, and like valley winds, move through the main valleys. Smaller scale winds of this type are called downslope winds. As the cool air moves downslope it settles in the valleys, which become cold air sinks where the temperatures may be significantly lower at night than on the ridges around them. This cold air is quick to condense any moisture it picks up on its descent, accounting for the abundant dew and frost of so many valley mornings. The presence of such cold air sinks is often evidenced by vegetation, as plants normally growing at higher elevations with cooler more moist conditions follow cold air drainages downslope to lower elevation valley floors. Many a traveler has avoided the cold, moist valleys by strategically camping on slopes and ridges a few hundred feet above the valley floor.

Snow further complicates such local thermally induced winds. During the day the air over large snowfields and/or glacial ice can cool significantly relative to the surrounding air. As it cools it sinks, diving beneath valley and upslope winds. At night these glacier winds join mountain and downslope winds as the cold air heads for the valleys. Thermally induced winds such as mountain and valley winds, upslope and downslope winds, and glacier winds are most prominent during summer, when the heat driving the winds is greatest. With the high number of clear, sunny days throughout the Sierran summer, it is no wonder that these winds are well-developed.

Non-local, or regional winds, primarily move across the Sierra Nevada from west to east. As these winds are forced over the mountain barrier, they are modified. Chinook, or foehn winds occur on the lee side of barrier ranges, on the east side of the Sierra Nevada. These winds are caused by the warm, dry, descending air as it blows into the eastern basins and desertifies the region. Lee waves form as wind flow is obstructed by the mountain barrier, and a train of waves is created that extends downwind. Waves vary greatly in their spacing and vertical amplitude, ranging from one to twenty-five miles in length and 0.6 to three miles in depth, depending on wind speed and the shape and height of the mountain barrier. Lenticular clouds, restricted to the lee sides of mountain ranges, form at the crest of lee waves. Their flat bottoms indicate the condensation level, while their rounded tops are shaped by the contour of the wave. Lenticular clouds may occur in vertical stacks, each cloud representing different wave levels, or they may extend horizontally, like a fleet of flying saucers, indicating successive waves. In both cases, they tend to be stationary, moving only if changing wind speeds alter the wave pattern. In addition to lee waves, roll-like circulations of air called rotors develop on the immediate lee side of mountain barriers, forming beneath wave crest. These rotors spin toward the base of the mountains and away from the crest, so that if you were to stand facing north on the east side of the Sierra, they would appear to be turning clockwise. The east side is notorious for its rotors, eagerly sought after by hang-gliders for the excellent rides they offer.

Alpine winds leave the marks of their presence all over the mountains, shaping and manipulating the landscape to reflect their passing. The sculpting of the wind is most easily recognized in malleable substances, particularly snow, and among the plants of the alpine zone. Snow may exhibit drifts, ripples, small rollers, and cornices. Cornices, well known by mountaineers, form as the wind drifts snow up and over ridges, forming overhanging edges of snow at the tops of steep, leeward slopes. Gravity often curves cornices downward, so that they resemble the shape of a wave about to break. They may be stable or soft, depending on conditions at any given time. Other types of frozen precipitation also reflect the wind. Rime ice and hoarfrost form as tiny supercooled water droplets in the air freeze upon contacting a solid object. These frozen droplets accumulate on the windward side, often forming horizontal stalactite-like appendages of ice onto objects exposed to the wind.

Among alpine plants, those that are truly alpine typically avoid the wind by either growing low to the ground or in sheltered areas. The trees of treeline, however, are known for their sculpting by the wind, and exhibit an array of twisted, gnarled-looking forms. Most commonly, the windward side of the tree becomes pruned by wind-borne particles, and is devoid of branches, and sometimes even bark. The leeward side, protected at least somewhat by the trunk itself, has branches extending like flags in the direction of the wind. Often only the tip of the tree will have branches, the lower trunk bare due to ice blasting across the winter snow surface. The main vegetative mass of these trees usually survives as a cushion, or skirt, around its base, below the flagpole. Other trees exhibit stunted, dwarfed, or prostrate forms, sometimes growing together in tree islands for optimal protection from the wind. Such tree islands may remain in place or move steadily in a leeward direction, as the windward sections die off and new roots are put down on the lee side. In the Alpine Sierra, alpine willow is the extreme case of this phenomenon, growing so low that it often resembles a well-kept lawn.

Even in the midst of a moment of stillness, the alpine landscape suggests that wind is not far off. Be it warm air rising and cooling as a valley wind, cold air falling and warming as a mountain wind, the decimating sink of a chinook, or the ride of lee waves, the mountains are tuned to the quickened air. As wind moves through the instrument of the landscape, the mountains sing their song in full glory.

The Great Snowy Range

Snow Dynamics

It was for good reason that Father Pedro Font dubbed the mountains "una gran sierra nevada." What he beheld was indeed a great snowy mountain range, spanning north and south as far as he could see. The Sierra Nevada are the snowiest mountain range in the contiguous United States, second only to the Cascades of the Pacific Northwest that get their first snows earlier in the fall and their last later in the spring. In addition, the Cascades are too far north to be protected from winter storms by the North Pacific High, and cyclonic storms during the summer months are not uncommon. In the Sierra the snow season is shorter, but still remarkable, leaving snows that linger all through the summer, watering much of the surrounding region during the summer drought.

More snow falls along the west slope of the Sierra than on the east, which is more sheltered from precipitation by the rain-shadow effect. Overall precipitation on the west slope varies from twenty to eighty inches per year, depending on elevation and latitude, versus ten to thirty inches per year on the east slope. On the west slope, snow accumulation is greatest between 6,000 feet and 10,000 feet. Within this snow belt, over thirty feet of winter snowfall is common, reaching maximums of over seventy feet in some areas. The snowpack never actually reaches such depth, as the snow is constantly settling and consolidating, though it is not uncommon for snowpack to exceed ten feet. In alpine areas, observers generally assume that snowfall is less, though there have been few studies that actually document this. The reason for this assumption is that most of the water vapor in air masses has already condensed by the time the air masses reach the higher elevations of the alpine zone. Snowpack in alpine areas is notably less, but this is largely due to wind action which shifts the snow around, resulting in deep drifts in some areas and virtually snow-free patches in others.

Whenever cloud temperatures dip below zero there is a potential for snow. Under any temperature conditions, for moisture vapor to condense into liquid form it requires a condensation nucleus, a speck of dust or other atmospheric impurity to cling to and form around. Such particulates are relatively common in the atmosphere. For freezing to occur, however, a second nucleus is required, which is much less common. Typically, water that freezes forms a primitive snowflake, an embryonic ice crystal. As freezing occurs, the vapor pressure around the freezing body is reduced, and supercooled water droplets that have not yet frozen begin to coalesce around the new nucleus, crystallizing onto it. This process results in a magnificent array of pure crystals, including stellar crystals, plates, columns, and needles, that are the subject of intrigue among so many winter enthusiasts. More typical than such uniform coalescence, however, is random collision among ice crystals and supercooled water droplets. This process results in riming, which accumulates around the crystal and encrusts it in a sheath of white, fine-grained ice. Coalescence and pure crystal formation are most prominent in regions that experience colder, continental climates, such as the Intermountain West of North America. Riming is more typical of milder maritime climates, such as the Sierra Nevada. Sleet and hail are formed by processes of their own; the former by water droplets freezing on the outside,

Hoarfrost. Photo: Andy Zdon

and the latter by a solid core accumulating ice layers by circulating up and down huge thunderheads.

The maritime influence on the Sierra Nevada usually prevents temperatures from being cold enough for actual snowflakes to form. More typical are the various types of graupel (snow crystals encased in a layer of rime ice) and soft hail, collectively referred to by backcountry travelers as "Sierra cement." Cyclonic storms out of the north tend to bring less precipitation than those from the south. These tropical storms, commonly called "pineapple express," bring warm air loaded with moisture to the Sierra region. The mountain barrier may block these storms from passage for days on end, as heavy, dense snow blankets the high country. In autumn the snow from these storms tends to melt off until the latter half of November, when the ground becomes cold enough to promote accumulation.

Newly fallen snow settles on the surface as loose crystals and soon begins metamorphosing and compacting to form layers within the snowpack. Such metamorphosis does not require temperatures above freezing. Even before a crystal hits the ground, it begins changing on both a mechanical and molecular level. Essentially, the crystal slowly but surely collapses on itself as molecules head towards concavities. As pore space becomes filled by extremities, the crystal takes on an increasingly rounded shape. This process is generally referred to as destructive metamorphism, or equitemperature metamorphism, but has most recently been renamed by Japanese researchers "radius of curvature metamorphism."

Other types of snow crystal metamorphism occur when temperatures start changing. Temperature gradient metamorphism, also called constructive metamorphism, occurs as warmer molecules move towards colder molecules, creating a totally new kind of crystal. The newly created crystals do not bond well with other crystals, and the result is "sugar snow," composed of powdery, faceted crystals nearly impossible to pack into a snowball. Such snow rarely occurs in the Sierra Nevada, and is more typical of continental regions such as the South San Juans of Colorado, renowned for both sugar snow and coincidental avalanches. More common in the Sierra Nevada is melt-freeze metamorphism, also called firnification. Considering the mild climate of the Sierra, this process may occur anytime of the year, though it is most prominent during the spring. Due to repeated melt-freeze cycles, smaller grains lose mass to larger grains. Pores are diminished and the snow increases density, gradually becoming the hard corn snow that has made the Sierra famous among springtime backcountry skiers. If this snow survives the entire snow season it becomes firn. Eventually, firn may continue to metamorphose into glacial ice.

The strata of metamorphic crystals within the snowpack are dependent on the weather conditions at the time of the storm, the subsequent air temperatures, and the subsequent layers of snow atop. Interstorm periods with air temperatures that exceed the freezing point result in freeze-thaw cycles at the snow surface, creating more dense surface layers. The snowpack deepens as long as accumulation exceeds meltoff, usually until mid-March. The snowpack then lessens with spring, as storms taper off and the days grow longer and warmer. During this time meltoff exceeds accumulation, continuing through the summer months and into the fall, when ground temperatures once again become cold enough to prohibit meltoff. Most alpine lakes remain iced-over through May, sometimes even into September. Occasionally, a particularly high, shaded glacial tarn will remain ice-covered through the entire year.

Snowmelt is a result of heat being applied to snow. The primary heat agents responsible for melting are insolation, warm air, and rain. If the air (or rain) is warmer than the surface of the snow (always at or below freezing), the air will lose heat to the snow. If the snow is warmer, then it will lose heat to the air. As insolation, rainfall, and/or winds (which bring warm air) increase, so will meltoff rates. A six-year study in the Tahoe region showed that rainfall was significantly correlated with outflow of meltwater from snowpack, and further, that late spring flooding was directly related to rainfall on snow. Insolation alone may account for sixty-six to ninety percent of the energy available for melting. Soil conduction and advection also influence meltoff, accounting for as much as twenty percent of meltoff from the base of the snowpack during winter, but relatively little during the actual spring thaw. Other objects such as rocks, dirt, and other debris, along with projecting vegetation, also aid in meltoff by absorbing heat and reradiating it out to the

surrounding snow. In the alpine zone, areas with the most exposure to sun and winds, such as south and west-facing slopes
and open areas, are the first to begin meltoff, followed by north
and east-facing slopes and sheltered areas. In addition to horizontal subsurface channels, water also moves through vertical
flow channels, or "fingers" within the snow strata. As the spring
thaw progresses, snow may continue to melt at a rate of one to
four inches per day.

When spring metamorphoses snow into water, remarkable
changes take place on the surface of the snow. As grains continually melt during the day and refreeze at night, they turn into
the coarse-grained corn snow that the Sierra are known for in
the spring. As irregularities form in the snow surface, its ability
to reflect light lessens. The snow surface heats and melts more
and more unevenly, forming deep scoops in the snow surface,
divided by angular ridges. These hollows, called snowcups,
create a topography on the snow surface that is much like a
miniature version of the Alpine Sierran landscape, complete
with miniature cirques, aretes, and horns, all made of melting
snow. The snowcup topography perpetuates itself, and snowcups become deeper and deeper as the snow continues to melt
irregularly. On the snow surface, meltwater and precipitation
leave evidence of their presence as runnels, eventually developing into rills of running water. As meltwater channels beneath
the snow surface widen while the snowpack itself thins,
snow collapses into the meltwater cavities, forming rotten snow.
On steeper slopes, usually exceeding thirty degrees, upper
layers of snow may break away from rotten snow beneath,
resulting in slab avalanches. These have an obvious fracture
line at their upper end, and are characterized by a large body
of snow that is released and moves suddenly at the same time.
On even steeper slopes, the sheer weight of the snow may

succumb to the pull of gravity, resulting in a loose snow avalanche. These avalanches start at one point and grow as they move downslope. Both types of avalanches may also be triggered by sound, movement, or falling debris. Avalanches pose a serious hazard to backcountry travelers, and in-depth knowledge of their dynamics is critical to safe snow travel in the alpine zone.

As summer approaches, many snowfields in the Alpine Sierra persist. Some of these remain all year round, year after year, straddling the delineation between glacier and perennial snowfield. Given enough time and cold enough temperatures, all of the snow that falls on the Sierra would eventually meta-morphose into glacial ice. As you travel the alpine country in spring, it seems much easier to imagine such a change taking place then it does to imagine that beneath all the snow are tiny wildflowers, lying in wait. Someday perhaps they will see the sunlight no more, as the snowpack settles, compacts, melts and refreezes, and begins its slow, steady flow of ice down the sides of the mountains.

C h a n g i n g   T i m e s

Climate Change and the Sierra Nevada

As we know, the Sierra have not always been what they are today. All of the factors contributing to the present-day weather and climate of the mountains, including latitude, continentality, altitude, insolation, and winds, have fluctuated throughout the geologic history of the range, and continue to do so today. What was once ocean became land; what was once barren volcanic soil sprouted a lush subtropical forest; mountains higher than today's Sierra Nevada became low, rolling hills, then high mountains once again; and where there were once glaciers, there are now carpets of wildflowers, gardens of rock, and glistening lakes. Throughout this time, the Alpine Sierra has come and gone, at times completely inundated by the rising tide of trees, and at other times much more widespread than today. What we revel in today is but a moment in time, a blink of the geologic eye, a fleeting glimpse of beauty in a world of constant change.

Though the mechanisms that induced global climate change and resulted in the Pleistocene glaciation are not fully understood, there are a few factors that seem to have undoubtedly contributed to global cooling. These include the position of the continents in relation to the poles, global circulation of ocean waters, weathering rates of land masses, uplift of mountain ranges, and atmospheric carbon dioxide levels. It is important to consider that the chronology of the following events has not yet been deciphered, and is the subject of hot debate among geologists and climatologists alike.

Over 100 million years ago, during the Cretaceous period of the Mesozoic era, the whole earth experienced a prolonged and relatively warm spell. Throughout the characteristically warm, wet Cretaceous period, most of the continental land-masses were gathered around the equatorial regions of the globe. This allowed warmer ocean waters to circulate around the planet. At the poles, these dark masses of ocean waters were less likely to freeze due to continued circulation, as they absorbed and captured a tremendous amount of solar radiation and distributed it around the globe. This situation perpetuated an ice-free global climate. Temperature gradients between the equatorial regions and the poles were much less than today, and the planet experienced a warm, moist period of rela-tively few temperature extremes. As the dinosaurs waned, primitive insects found nectar left for them in open, colorful plant appendages, and flowers changed the world.

Around forty million years ago, during the Oligocene epoch of the Tertiary period, the warm-wet dynamic of the Cretaceous began to change. Antarctica was skating towards the South Pole. The landmass, lacking the heat-holding capacity of water, cooled things off significantly and began accumulating ice. Soon the ice itself mirrored heat back out to the atmosphere, and one of many feedback loops led to the encasing of Antarctica in glacial ice. As the continents continued their drift away from the equator, things cooled down even more. As polar ice caps built up, sea levels dropped. As sea levels dropped, land bridges between continents were exposed, cutting off arctic ocean waters from warmer replenishment in the south. These isolated waters got colder and colder, freezing into an ice shelf that covered the polar regions to the north. Woolly mammoths and giant ground sloths made their debut.

As the continents approached their present positions, ocean basins that had been expanding since the break-up of Pangea reached their maximum volume and the fixed amount of ocean water on the planet couldn't quite fill them up. The result was lower sea levels and more exposed landmass. As this was happening, world-wide uplift of land surfaces occurred throughout the Late Cenozoic era, including the Himalayas, Alps, Austral-Pacific Ranges, and the Andes, not to mention the many ranges of the North American Cordillera. These major uplifts, among many other factors, may have resulted in wide scale climatic change, altering air circulation and weathering rates across the globe. Increased weathering required an increase in carbon dioxide consumption, thus decreasing the greenhouse effect and reflecting less heat back to the earth. The result was global cooling. As the planet cooled, temperature gradients at the poles became greater than at the equator. Air and water began to shift around to compensate, ultimately leading to stormy weather all across the globe. As the snow and ice came down over the poles and high mountains, it collected and compacted over many years to form the huge glaciers of the Late Pliocene and Pleistocene epochs.

The ice grew. A third of Eurasia and half of North America were inundated. By three million years ago, at the close of the Pliocene, the first glacial ice appeared at the mid-latitudes, including the Sierra Nevada. The ice age slowly wrapped itself around more and more of the earth's surface. This was not the first large-scale glaciation of the earth. Evidence in Africa and South America indicate that large-scale glaciation occurred in the Paleozoic as Gondwanaland rode over the South Pole on its way to becoming part of Pangea. Before that, Rodinia held substantial glaciers of its own as parts of it encountered polar latitudes. Conclusion: stick a continental landmass over a pole and things get chilly.

Between fifteen and twenty glaciations are thought to have occurred throughout the Pleistocene epoch, each averaging about 100,000 years long. Average global temperatures during these glaciations were five to fifteen degrees cooler than during interglacial periods. Although evidence is scant concerning the earlier glaciations, it is believed that they were of about the same extent as the more recent glaciations. Between each glaciation were warmer interglacial periods during which the glacial ice melted wholly or partially off. During these times, Pleistocene conifer forests rose up the flanks of the mountains, squeezing the alpine areas up to even higher elevations, only to be chased down by the alpine tundra as the climate cooled once again. During cooler periods, when it would seem that the alpine habitat would expand the most, glaciers covered the landscape, again contracting the alpine habitat to the highest unglaciated peaks and plateaus. The Alpine Sierra fluctuated greatly, even as the Sierra Nevada continued to heave upward throughout the Pleistocene.

Since the end of the last major glaciation around 10,000 years ago, the climate in the Sierra Nevada has continued to fluctuate in correspondence with the greater climatic fluctuations of the planet. The warming period of 8,000 to 6,000 years ago (called the "climatic optimum" by climatologists) wiped the region completely clean of glacial ice. Treelines raised significantly during this time, though soil development was slow in the wake of the glaciers. This "climatic optimum" did not last long, and was followed by a series of four small-scale glacial advances beginning around 5,800 years ago. The most notable (and most recent) of these was the Little Ice Age (1350-1850), during which all of the remaining glaciers in the Sierra Nevada, and many that have since ablated, advanced significantly. The Little Ice Age was caused by increased atmospheric circulation, which shifted the polar front southward by five to ten degrees, allowing wetter weather to bombard Western North America with precipitation. As temperatures worldwide averaged one to two degrees colder than at present, snow levels dropped 300 to 500 feet throughout the Northern Hemisphere, causing glaciers across the globe to grow and sea ice to expand. A warming trend in the mid-1800's brought a close to the Little Ice Age, and glaciers all over the world retreated rapidly.

Recent years have been no exception to the rule of climatic fluctuations in the Alpine Sierra Nevada. Studies of tree rings in the alpine zone indicate that the last century has brought both severe drought (1910-1934) and a long period of relatively high precipitation (1937-1986) that has been exceeded only twice during the last 1,000 years. The Sierra Nevada are still in a period of a high precipitation anomaly, though shorter drought within may partially disguise this little known fact. Climate change over the last 2,000 years, including the recent global warming of the late twentieth century, may be attributed to the amount and quality of insolation in the Alpine Sierra, due in part to the Milankovitch cycles. Other influences may include volcanic activity, global air circulation, and shifting landmasses.

The interplay between what is occurring both beneath and above the surface work together to determining what happens above. For the Alpine Sierra, this has meant constant expansion and contraction ever since its birth during the Tertiary period. Since then, the land has seen conifers, ice, bare rock, soil, bright-eyed wildflowers, and countless walking and flying creatures, all chased in and out of the top of the range by the winds of change. The present day climate is the determining factor of the size and extent of the Alpine Sierra, delineating and maintaining its boundaries. A few million years may well bring both forests and ice to the region, then back to fell fields, lakes, and flowers as one of the many concentric cycles completes itself yet again.

Part Two

Alpine Ecology

Into the Cold
Alpine Ecosystems

"The high mountain crests showing roseate in the light of the setting sun, then fading to gray, then glimmering obscurely in the moonlight. Flowers, flowers almost everywhere."

Norman Clyde (journal entry from Alta Peak)

Mt. Ritter

It was one-thirty in the afternoon when I set out from camp along the ridge between Davis and Thousand Island Lakes. With the opportunity to be alone for the half a day, I left my students to their Sierra Nevada natural history and ecology studies, and made my way due west and south towards North Glacier Pass, to find my way up Mt. Davis by way of a back door. I trod my way downslope, between twisted whitebark pines, prostrate alpine everlasting, Brewer's lupine, and red mountain heather, across streamlets lined with blooming corn lilies, sweet willows, and hundreds of crimson red paintbrushes, over rocks of all sizes and mysterious metavolcanic origin, across the chunky talus and old snow to the bottom of the pass.

As the climbing got steeper I resolved to continue to the top of the pass without stopping, feeling good and strong after a night and a half-day of rest. Many steps later, I reached the top of the Little Ice Age moraine that makes North Glacier Pass. I was breathless, but reinvigorated by the sight of the deepened sapphire waters of Lake Catharine, gem among gems, as house-sized chunks of ice and snow gave themselves to her unfathomably deep waters: the inner eye of the mountains.

I kept moving, scrambling up the steep talus to the north of the pass, decorated elegantly with pink Sierra primrose. To the south of Mt. Davis, were the dark looming silhouettes of

Alpine ecology page: Coville's columbine *(Aquilegia pubescens)* by Martha McCord.

Mts. Ritter and Banner. Looking over at them, I wondered how I could possibly get to the top of either one before dusk. Soon, I arrived atop Davis' rolling plateau, and began heading toward its summit, contemplating the long slog through talus and snow between myself and that strange, almost lopsided-looking peak. Without stopping, I crossed the wide back of the plateau in search of the highest point. My energy seemed unebbing as I pumped myself up the summit ridge to the high seat and for the first time since I left camp, took the weight off of my legs.

I was momentarily transfixed by the white swath of the east Davis glacier several hundred feet down, and had a short-lived fantasy about free-falling down to its frosty slope, then riding the great white bib all the way down to upper Davis Lake and flying straight into the cold waters. Snapping out of it, I shifted around for another look to the south. Ritter and Banner stood like dark towers of impregnable austerity, beautiful in their simplicity, yet awesome in their majesty. Something seated deeply in my being was driving me to go there, though I had planned to visit those lofty heights the next day. An inner voice called, saying, *the time is now, or perhaps, never.*

In a short time, I was off Davis and back down to Lake Catharine, stopping only to fill my bottle with the icy waters coming off the Davis plateau snowfield. I tinkered along the bulky moraine of North Glacier Pass, then traversed the rock and snow along the upper south shore, and finally hopped over the small lateral moraine near the terminus of the ice and set my soggy feet down onto the firn of North Glacier.

Looking up that big white tongue of ice framed by the incredible hulks of Ritter and Banner on either side, I felt genuinely tired for the first time all day. I knew I had to get up and beyond what appeared to be the top of the snow, and do so quickly. The glacier was a grunt only worsened by the fact that the sun cups deepened the higher I climbed. I knew I was pushing it by the dizziness in my head and the leaden feeling in my limbs. I stumbled and slipped, a sign of a weakened body and neglected mind. Nevertheless, I hauled myself up onto the saddle rocks, fell onto my back and just breathed for awhile. Then, I noticed a figure moving down the talused ridge from Banner.

It was Heather Gates, my teaching assistant, who had left camp just after me with the intention of climbing Banner Peak. Under the guise of scouting out Mt. Ritter for tomorrow's potential ascent, I called to her to come off of Banner and down to the saddle. As she carefully descended Banner's notorious talus, I listened for the clinking sound of moving rocks that would indicate her coming. By the time she was in near view I was already making my way up the finger of glacier that tickled the east flank of Ritter. From my perspective (and no doubt hers), my line led up to a definitely vertical, undoubtedly loose and unscalable chute of rock that, according to legend, led up to the summit ridge. Unable to see the ridge itself, I doubted that it was even possible, especially given the fact that we were free-tramping without any technical equipment.

By this time of afternoon, the east side of Mt. Ritter was in shade, and the snow on which I was climbing had begun to harden. This actually proved for the best, because as the slope reached a maximum angle that seemed to exceed fifty degrees, I needed all the help I could get to find adequate steps. The cups and small frozen hogbacks in the snow proved invaluable for this purpose. Soon, I developed a different concern. Looking into the deepest pockmarks, I noticed that each of them held in their bottom a dark chunk of rock. Looking around, I soon realized there were hundreds of them, rockfall from above was littering the snow surface. I looked up into the chute, half expecting the whole thing to come tumbling down as a sudden earthquake sheared off the entire east side of Mt. Ritter. I shook my head. My hands were getting cold. I had to hurry up and reach the rock.

From those last steps on the hardened snow, I reached up and grabbed at relative security: frozen magma instead of frozen water. It felt good. I climbed up to a steady perch and tried to find Heather. I called to her. She called back.

"Is that you?" echoed through the notch.

"Yes," I said. "Are you coming up here?"

"What are you doing?" she yelled.

"Checking out the route!" I shouted back. There was a pause. I think she realized what I really had in mind.

"Are you going for the top?" she asked, as if there were ever a question in either of our minds.

"Are you?" That was it. She was moving. Halfway up, she reached where I had left my shoulder-bag in the snow. "I don't have my long johns or shirt with me," she said, concerned.

"In my bag, grab my parka."

When Heather got up to the ledge, she had a kind of mad, confused, even excited look in her eyes. Everything was happening dizzyingly fast.

"This is it," I said convincingly. "There's no other time but right now. Get ready for the quickest mountaintop satori of your life. We're finally going up the mountain we've both dreamed about."

The chute looked treacherously loose, so I chose a smaller, more solid run to the right. We followed the line upward several hundred feet, hard but sturdy class three climbing all the way. Eventually the chute spit us out and onto a series of tricky class four moves that looked as though they were leading to even more dangerous climbing. Heather suggested traversing back to the left, which would put us at the top of the main chute.

Mt. Ritter (13,157') from Davis Plateau. Photo: David Gilligan

Her idea seemed better only after I made a few foolhardy moves and almost got myself stuck out on a narrow ledge. I worked my way back down and followed her over to the main chute.

Once safe, we continued up and across, tending south, to our left. After a series of hand and foot moves I worked my way up to a small notch between two standing stones, then passed between them. Before me was a narrow ledge below a dark, vertical wall. The ledge led to a steep, narrow chute choked with snow and ice. Above the chute I could see the waning light of day, and the waiting steps of the summit block. Finally I was sure that we could make it. I called back to Heather, "It's here! It's here!"

We crossed the ledge, then ascended, wedging our bodies between ice and rock and squeezing our way up the chute one at a time. This was a fitting finale to an outstanding climb, one that required every ounce of my attention the entire way. Upon reaching the top of the chute, I called down to Heather, telling her to begin her ascent. Then I sat down, my body finally free to release a head full of endorphines. I sat there dazed and elated, feeling my pulse in every minute corner of my body. Then I looked up, only to see the slender, furry face of a weasel. It was soft but fierce, conspicuously masked with cream-white across an otherwise brown head. It stared right at me with unreadable eyes, and I stared back. After a few seconds of this, it turned and wove its way back into the rocks. The presence of the weasel surprised me.

I wondered, given the circumstances and my state of being, what a weasel would be doing all the way up here at 13,000 feet above sea level. My best guess was that it was assigned this position to provide borderline mystical experiences for early evening exhausted mountaineers in search of boons and totems. My second guess was that it was making a fine summer living off of rosy finch eggs and nestlings, and would move off the mountain when the breeding season ended. Both guesses probably had some truth to them. Either way, I was going to follow that weasel all the way to the top of Mt. Ritter.

With Heather on top of the chute and me a touch less lucid, we skipped across the ridge to the tip-top of one of the largest hunks of rock in the central Sierra: Mt. Ritter, a mountain even among mountains. So filled was I with the strange energy of near dusk that I threw my head back and unloaded what was left of my lungs to the mountain air. A hoot of such brilliant volume and pitch had never before issued forth from my body—my throat wide open and diaphragm contracted in an effort of trancendental expression. All around us the silver-white snow of the alpine landscape was tinged with the slightest hint of gold. Consciously aware that my time here would be short, I opened my senses wide, as if turning my body into an open hole into which the experience of 13,143 feet in the golden evening, euphoria, and the dizzy drama of the fastest, hardest, most liberating climb of my life all flooded into my being like an ocean entering into a small but sturdy vessel. My ideas of containment were shattered and in their place came an epiphany.

There was no boon here for me to collect and return with. No noble truth awaited me. There was no seeing through nature and into something deeper, for the depth of nature before me was infinite in itself. This was no platonic shadow of reality cast upon the wall of a cave. I was not a victim of illusion chained to the stone of such a dark place. My vision was simply that of what was around me, blinding in its reality. There was no need for the supernatural here when the natural was hitting me across the face with a billion tons of rock, saying, "This is all there is, and all there needs to be."

I think Heather and I were both feeling something like this as we sat beaming and laughing out loud, gulping down fresh snowmelt water and eating dried mango slices. People often say you only live once. Whether the Hindu and Buddhist ressurectionists have had it wrong or right all this time, I can conceive of no other way of living this precious life than as if it were both the first and the last time I will have to kiss the raw bones of the earth, shaken upward in a stone embrace with the alpine sky. As John Muir said, going to the mountains *really is going home.*

Tip-toes and falling rocks on the descent, then we slid across glaciers and snowfields, hopped boulders and jumped streams as the light grew deeper golden, then orange-peach, then rose, then crimson-red. Altocumulous clouds were strung across the sky like illuminated necklaces of jewels. To the east rose the glowing orb of the full moon, initiating the night. Shadows returned and lengthened. One last uphill climb, and we returned exhausted, emptied, and spent. I stumbled to the sweet-smelling grass, and eventually crawled like a baby to the warm cocoon of my sleeping bag. The day was done.

Alpine   at   Last

Alpine Environments

As you ascend into the high country, everything about the alpine zone seems to make it a world of its own. The evergreen slopes of the montane forest below give way to stark, open country. The air is brisk, cool, and thin, valuable to breathe. The light is sharp, illuminating the world with meticulous clarity. The land is angular and steep, its contours seemingly over-stated. The plants are shrunken, dwarfed, lying low beneath the prevailing influences of wind and snow. They are compact and efficient in all ways, able to survive in a land where growing conditions persist for little more than two months out of the year. The ground is decorated with patterns of rocks and vege-tation, like hieroglyphs telling the tales of the mountains. Miniature deserts and soggy bogs border one another, hosting plants that are found in the arctic next to those that are found in the deserts below, along with varieties that grow nowhere else on earth but in the Alpine Sierra. Visiting birds pick stranded insects out of the snow while fat, furry mammals bumble their way across the boulder fields. The alpine zone hums with life for a short summer before the snows of autumn plunge it back into its trademark quality, the cold. This is the alpine zone, the land of extremes, in all its brightness, whiteness, and wildness.

Alpine areas across the globe are so named because of their close affinity to the Alps of Europe. The word alpine derives

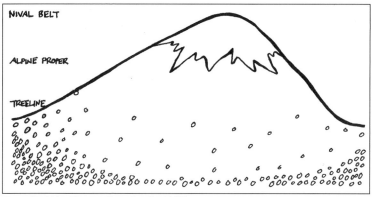

Figure 10. Alpine lifezones. Illustration: David Gilligan

from the Latin for "white," used during the high days of Rome
in reference to the snow-covered treeless peaks of Northern
Italy, and later used to describe the inhabitants of this region.
Eventually, the word found wider use, and has since been used
to describe similar snow-covered mountains all over the world.
But what are the similarities that these mountain regions share?
What are the criteria that make a place truly alpine?

Simply stated, alpine areas are those that are found at and
above the upper treeline (also referred to as the cold, or alpine
treeline) of the greater region in which they are set. The distinction between what is truly alpine and what is not, however, can
be far more complicated than this single criterion would suggest.
It is not enough to simply say that the alpine zone begins where
the trees end. Upper treeline, though a pronounced ecological
boundary, is rarely a definable "line," and more typically forms
a transitional zone, or ecotone, between the more distinct communities of the montane forest below and the alpine zone above.
The effects of alpine conditions are evidenced in the growth
forms of trees, which exhibit remarkable adaptations to extremes
of cold and wind, persisting upward from the montane forest

and into the open lands above. While many consider this upper treeline ecotone a separate "subalpine zone," it also represents both the lower reaches of the alpine zone, and the upper reaches of the montane forest. As the alpine influences are readily apparent here, we will consider it the lower reaches of the greater Sierran alpine zone.

Alpine areas of mid-latitudes, including the Alpine Sierra, may be considered as composed of a series of lifezones, much like the forested slopes below, based on the effects of increasing elevation (Figure 10). The lowest lifezone of the greater alpine ecosystem, as discussed above, is the transitional belt of the upper treeline. This zone extends from the upper extent of the continuous forest to the point above which no trees, however adapted to alpine conditions, can grow. Above the transitional belt is the alpine proper, characterized by the total absence of trees and the dominance of prostrate, dwarfed, vascular plant life. Still higher is the aeolian belt, or nival belt, distinct from the alpine proper because it occurs above the upper limit of vascular plant growth. The delineation between the alpine and nival belts typically coincides with the permanent snow level, though there are many exceptions to this. Life is largely restricted to lichens, making a sparse living among the true rock and ice of high altitudes and latitudes alike. Nutrition comes to the few inhabitants of these areas via windblown organic matter. The Alpine Sierra does not presently have a distinct nival belt, the closest example being just north, atop Mt. Shasta. Representatives of nival habitats do, however, extend down into the alpine proper, where smaller patches with nival conditions persist.

Alpine vegetation is often referred to as tundra. The word tundra comes to us from the Finnish language, and was used to refer to the treeless regions of northern Eurasia. With European immigration to North America, the term tundra was accordingly tagged onto any region that resembled the Eurasian original. While the tundra of alpine areas is determined by increased elevation and associated climatic conditions, the tundra of the polar regions is determined by increased latitude, emulating similar climatic conditions. The polar tundra is called arctic tundra, after the Greek word arktos, meaning "bear." The Latin equivalent is ursae, meaning "bear," as in ursae minor and ursae major, the bear constellations used to locate Polaris, the north star. Arctic has come to refer to the high northern latitudes.

All tundra, be it arctic or alpine, shares only one thing: low mean air temperatures during the growing season. All other environmental factors have their own gradients. The tundras of the world may be considered as three types: arctic, alpine (generally considered mid-latitude), and equatorial. Alpine and equatorial tundra are distinct from arctic in that alpine and equatorial tundra boundaries are determined by altitude rather than latitude. At both ends of its range, alpine tundra may overlap with that of the poles and the equatorial regions, such as the Brooks Range of Alaska, and the Andes of South America.

There are many generalities concerning all tundras. In general, the growing season increases closer to the equator. Polar desert tundra of the higher latitudes (75-90 degrees) consistently has the shortest growing season in the world, though diurnal temperature fluctuations during the growing season are relatively low due to the low elevation and round-the-clock insolation. Tundras of the equatorial regions, in contrast, have a year-round growing season, with high diurnal temperature fluctuations due to high elevations and extreme variance in insolation levels, often resulting in extreme heat by day and killing frosts by night. Alpine tundra, spanning the mid-latitudes between these extremes, has the most unpredictable growing season of all tundra types. Here, though average summer temperatures are higher than the arctic, the growing season may actually be shorter due to the effects of lingering snowpack. Other years, when snowpack is less, the growing season will be longer. Most years, however, it is both, as one shaded site remains snowbound through mid-August while an adjacent site flowers in mid-June.

The diversity of life varies greatly among different tundra types. In general, biological diversity decreases as latitude increases. Accordingly, arctic tundras tend to have low diversity and high numbers of individuals within each species, while equatorial tundras tend to have high diversity and lower numbers among each species. Alpine tundras almost always have higher levels of biological diversity than arctic areas of the same size due to slightly higher summer temperatures, diversity of habitats (due to topography), and inward migration pathways from both the arctic and the adjacent lowlands. Among all tundras, the subject of biological diversity is further complicated by climatic change and associated glacial histories. Glaciated areas tend to have lower diversity than non-glaciated areas of similar latitude, such that an unglaciated tundra further north may have a more diverse flora than a glaciated (or previously glaciated) area far to the south.

Alpine tundra exhibits condensed microclimates due to the effects of minute topographic variations on moisture availability. Combinations of topographic and moisture gradients are referred to by alpine ecologists as "mesotopographic gradients." These gradients are created in the alpine zone by snowmelt throughout the summer months, which supplies an abundance of surface water to lower areas, while ground only inches higher may remain relatively dry throughout the growing season, and thus support entirely different vegetation. The result is a compressed, miniature mosaic of specialized natural communities formed in response to moisture availability and soil. Waterlogged snow-bank communities may border communities with desert conditions throughout the growing season, each tiny topographic area seemingly starving for the relief that the adjacent patch of ground has to offer. In actuality, the plants of each of these communities are specifically adapted to the amount of available water and soil conditions of the area. Though species may differ from place to place, growth forms are the same along these mesotopographic gradients. Where moisture is not limiting, such as below snow drifts, and along bogs and streams, grasses, sedges, and rushes tend to dominate, along with willows. Drier areas such as ridges, gravel flats, and rock crannies are characterized by cushion-like plants and stemless rosettes: skirts of leaves growing out from the center of the plant in all directions. Prostrate mats and shrubs may range across all gradients.

As we know, the Alpine Sierra is a mid-latitude alpine ecosystem, extending in a narrow northwest-southeast strip 150-200 miles in length by 10-20 miles in width, experiencing a tempered Mediterranean-maritime climate regime. It is primarily a granitic mountain range, with a complex, rich geologic history, including extensive glaciations throughout the Pleistocene, resulting in repeated compression and expansion of the Sierran Alpine zone. Presently, the alpine zone consists of a transitional belt and an alpine belt, with not enough altitudinal span to allow for a nival belt, though nival conditions do exist within the alpine belt. The Alpine Sierra Nevada is warmer than any other alpine area of comparable latitude in North America, drier than most during the growing season, and wetter than most during winter. As such, it is like no other alpine area in the continent.

Patterns in the Ground

Frozen Ground Phenomena

Looking closely at the alpine ground, you will begin to see patterns emerging from the land. Grasses grow in concentric circles, heart-shaped wreaths, and hummocks balding on top. Rocks are piled together, or strung out across the ground, forming streams and streaks, garlands, hoops, and rings. Slopes seem to sag, the thin veneer of soil pulling away from the bedrock beneath. An assortment of rocks in a low-lying depression appears as a miniature field of monuments, seemingly random in their placement, fist-sized stones strewn across a staccato carpet of sedges.

Due to the combination of geology and climate, soil development in the Alpine Sierra Nevada is slow compared to that of other alpine regions. The primarily granitic parent material is extremely resistant to degradational forces relative to other rock types. Extreme summer aridity augments what are already slow decomposition rates. The extensive glaciations of the Pleistocene scoured away existent soils and polished the granitic rock surfaces to a hard sheen. The shortened growing season of the alpine zone decreases the rate of soil development still more. Late lying snow patches prevent soil development in many areas by impeding the organic processes necessary for decomposition. These factors combine to result in Alpine Sierran soils which are thin, gravelly to sandy, and low in organic matter.

Heart-shaped grass–frozen ground in Humphreys Basin. Photo: Martha McCord

Soil scientists call such soils lithosols when they are undevel-oped and are lacking distinct, layered horizons, and entosols when horizons are minimally developed.

In addition to having rudimentary soils, the alpine ground is subject to repeated freezing and thawing throughout the year. Freeze-thaw cycles are most frequent and intense during spring and fall, when diurnal temperature fluctuations are the greatest. Although permafrost is not widespread in alpine areas, and is in fact a rarity in the Alpine Sierra Nevada, frozen ground phenomena are widespread. Frost action is the main weathering agent in the alpine zone, reducing boulders to talus, talus to scree, scree to gravel, and gravel to sand and soil. Within the soil, repeated freezing and thawing of water results in patterns in the ground, among rocks, soil, and vegetation alike.

When water within the soil freezes it expands, increasing the volume of the soil and exerting pressure on other objects, thus forcing them to shift around to accommodate the growing ice. Weathered, broken bedrock, as well as buried rocks are slowly moved to the surface, where they are pushed to the outside of hummocks. This process may form rock piles, stripes, and nearly symmetrical circles. These are easily confused with rocks that have dropped out of melting snowbanks. Dropped rocks are more often scattered randomly across saturated depressions left by the sagging weight of the late-lying snow, and rarely exhibit the classic patterns of rocks that have been pushed to the surface by freeze-thaw cycles.

Ice in the soil often forms needle ice, a phenomenon that also occurs at lower elevations. These thin, vertical columns of ice are most visible when the crystals actually raise the soil surface. Needle ice only forms in wet soils, where temperatures drop slowly below the freezing point. It begins forming when a thin layer of ice forms parallel to the soil surface. Perpendicular needles form as the developing ice pulls water up from the saturated soil below. As the ice continues to form, the increasing volume raises the soil surface. As the mound elevates, seedling roots are torn and rocks are displaced. As the ice melts, it leaves behind dead seedlings, displaced rocks, and mounds as evidence of its occurrence.

Hummocks form due to freeze-thaw cycles in bogs. The cycle begins when the tops of larger hummocks lose their snow protection and are ravaged by the elements, denuding them of their vegetative cover. Needle ice is then free to crumble the soil, which in time is also blasted away by the wind. Frost action moves buried rocks upward, displacing them on the outside of the hummock, leaving the center a convex, frost-heaved depression. As soil develops along the outer perimeter of the hummock, plants become established, keeping the soil in, eventually leveling and stabilizing the center. As plant cover becomes complete, the mound is raised again, and the cycle begins anew.

The melting of ice can be equally as influential on the alpine landscape as the formation of ice. Melting ice within soil causes the soil to become saturated, resulting in solifluction: the differential slump and creep of soil layers on slopes due to thawing. The sheer weight of many late-lying snowbanks creates and exaggerates depressions in the ground. These depressions capture the meltwater of the melting snow and hold it like a shallow bowl. Thus, snowbank depressions, once free from snow, are classically wet, soggy troughs. Saturated soils, in combination with subsequent freeze-thaw cycles, make snowbank depressions unique and interesting habitats for plants to live in.

The alpine ground is a unique aspect of the alpine ecosystem. In the Sierra Nevada, thin gravelly soils, freeze-thaw cycles, rock patterns, needle ice, hummocks, solifluction, and snow bank depressions all contribute to the diverse character of the ground. Aspects of the region's geologic history, geomorphology, weather and climate, and ecology all come together to influence the changing veneer of soil and stone that temporarily covers the bones of the mountains. Rocks break down to soil as ice heaves upward at the surface. Soil blows or slides away as new material takes its place, an ongoing cycle of the mountains shedding their skins, over and over again.

Precipice Lake, an example of an oligotrophic water body. Photo: Martha McCord

P l a c e s   t o   L i v e

Alpine Habitats

Looking across an alpine basin of the Sierra Nevada with a trained eye, you will notice a quilt of little worlds that together comprise the greater alpine community. Flowers poke out from beneath a lingering snowbank next to a broad slab of granite, ground and polished to a dance floor sheen. A meltwater stream winds through a wet meadow while a sprawling cushion plant a few feet away lies parched in a miniature desert. Rock faces barely support leathery lichen while wildflowers peek out from crevices among the boulders. Underground, animals turn back the hand of time. Bite by bite, a rich meadow becomes a dry gravel flat. The Alpine Sierra is full of such subtleties and nuances.

The Sierran alpine zone is by no means a homogeneous ecosystem. All alpine tundra exhibits mesotopographic gradients due to the effects of minute topographic variations on moisture availability. In the Sierra these gradients are amplified by the Mediterranean climate. Winters are exceptionally wet, bringing heavy snows and deep snowpack, which linger throughout the summer months. Summers bring drought conditions. The result is a dramatic juxtaposition between wet and dry microclimates, more dramatic than any other alpine region in North America. Miniature deserts and wetlands stand just inches away from each other, and plants of drastically different worlds grow in close proximity to one another, mingling ever-so-slightly along relatively strict moisture bound-aries. While at first glance the alpine ecosystem appears small and simple, closer inspection reveals great diversity.

In the Alpine Sierra Nevada, where drought conditions persist throughout the summer, plants are dependent on melt-water streams and lakes for moisture. Thousands of lakes and streams dot and cross the high country, fed by the heavy snows of winter as they melt away into the familiar snowfields of the summer months. The snowmelt surge of late spring and early summer brings moisture to many locations that dry up as the growing season matures. In general, moisture availability becomes increasingly limited to streamsides, lakeshores, and snowbank communities as the summer progresses, leaving only brief, infrequent thundershowers for the higher ground: scree and talus slopes, boulder fields, rock crannies, and gravel flats. Under such conditions, a few inches of elevation mean the difference between plenty of water or none at all. A site can be completely submerged beneath a meltwater stream, or just out of water's reach for the entire growing season.

Streams and lakes, being aquatic, are the wettest habitats of the alpine zone. Alpine streams vary according to their source, temperature, volume, and water clarity. Streams fed directly by glacial meltwater are called kryal streams, and are characterized by low temperatures (thirty-nine degrees Fahrenheit and less), fluctuating volume, rocky channels, and water ranging from clear to turbid, depending on the amount of suspended glacial flour. They have the shortest growing season of all alpine streams. Higher plants and animals such as fish are absent due to limited food sources which include algae, cyanobac-teria, or other organic matter blown in by the wind. Streams fed by snowbanks, lakes, and runoff are called rithral. These streams are similar to glacial streams, but tend to have slightly warmer temperatures (41 to 50 degrees), more consistent water clarity, and a longer growing season, thus supporting a richer aquatic flora and fauna, including mosses, algae, lichen, and occasionally trout. Streams fed by groundwater are called krenal, and are less common in the Alpine Sierra. These streams have temperatures corresponding to the mean air temperature of the region (32 to 46.5 degrees), thus are relatively cool in the summer and warm during the winter, and less subject to freezing than other stream types. Since these streams originate from springs, flow is relatively low volume, but consistent and clear. This relatively stable habitat supports the most diverse aquatic flora and fauna of any alpine stream type, including abundant algae, aquatic invertebrates, and char (introduced to the Sierra).

Lakes in the Alpine Sierra are the result of glaciation. All alpine lakes have a continuous inflow and outflow, and water circulates throughout the body of water. Temperatures range from 40 to 50 degrees Fahrenheit when lakes are not frozen over. The clear, blue-green water gets its color from glacial flour and other minute particles in suspension, reflecting blue and green light. The organic input into these lakes is low due to the nature of their sources: cold, fast-moving meltwater streams. Thus, organic growth is low, further contributing to the clarity of the water.

The lakes of the Alpine Sierra have been slowly but surely filling in with sediments since the last big ice sheets pulled back. Generally, lakes at higher elevations are slower to fill than those at lower elevations, due to the combined factors of smaller watersheds, shorter ice-free periods, shorter growing seasons, and slow soil development. Also, high elevation lakes are the most recently exposed by retreating glaciers, some being glaciated as recently as a few hundred years ago, during the Little Ice Age.

Accordingly, the lower and older the lake, the more filled it should be. These sediments may be dissolved in solution, suspended, or remain for the most part at the bottom of lakes and streams. As sediments increase, nutrients are added to the lake water. Water temperatures also increase, as there is more material in the water to hold heat. Overall, biological productivity increases as the lake fills in, a process called eutrophication, meaning "good," or "improved nutrients."

A somewhat predictable succession of ecological changes takes place as a Sierran lake undergoes eutrophication. These processes vary in different geographic regions of the world, and even within the Alpine Sierra may vary greatly. Generally, as the depth of the lake becomes less the water is displaced outward, resulting in an increasingly wide and shallow body of water. As water levels fluctuate seasonally, well-adapted plants may eventually move in and inhabit the fringes. Soon the lake becomes shallow enough that rooted aquatic plants can potentially move in from the periphery. All of these plants help stabilize the soil, and incoming sediment is less likely to wash out the outlet, and thus collects still more rapidly. As the cycle continues, the lake may evolve into a soggy wet meadow, inhabited for a few thousand years by those plants that can handle inundation by standing water throughout the growing season. At treeline and below, lodgepole pine seedlings may establish themselves where pocket gophers have churned up fresh mineral soil. Slowly but surely the trees move in, until an avalanche or insect infestation wipes them out. In the past and probable future, the ice comes back, wiping the slate clean and beginning the cycle anew.

As eutrophication occurs, alpine lakes vary according to their elevations and volumes. Higher elevation lakes remain frozen longer, have shorter growing seasons, and smaller floras and faunas. These lakes are called oligotrophic, meaning "slight nutrients," and are typically clear and cold, with low organic input and high oxygen levels. These are your classic glacial tarns and upper paternoster lakes, held in a bowl of car-sized frost-riven rocks, and offering both the most intimidating and the most rewarding swims. Moving down in elevation, lakes thaw progressively sooner and freeze later in the year, have a longer growing season, thus relatively rich floras and faunas. Such lakes are called mesotrophic, meaning "middle nutrients," and are characterized by slightly warmer waters with greater sediment input and a higher level of organics. These lakes are typically fringed by sedges, rushes, and willows, as well as lodgepole pines and alders at treeline. Few alpine lakes have reached further stages of eutrophication, as sediments have only been accumulating for some 10,000 years.

Two human-induced factors have had further influences on alpine lake communities. Acidification of lake waters, commonly a result of acid rain, has been shown to have detrimental effects on the microscopic animals that form the base of the food chain in the aquatic ecosystem. The introduction of non-native trout and char has been linked to the dramatic decline of native frog and toad species throughout the Alpine Sierra, as the fish not only compete with the amphibians for food, but also prey on the frogs and toads directly. Prior to these introductions, only west slope streams supported native rainbow trout, and a few streams of the southern High Sierra hosted native golden trout. Alpine lakes have never provided an abundant enough food source to sustain ongoing fish populations. For this reason, most higher elevation lakes are restocked every year.

Moving onshore, moist alpine habitats occur along lakeshores, stream banks, benches, near seeps, and downslope from snowbanks. Such habitats are called mesic, meaning that they are in

Mountaineer's shooting star (*Dodecatheon redolens*). Photo: Martha McCord

the middle of the moisture gradient. Accordingly, the plants that grow in mesic conditions are called mesophytes. These sites support wet and moist meadow communities, distinguished from dry meadows by the fact that they remain green and unwilted throughout the growing season. They thus have a higher overall productivity rate than dry meadows. Wet and moist meadow communities are dominated by sod-forming sedges and grasses which reproduce vegetatively via root networks. The fine roots of these plants often extend over a foot into the soil, altering the soil's parent material and perpetuating soil development. Soils are characteristically cold, acidic, and poorly aerated due to saturation. Frozen ground phenomena are common and evident due to the abundant moisture in the soil. In addition to sedges and grasses, broad-leaved herbs and shrubs may inhabit meadow communities. Shrubs form dense, low-lying thickets and prostrate mats. Representative species include arctic willow, bog kalmia, alpine, subalpine, and mountaineer's shooting stars, greater and lesser elephant heads, Lemmon's paintbrush, and tufted and alpine gentian (blooming later in the season). On slightly dryer sites adjoining wet and moist meadows, red mountain heather and white mountain heather garnish the edges.

Snow distribution is the single most influential factor in alpine plant distribution. The presence or absence of snow determines both the length of the growing season and the amount, location, and timing of available moisture. Snowbank habitats support specialized plant associations due to the especially steep mesotopographic gradients over a relatively small area associated with slow summer melting. Many plant species are restricted to snowbank areas because of the winter protection the snow offers, as well as the protection from summer drought offered by cold, soggy, acidic soils. The costs are the sheer weight of the snow compressing vegetation and restricting growth, colder soil temperatures, increased damage due to frozen ground phenomenon, and a shorter growing season.

Snowbank plant associations usually develop a zonation of concentric rings, the snow melting from the outside in. The outer rings are higher, drier, and snow-free longer than the center, which bears snow the longest. Growth and productivity are greatest in the outer rings of the zonation, and decrease as the growing season shortens in the innermost rings. The central ring, if not completely dark and empty, supports the most mesic plants, including a few specialized varieties of sedges and rushes. Snow may be so late-lying that plants are only exposed for a few days in some years, and, in the most extreme cases, may remain covered with snow all summer. Plants must be able to reproduce vegetatively if they are to persist under such conditions. Surrounding the center of the snowbank community is a ring of lichen and sibbaldia. Sibbaldia is a key indicator plant of late-lying snowbanks, and is found in alpine regions throughout the northern hemisphere. Moving outward, beyond the sibbaldia are grasses, and finally, willows.

The drier habitats of the alpine zone include boulder fields, rocky slopes and associated rock crannies, gravel flats, and dry meadows. These habitats are called xeric, meaning that they are the driest along the moisture gradient. Accordingly, plants adapted to xeric conditions are called xerophytes. Boulder fields and rocky slopes have rock crannies, which offer a more protected environment than do slopes and flats. The majority of the surface area is bare rock, habitable only by lichens. Plants are limited to the spaces between, which offer protection from wind and cold due to snowpack throughout the winter. Well-developed, well-drained soils in crevices allow for at least some moisture year-round, without the saturation of meadow soils. Representative plants in the Alpine Sierra include rock fringe, Davidson's penstemon, mountain pride, alpine gold, Lemmon's draba, Coville's columbine, mountain sorrel, dwarf daisy, granite gilia, showy polemonium, and sky pilot at the highest elevations.

Gravel flats and scree and talus slopes are the most xeric alpine habitats. They occur where frost action has created a jumble of fractured rock material, including everything from boulders to gravel and sand. These areas are often blown free of protective snow cover during the winter, and so offer no protection from wind and wind-borne debris. Wind also wafts away soil particles, leaving wide floors of exposed bedrock. Soils that remain tend to be rudimentary at best, gravelly to sandy with little organic material. Such coarse soils drain quickly, and are usually dry by midsummer. Widely-spaced bunch-grasses, cushions, mats, and rosettes are characteristic of such areas, and many of these plants have counterparts in similar desert-like areas of lower elevations. Representative species in the Alpine Sierra include pussy-paws, oval-leafed eriogonum, alpine everlasting, Muir's and Gordon's ivesia, Coville's phlox, and alpine fescue.

If these communities are left undisturbed for hundreds, sometimes even thousands of years, they will eventually succeed into alpine turf, or dry meadows. Dry meadows are distinguished from wet meadows by the fact that they dry up by mid July, and their plant inhabitants must complete their reproductive cycles by this time. For this reason, dry meadow plants have especially rapid productivity, though overall it is lower than that of wet meadows, which continue to produce through August. Their species composition is markedly different from that of wet meadows, and includes more xeric-adapted graminoids (grass-like plants) and perennial herbs. Representative species

Alpine gold *(Hulsea algida)* Photo: Martha McCord

include Brewer's lupine, Sierra penstemon, alpine everlasting, and several species of bunch grasses. Red mountain heather and white heather often line the fringes here, where additional soil and moisture collects around rock edges. In the Sierra Nevada, these communities are presently on the decline, while those of gravel flats are expanding, largely due to rodent disturbance and erosion. The shift from dry meadows to gravel flats may also be attributed to a climatic shift toward greater aridity.

Pocket gophers and other rodents are a chief cause of disturbance among alpine dry meadow communities. They are responsible for both preventing gravel flats from succeeding into meadows, and meadows turning back into gravel flats. Pocket gophers are rat-sized underground dwellers, feeding on the succulent roots of graminoid plants year-round. Their effects on meadows are numerous. The sedges and grasses that dominate the plant community gradually die off as their root systems are destroyed. Cushion plants, which are not fed on by pocket gophers, are then free to expand. The dirt mounds left by pocket gophers may smother small surface plants. In winter, when the ground is frozen, they burrow through the snow, leaving behind telltale miniature eskers in the spring when the snow melts away. Both mounds and eskers are eroded by wind, which blows the finer soil away, and water, which washes it downslope, leaving coarse gravel and sand. The porous soils that remain drain too quickly to retain water, and the available moisture in the community plummets.

Pocket gopher tunnels may be reinhabited by meadow voles. These mouse-sized rodents feed on sedges and grasses above ground, and may even graze on the expanding cushion plants in times of population stress. They concentrate on the center of the cushion, leaving a distinctive outer ring of living plant material surrounding a denuded center. The cushions will live on as long as their taproots are not severed, which sometimes occurs due to pocket gophers tunneling underground. Eventually, as the graminoids die off, the cushions expand, the soil becomes coarse and the habitat more xeric, and the meadow reverts back to a gravel flat.

From the clear, cold waters of the deepest alpine lake to the highest, most arid gravel flat, the Alpine Sierra Nevada is a varied environment composed of diverse plant communities. As with other alpine regions, moisture availability, governed by topography and soils, is the key factor in determining plant associations for a given site. This results in a compressed assemblage of plant communities, each composed of species with specialized adaptations according to the habitat's position along the mesotopographic gradient. In the Alpine Sierra, moisture gradients are accentuated by summer aridity. Aquatic, mesic, and xeric communities border one another, all existing within a few square yards, and little mixing takes place between them. Some habitats may undergo succession, only to be turned backwards by disturbances. It is a land of great and subtle wonders for the eye to behold.

Twisted Wisdom
Treeline Ecology

"These trees, barely resembling their montane counterparts, are testaments to 'adaptation.' Here, individuals and groups of individuals have broken the ranks and placed themselves in circumstances allowing them to experience a higher risk reality. Although scarred, deformed, and weathered by the events, they have gained the ultimate strength, character, and beauty. We should endeavor to live krummholz lives."

David Lovejoy

Transitions

The Treeline Environment

At treeline, the comfort of the forest below and the intimidation and exhilaration of the open country above merge to become one. Trees similar to those that stood straight and tall at only slightly lower elevations are twisted here, beaten down, bent and contorted like the features of the oldest age. They grow dwarfed, deformed, prone to the will of wind and snow, sprawled across the ground like groping fingers reaching for security. Others seem to defy the law of wind and frozen water, standing erect until they can stand no more, stripped nearly completely of their bark hide, revealing wood tough enough to crack stone wide open. Others are torn, pruned, pushed, or otherwise persuaded to grow as flags, banners, brooms, and skirts, the elements seemingly stretching their lives out, pulling them in the direction of the whipping wind. These trees are made for this. As experts in a land of uncertainty, they tenaciously make a living where no other trees can. They straddle a boundary between two contrasting landscapes, and specialize in dealing with the conditions of both. This is the borderline, the transitional zone of the alpine treeline.

Treeline is the ecotone between the upper montane forest and the alpine zone, and further, the lowest lifezone, called the transitional zone, of the greater alpine ecosystem. As such, it includes elements of both of these distinct ecosystems. Treeline is the place where the distinctions between the forest and the alpine zone come together and mingle, defying their usual categories and resulting in an ecological association worthy of its own discussion.

Relative to other ecological boundaries, alpine treeline is one of the most distinct boundaries found in nature. Even arctic treelines (also cold treelines), which are created by similar ecological conditions, may be dozens of latitudinal miles wide. Alpine treelines, in comparison, are compressed by topographical factors, and rarely span more than a few thousand vertical feet. From just about anywhere in the Alpine Sierra, if you look down into the valleys you will see the place where the open country ends and the trees begin, thickening to seas of green below. Distance provides a perspective that suggests the "line" that the word "treeline" implies. Closer inspection, however, reveals that this 'line' is not so definitive. While in some places the trees do seem to give way quite suddenly to the open country, this is the exception and not the norm. More typical is a broad belt of trees exhibiting adaptations specific to straddling the forest-tundra border, ranging over a thousand feet in elevation between forest below and the alpine belt above.

The transitional zone of the treeline belt reflects the limiting factor of tree growth: cold. It is not the cold of winter that limits the growth of trees, however, but the cold of summer. The trees of the Sierran treeline can withstand temperatures colder than what the Sierra Nevada typically experience in winter, but none of them can withstand it year-round. During the summer growing season, average temperatures must exceed fifty degrees Fahrenheit to allow for tree growth. Where average July temperatures exceed fifty degrees, if all other conditions are favorable, trees will grow. Conversely, where average July temperatures remain below fifty degrees, regardless of other conditions, trees will not grow. The fact that treeline can span over a thousand feet of elevation reflects the flexibility of this ecological criterion.

Treeline occurs at an increasingly lower elevation as you travel north through the Alpine Sierra, corresponding with the increased cooling of air as you move further north from the equator. Within the 200 miles of the Alpine Sierra, treeline lowers from 11,000 feet in the south to 9,500 feet in the north. Continuing north of the range, treeline continues to lower, down to about 6,000 feet in the North Cascades, all the way to the Brooks Range of Alaska, where the alpine treeline catches up with the arctic treeline, north of which tundra grows down to sea level. South of the Sierra Nevada, through Mexico and Central America, the equatorial treeline finds its maximum at around 16,000 feet.

Within the Sierra Nevada are several other types of treelines which are created by different environmental conditions than those which create the alpine treeline. Down in the middle-elevations (6,000-10,000 feet), montane forests frequently border wet meadows, forming "wet" treelines, where soils are not aerated enough to allow for tree growth. In other areas, especially along the west slope, such as in Yosemite Valley, gargantuan granite monoliths dominate the landscape, often times completely devoid of trees. Here, lack of suitable soil is the factor limiting tree growth. Even lower in elevation, where the flat bottom of the Central Valley first tilts upward to the lower foothills of the Sierra Nevada, there is a lower treeline, or "dry" treeline, where a lack of water limits tree growth. Among both alpine and arctic treelines, cold, rather than soil or water, is always the limiting factor, and it is this criterion that distinguishes cold treelines from other treeline types.

In addition to cold, two other main factors contribute to the ecological dynamic of alpine treelines that are of less concern among other treelines. These are wind and snow. High-speed

Looking down to the forest limit in upper Spiller Canyon. Photo: David Gilligan

winds put an additional stress on trees in two ways. First, it may inflict actual mechanical damage to trees by the sheer force of the wind itself, or by wind-borne debris, such as snow, ice, dirt, and dust, resulting in flagging and dwarfing, if not death. Second, wind may also inflict damage by dessication, as the dry, thirsty alpine air moves across trees and draws the moisture out of them. Wind is an especially important factor in exposed sites in alpine treelines of the mid-latitudes, such as in the Sierra Nevada, but less of a factor in arctic and tropical treelines.

Snow has both advantages and disadvantages for tree growth. The sheer weight of snowpack can break branches and even entire trees. As snow shifts downslope it can pull trees with it, often times resulting in trunks bent downslope, called snow knees. Wind-borne snow and ice act as abrasives, accentuating the damage done to trees by wind. On a larger scale, avalanches may take out entire stands of trees. Late-lying snow can also inhibit tree growth in an area that might otherwise support trees. In the Sierra Nevada, snow mold fungi frequently degenerate whitebark pines. The fungi's most favorable growing conditions are just at freezing point, which is the temperature of many late-lying snowfields. The fungi most often affect the lee sides of the trees (or group of trees), killing lower limbs first and eventually moving up into the crown.

Snow also benefits trees. It provides a layer of protection from the harsh elements of winter, sheltering trees from the extreme winds and repeated cycles of freezing and thawing that take place above the surface. Trees growing lower to the ground are best able to take advantage of such protection. When spring comes and melt-off proceeds, such low-lying trees, often growing close to one another for added protection, absorb greater amounts of insolation due to their darker color, and so cause increased meltoff around them. This phenomenon is known as the "black body effect." Snow is less of a factor in both tropical and arctic treelines, where snowfall is typically less abundant than in the alpine treelines of the mid-latitudes.

Alpine treelines are bound on either end by ecosystems remarkably distinct from one another. The lower limit of the alpine treeline is the upper limit of continuous forest cover. It is called forest line, or forest limit. Forest limit, as referred to here, is itself an ambiguous ecological boundary, especially in the Sierra Nevada, where arid conditions persist throughout the growing season. Forest cover is already discontinuous in many places, due to a combination of thin soils, little available moisture throughout the summer months, and an abundance of exposed rock. The delineation of forest limit is further complicated by topography and related microclimates. Forest limit is higher on south and west-facing slopes than on slopes facing north and east. The warmer slopes also tend to be drier, however, and thus tree cover is often sparse to begin with. Wind also plays a prominent role in determining forest limit. Sites protected from its effects will support forests at higher elevations if all other conditions are conducive.

The upper limit of treeline is more easily discernable than the lower. It is simply the elevational point above which trees cannot grow, no matter how adapted they may be to alpine conditions. Various sources refer to this ecological boundary as tree limit, or krummholz limit ("krummholz" being German for "twisted tree"). Krummholz limit refers more specifically to the growth form that many trees exhibit in alpine habitats. Other trees, such as the foxtail pine of the Sierra Nevada, do not commonly grow in krummholz form. Tree limit is a more inclusive term, and in the case of the Sierra Nevada it is a more accurate one. Although tree limit may seem more observable, and thus a more pronounced delineation than forest line, it also varies greatly due to topography, soil, and available moisture. In warmer sheltered sites, the last vestiges of tree growth may hang on over a thousand feet above the last trees found in more exposed areas, a kind of mountain arborial oasis.

In addition to the effects of topography on insolation, other topographical factors influence both forest limit and tree limit tremendously. Windward slopes often have lower tree limits than leeward slopes, where drifted snow collects, protecting the plant life beneath it. In other cases, when snowfields repeatedly melt exceptionally late in the season, or not at all, tree limits may lower on leeward slopes. Basins may have lower treelines than the higher ridges surrounding them due to cold air sinking into the basins at night. This can result in an inverted treeline, where a basin is devoid of trees and the ridges around it support tree growth, creating a "bathtub ring" of trees around the basin.

Precipitation is not a key factor in determining alpine treelines. It is, however, very important in determining which trees
make up the treeline assemblage. For overall tree growth, moisture requirements vary according to other ecological factors
including temperature, soils and local geology, and climatic
regime. In the mid-latitudes, twelve to eighteen inches is typically required, depending on the soil type.

Soils vary greatly in alpine areas, reflecting the local geology
and influencing the local treeline dynamic. Most soils in the
Alpine Sierra are derived from granitic rock, and are characteristically sandy, gravelly, and low in organic debris. Water
tends to percolate through such soils relatively quickly, so trees
not growing in close proximity to standing water must be
adapted to drought conditions in order to survive the dry
summers of the Alpine Sierra. Generally, conifers are adapted
to such conditions, preferring coarse-textured soils into which
their deep extensive roots can penetrate, seeking out any available moisture. As a result, conifers are mostly absent from areas
with finer soils: bottomlands, stream channels, and basins. In
such areas, grasses and their relatives are the dominant plants.

Treeline areas of the Sierra Nevada typically have sparse
understories. Like the alpine belt above the trees, diverse habitats are found among treeline ecosystems, in response to topographic and moisture gradients. Both wet and dry meadows,
rocky slopes, outcrops, and crannies, lakeshores, and streamsides all abound at the lower edge of the alpine zone, creating
a mosaic of places to live among the stunted trees. Some representative understory species of treeline include arctic willow,
red mountain heather, Labrador tea, bog kalmia, and an assortment of grasses and sedges.

Plant succession at treeline is markedly different from the
montane forest below. When disturbance occurs in the montane

forest, herbacious plants, such as grasses, are the first to move in. These are classically followed by shade-intolerant, sun-loving tree species, which are eventually succeeded by shade-tolerant "climax" species. While this simplistic model works for some forest communities, such as those of the west slope of the Sierra Nevada, it does not apply so neatly to the higher slopes of treeline, where disturbances such as avalanches, volcanic activity, glacial movement, and an occasional fire may wipe the slate clean for primary succession, the initial colonization of unvegetated sites, to occur. Such colonization usually occurs in cracks and crevices in rock surfaces, where moisture, and the rudimentary beginnings of soil can collect. In many cases of disturbance at treeline, however, tundra succeeds where trees once grew, and the treeline species find it difficult to regain a foothold. Secondary succession, the colonization of sites already vegetated, may take hundreds of years, especially in the case of fire, where tundra may succeed burns for up to 3,500 years before the trees move in again. When succession does occur, any pioneering species adapted enough to make a living is usually there to stay.

Treeline in the Sierra Nevada has fluctuated greatly throughout time in response to varying climatic conditions. As previously discussed in the chapters on geologic history, alpine geomorphology, and mountain weather and climate, the treeline of today is but a snapshot of ecological conditions in motion, riding the stream of time. The treeline of tomorrow may recede, greatly expanding the alpine zone of the Sierra Nevada, or it may rise, inundating the alpine zone in a rising sea of trees.

To Bend or Break?

Treeline Adaptations

The treeline factors of temperature, wind, precipitation, snowpack, soils, and local geology all work together to push trees literally to the edge of their limits. In response to this, treeline species have developed specialized adaptations to cope with alpine environmental conditions. In the Sierra Nevada, the usual condition of a short growing season at treeline is coupled with that of summer drought, resulting in a unique assemblage of timberline species which exhibit adaptations held in common with other alpine treelines all over the world. These adaptations are evident in both the growth forms of trees and their methods of reproduction.

The short growing season typical of the treeline environment leaves little time for trees to prepare themselves for winter. Regardless of their reproductive strategies, all trees grow and ripen new shoots during the short weeks of summer. Treeline species are able to undergo maximum photosynthesis at lower temperatures than other trees, and will continue to photosynthesize substantially as long as leaf temperatures are above 46 degrees. During this time new cells grow, cell walls mature, and the new shoots gradually lose their youthful succulence. As the new shoots ripen they develop a thick cuticle and become "hardened off," attaining tolerance to cold and wind damage with maturity. When the snow falls, if shoots have not matured they will be killed off by frost damage or wind action. Additional winter dessication occurs when the pores on the leaf surfaces, called stomata, do not have time to close before the growing season ends. Frozen roots throughout the winter prevent the tree from intaking any new moisture, while all the moisture it holds is lost through the open stomata. The result is dessication, evidenced by orange and brown shoots exposed to wind and sun.

The growth forms of treeline species vary greatly from large tree forms over fifty feet in height to dwarfed forms resembling a well-kept lawn. Most trees show at least partial stunting due to the alpine conditions. Stunted forms are those that are less than fifty-feet high at maturity. They are often skirted by extensive horizontal branches growing outward from the trunk, below the protective level of the winter snowpack. These branches often intertwine with those of other trees, creating tree-islands as trees cluster together for protection from the alpine winter. Such tree-islands provide shelter from the wind, mechanical support, moderation for temperature extremes, and higher humidity levels. In addition, the mass of trees has a black body effect, thus a lower albedo than the surrounding snow, resulting in earlier snowmelt within and around the tree island.

Many treeline species are able to reproduce vegetatively by layering. When a branch is in contact with the ground long enough, given the right conditions it will form roots and begin growing on its own. A tree island a hundred feet wide, which appears to be composed of many trees, may actually be all one organism. As the island itself creates a protective microclimate, new growth will typically occur on the leeward side. Eventually, the harsher conditions of the windward side may cause the vegetation to die back, resulting in a moving tree island, slowly shifting year by year in the tide of the wind. In other cases, the original pioneer tree dies of old age, leaving a hole in the island, resulting in a timber atoll.

Krummholz is a more extreme case of stunting. As with any type of horizontal growth, a species' ability to grow in krummholz form is determined by its genetic makeup. It occurs when a tree is so twisted and deformed that the only growth form it can achieve is that of a cushion, formed by continuous vegetative reproduction via layering. Krummholz cushions may have flagged branches extending upward from the cushion itself. While the cushion remains protected throughout the winter, the vertical branches are subject to continual wind and ice blasting. Krummholz may also creep in the leeward direction, or wind cropping may cause it to stay in one place. If it creeps, eventually snow mold fungus will develop on the leeward side, leading to the death of the tree. Another type of krummholz, called prostrate krummholz, occurs when a tree grows with a definite single trunk (as opposed to a cushion with many trunks), but grows totally horizontally (as opposed to a flag or tree island). In the Sierra Nevada, alpine willow gets down the lowest, to the extreme that it resembles a lawn. Its branches are typically in the soil, with leaves and catkins only projecting up one or two inches.

In addition to growth forms, treeline species' adaptations to the alpine environment are also evidenced among reproductive strategies. The shortened growing season of treeline is not long enough for trees to complete their entire reproductive cycle every year; thus seed crops at treeline do not occur with the regularity that they do in the lowlands. At forest level, trees may seed one year out of every three to ten. Moving upward, seeding is even more infrequent. Because of the uncertainty of reproduction that results from this dynamic, most treeline species augment sexual reproduction with vegetative reproduction. While vegetative reproduction provides much immediate insurance against demise, it is not a healthy alternative in the long run. Unlike sexual reproduction, there is no exchange of genetic material in vegetative reproduction; thus offspring are genetic clones of their parent tree. If this were the only means by which treeline species could reproduce, their gene pools would soon lose the diversity that give a species potential to be resilient to disease and infestation. Without the ability to adapt, these species would die out. A combination of sexual reproduction and vegetative reproduction among treeline species is their answer to both problems at hand: insuring regeneration and maintaining genetic diversity.

Cast   of   Characters

Alpine Sierran Treeline Species

Three species dominate treeline in the Alpine Sierra Nevada: foxtail pine, whitebark pine, and mountain hemlock, and each dominates the treeline landscape in different areas of the range. In addition to these dominants, lodgepole pine, limber pine, western white pine, and western juniper also occur as associates, but are more limited in their distribution and abundance. Each of the treeline species of the Sierra Nevada copes with the alpine conditions in a slightly different way. By looking around at what trees are where, one can tell a lot about a given place. The Alpine Sierra, which spans some two hundred miles, is a meeting ground for diverse conditions. Latitudinally, it incorporates ecological elements of the cool, moist Pacific Northwest to the north, and the hot, dry Mediterranean regions to the south. Longitudinally, it both separates and incorporates ecological elements of maritime California to the west, and the desert regions to the east. Accordingly, the composition of treeline species reflects this incorporation.

The quintessential treeline species of the Sierra Nevada are the whitebark pines. In the lower part of their range, they may grow straight and tall up to forty feet in height, with rounded crowns, to over a thousand years old. More typically, however, they grow as tree islands and various forms of krummholz, where they may still attain a venerable age.

The whitebark pines are the most common treeline species in all of the Sierra Nevada. They are a true treeline tree, rarely found below forest limit, ranging at treeline throughout the interior mountain regions of westernNorth America, spanning nearly the entire length of the Alpine Sierra. As a continental species, they are adapted to short, sunny summers and bitter cold winters, capable of withstanding radical temperature fluctuations both seasonally and diurnally. The genetic ability of the whitebarks to grow horizontally means that they avoid, rather than endure, the hardships of the alpine winter. Rather than hold snow without breaking, the flexible branches of the whitebark pine simply shed it off.

Unlike those of most pines, the seeds of the whitebark pine are large and heavy, lacking a membranous wing to aid in dispersal. As such, they are an attractive food source for birds and mammals alike. Thus whitebark pines have evolved to be dependent on animals for seed dispersal. These animals include deer mice, chickaree squirrels, chipmunks, and the Clark's Nutcracker.

These trees have developed a co-evolutionary ecological relationship with the Clark's Nutcracker in particular. The birds begin feeding on the whitebark seeds in late summer. At first they strip the new purple cones, then the dry brown ones. Some of the seeds they eat on the spot, but the majority of them fall into a special pouch at the floor of their mouth, called a sublingual pouch, which can hold up to eighty-two whitebark pine seeds at once. The nutcrackers then fly off to their favorite cache sites: south-facing slopes, the first areas to be free of snow when the hungry birds return the following spring, and ridges with exposed soils where hole-digging is an easy task. These are also the ideal soil conditions for the seeds of the whitebark pines to germinate. They dig their cache holes, inserting one to fifteen

Foxtail pine (Pinus balfouriana ssp. austrina) at Matlock Lake. Photo: Richard Coons

seeds in each hole, approximately one inch below the surface. Then, they cover the holes by raking dirt and debris back over them. Clark's Nutcrackers will regularly cache up to 30,000 seeds per year, and studies of the bird-tree relationship in Wyoming found birds caching up to 98,000 seeds. The nutcrackers live off of the stored seeds until the next summer's crop, migrating around the high country as different areas produce seed in

different years. Studies have shown that they are typically able
to relocate sixty to ninety percent of their cache sites. This
still leaves plenty of seeds for germination, however, and the
whitebark pine groves of today frequently indicate forgotten
cache sites of yesterday.

The dominant treeline species of the southern Alpine Sierra
is the foxtail pine. They form open, park-like groves of large
trees, and may exceed fifty feet in height all the way up to tree
limit. These groves are devoid of understory, and each tree is
separated by ten to fifty feet of bright, gravelly, granitic soil.
The word forest does not apply here, as the sun floods into the
foxtail groves and illuminates every nook and nuance. It is
more like a treeline savannah: widely spaced tall trees separated by fields of granite. Krummholz is not found here, where
foxtails typically are the only tree species growing.

Although they are well adapted to arid conditions, foxtail
pines require some moisture throughout the summer months,
which their deep and spreading root systems take in through
the coarse, gravelly granitic soils they prefer. In the Sierra
Nevada, they occur between 10,000 feet, well below forest level,
and 12,000 feet, at tree limit, in the vicinity of Sequoia-Kings
Canyon National Parks and the adjacent Inyo National Forest.
Summer thundershowers and an occasional storm system up
from the Gulf of California bring slightly more water to the
slopes than to the north, where foxtails are replaced by other
species. A second, disjunct population of foxtail pines occurs
one hundred and eighty miles away, on the highest peaks of
the Scott, Salmon, Yolla Bolly and Klamath Mountains of northern
California, where similar granitic soils abound, and some moisture is available year-round. Both populations are remnants of
the Late Miocene and Pliocene epochs, when ample summer
rainfall allowed for extensive subalpine forests in upland regions

amid a widespread mixed coniferous and hardwood forest of the lowlands. Subsequently, most species that were dependent on summer rainfall either died out or moved north.

In the Sierra Nevada, foxtail pines may grow to be up to 3,000 years old, approaching the age of their close relatives, the ancient bristlecone pines of the Great Basin. Even their needles may stay on the tree for up to seventeen years. Like all treeline species, they are extremely slow growing; a tree thousands of years old may be less than six-feet wide and fifty-feet tall. Growing upright under treeline conditions requires that foxtail pines are extremely strong structurally, as their tough, tight-grained, pitchy wood attests. They cope with snow load by being strong enough to withstand breakage beneath the weight. The high amount of pitch in the wood also makes the foxtails susceptible to lightning strikes, but fires don't often spread due to the spacing between the trees and lack of understory. The gnarled, half-dead appearance of most foxtail pines is not, however, because of lightning, but rather a special adaptation these trees have to deal with treeline conditions. Like their cousins the bristlecones, they are able to shut off sections of their cambium layer (the inner bark which transports nutrients and water to different parts of the plant) and maintain all of their functions through a strip of bark as narrow as a few inches. This is an extremely valuable adaptation to have if for growing upright at the edge of the alpine zone, where winds and wind-borne ice blast their way across the land on a regular basis. Many foxtail pines that would otherwise seem dead retain a narrow strip of bark through which life runs its course, sometimes supporting but one branch of green foliage on the entire tree. When winter comes, the water within the living cells of the tree drains out into the intercellular spaces, thus preventing the cells from bursting when the trees freeze and the water expands. foxtail pines have this adaptation in common with many other cold adapted trees.

The primary species of the northern Sierra Nevada treeline is the mountain hemlock. Near forest limit and below, these elegant conifers exhibit a tall, slender, spire-like growth form, with their terminal tip characteristically nodding over. Under treeline conditions, however, hemlocks have the ability for horizontal growth, and may form tree islands, flags, and various forms of krummholz.

Although more typical of the northern Sierra, mountain hemlocks are found as far south as Sequoia National Park. They form an important component of the upper montane forest, as well as treeline. South of Yosemite they are limited to shady, moist sites. The southernmost grove of mountain hemlocks in the Sierra Nevada (and in the world) is found near Silliman Lake, along a series of springs. Just above it, where conditions are drastically different, grows a stand of foxtail pines. To the north, the mountain hemlocks extend through Canada and into Alaska, keeping close to the coast throughout their range. As a maritime species, mountain hemlocks are adapted to cool, moist conditions, winds, heavy snowfall, and mild winter temperatures relative to the interior of the continent. Their flexible branches taper downward to shed snow. Their lightweight, winged seeds are dispersed by the wind. They are more drought-tolerant than the cedars and spruces with which they grow to the north, and are so able to withstand the conditions of the Sierra Nevada, where their usual neighbors cannot survive.

Other less prominent treeline associates in the Alpine Sierra include lodgepole pine and limber pine, as well as an occasional western white pine or western juniper. Lodgepole pines occur throughout the range, growing in a variety of forms, from tall trees to twisted, windswept dwarfs, although more often the

Sierran lodgepoles grow erect as high up as conditions allow. Their prolific wind-dispersed seeds can germinate in a variety of conditions, from lakeshores and wet meadows to dry post-fire sites. Although their relative abundance is far greater at and below forest level, they form a significant component of the treeline species composition.

Limber pine is a continental species, more typical of the colder mountains of the interior. In the Sierra, limber pines are typically flat, sprawling shrubs found in dry, rocky, windswept sites ranging from well below forest level to tree limit. They are limited to the dry east slope of the south-central portion of the range, except for along the South Fork of the Kings River, where isolated stands grow on dry, windy slopes to 12,000 feet. As both their common and scientific names suggests, limber pines are extremely flexible, able to give way to the harsh winds that frequent their sites.

The Good Life?

Alpine Inhabitants and Adaptations

"No peak is too high, too rugged or too exposed for rosy finches. To meet these weathered, confiding mountaineers in their breeding haunts, one must leave the timberline whitebarks far below. Among cirques and ridges, alpine lakes and meadows, sheer escarpments and eternal ice and snow, they pick insects from snowfields and harvest the seeds of alpine plants. They regularly visit the summits of the highest peaks, including Mt. Lyell (13,114'), the highest point in Yosemite."

David Gaines

Passing Through

It was early September when I first beheld the sun-washed expanse of the Alpine Sierra. I approached from the east, ascending Piute Pass and dropping into Humphreys Basin, where I have often since returned. At first sight the land was beautiful, though I did not have an immediate affection for it. The wide openness intimidated me. The giant scale of the mountains against the sky was almost crushing. There were no rounded hills, fertile fields, or shady groves of trees here; there was no lush, comforting soft green of the lowlands. Instead, there was hard rock, cold snow, and sharp sky. Life itself seemed smothered by the expansive presence of the land and sky, and the ever-changing interplay between these two. I instinctively looked toward rock walls, crevices, and the dwindling islands of twisted trees, seeking sheltered spots. Life was huddled here, presumably with the same idea as I, to find shelter from the elements. To spend the next five days up here, I would have to adapt, much like the plants.

I was not alone. I was traveling as a participant in the Sierra Institute, a field extension of the University of California. There were eleven of us, nine students, our teaching assistant, and our instructor. This landscape was new to almost everyone, as evidenced by the expressions on people's faces as they arrived at Piute Pass. The autumn wind whipped over the pass, hurling tiny balls of graupel down onto the smooth, polished granite.

We sheltered against the car-sized erratic boulder on the west side of the pass, waiting for all to arrive before continuing over to the site of our basecamp.

Three days later, it snowed in the basin once again. This time it came down heavily and we retreated to our tents, beating snow off the roof and walls along the way. As I settled in for the storm, I was uneasy in the stale air of the tent interior, and unzipped my vestibule to let the outside air (and snow) move through the tent more freely. My tent partner, Arya Degenhardt, and I stared out of this little window and watched the graupel cover the ground in white. Entranced for a time, my blank gaze was finally broken as the snowy ground itself seemed to be moving. As my eyes adjusted, focusing in on the movement, I distinguished the vague shape of four birds, about the size of small chickens, just five yards in front of the tent. They were huddled together, and seemed half-buried in snow. My first thought was that they were Blue Grouse, which occur in montane forests of both the Rockies and the Sierra Nevada. Arya and I consulted our bird book. Their size and shape were right, even the reddish-orange comb above the eye that suggested the male birds. Strangely, these grouse all seemed to have snow stuck to their undersides. I knew it was wet snow out there, but I had never in all my life seen snow so sticky that it would adhere to a bird's feathers. As we watched closer it began to make sense. It wasn't snow on the bird's undersides, but fluffy white feathers. These were not Blue Grouse; they were ptarmigan, still in summer plumage, not yet turned white for winter. But ptarmigan were not supposed to be here, so far south from the arctic. Nevertheless here they were as plain as day, White-tailed Ptarmigan atop the backbone of the Sierra Nevada.

The mystery was revealed to me as I flipped to the back of my bird book and looked through the maps. Along the Pacific seaboard, White-tailed Ptarmigan are not found further south than the northern Cascades, except for one spot—the central Sierra Nevada. As recently as 1972, the California Department of Fish and Game released ptarmigan here, in hopes of introducing a game bird for hunting to the Alpine Sierra. The first efforts were failures. The birds were dropped from the air, plummeting to their deaths on the rocks below. Thus the Fish and Game Department came to realize that ptarmigan, like all birds in the Phasianidae family, aren't the most able flyers. Subsequent introductions were land-based, and much more successful. By 1976, the ptarmigan had spread south to Mt. Williamson, and north to the Sawtooth Ridge. Presently, their range is still expanding. Feeding on arctic willow, the ptarmigan have an abundant food source readily available to them in the alpine zone, with few others in competition for it. Ptarmigan, as a non-native species, are presumed to bring negative impacts to the fragile ecosystem, though there is as of yet no documented evidence to support this. At the time, I was so intrigued with my new realization that it didn't matter where the birds came from. They were alive and mobile, and this was enough for me to identify with them.

As the ptarmigan slowly waddled away, Arya and I slipped into our warm clothes and left our tent for the big outside. The snow was still coming down, and the ground was now covered with a good four inches of fresh, wet, white snow. As the birds wandered off, we turned our attention to the broader picture of the changed landscape. We ran through camp and roused the others. Soon all eleven of us were out in it, throwing snowballs, making snowmen, dancing around with the falling white. We rolled snowballs four feet high and made ephemeral thrones, complete with footstools and armrests. We were like children out on the playground, making up games in an instant and changing the rules the next.

As the snow began to let up, the sky suddenly opened to

let in shafts of warming sunlight. Four of us ran down to the
icy waters of Lake Muriel. We jumped into the bright blue
void, without thought or reservation as to what might happen
next. The water seemed to repel us, throwing us back ashore
with the same equal intent with which we had thrown ourselves
in. Standing there, wet with glacial meltwater, I flapped my
limbs in the transient sun, trying to bring blood back into my
extremities. My head followed my body, now jumping, now
swimming, now trying to collect itself. This was all new; I'd
never felt anything like it before. The place, the storm, the birds,
the water, all together creating a scene that I was amazed to
find myself taking part in.

The storm was gone, leaving a temporary veneer of frozen
water on the ground, the last trace of its passing. Even the water,
which had left me tingling all over, evaporated off my skin,
and was gone. A few more days as a transient character in the
story of this land, then I would be leaving. I thought of the things
that occurred here, and how even this place was just a passing
occurrence. I was to the plants as they were to the rocks, as
they were to the stars, and beyond that, I could only speculate.
Though my stay in this place had left a permanent impression
on my being, five days was just not long enough for what I now
hoped to achieve. To really know this place would require delib-
erate time and effort, and I felt inspired enough to put in both.

Movement along the shoreline rocks caught my attention,
where I could hear a series of soft clucks. My eyes rested on a
solitary bird, a young ptarmigan, immature, walking through
the talus. I wondered why it was here, away from its kind,
alone, with nothing to eat. Did some maverick spirit coax it up
to this place to fulfill nature's obscure reason? Then again, who
was I to be asking such questions? Perhaps, like me, it was just
passing through, taking a look around, experiencing something
new for the very first time.

Small is Beautiful
Alpine Plant Adaptations

Harsh and unforgiving are terms often used to describe the conditions for life in the alpine zone, while the plants and animals that live there perceived by humans as barely "getting by." This is a common misconception, based on our lowland-centered idea of comfort and suitable living conditions. It is true that most of the lowland plants and animals we associate with on a daily basis could not survive in alpine conditions, but it is equally true that the plants and animals of the alpine zone would have a hard time making a living in the lowlands. The alpine environment has a specific set of ecological conditions that require specialized adaptations among the plants and animals that live there. Just as we have adapted to the rigors of human society, these plants and animals struggle no more or less than those that are specially adapted to life in various lowland conditions. The alpine zone is their home, and this is reflected in all aspects of their life.

While the species that inhabit the alpine zone may be well fitted to such a place, the ecological conditions of the alpine zone are still extreme relative to those of the lowlands. This is the place that within one year may be colder, windier, wetter, drier, sunnier, and snowier than the more "habitable" regions of the lowlands. Throughout the greater alpine zone, plant species have developed convergent adaptations in response to such extreme environmental conditions, resulting in many commonalities among alpine plants. Each species, however, exhibits its own unique combination of alpine plant adaptations which distinguishes it from others. The common factor among all alpine plants is that their growing season temperatures average less than fifty degrees Fahrenheit. Thus far we have focused our attention on the ecotone of treeline that reflects the flexibility of the fifty degree isotherm, as well as the tree species that straddle the forest below and the tundra above. Now we will look still closer to the ground, to the plants of the land above the trees.

Convergent adaptations among alpine plants are many. Alpine plants are typically perennial, meaning that they live for two or more years, rather than annual, meaning that they live for just one year. They tend to be shorter and more slender than their lowland relations, with a greater percentage of their vegetative mass below ground than above. They tend to have fewer branches and flowering stems, and fewer, smaller leaves. They have fewer flowers, though these are typically the same size as those of lowland relatives. This combination of dwarfed plants and seemingly oversized flowers accentuates the alpine bloom, where the showy colors of summer seem to jump out from the little green plants beneath. In spring and fall, many plants exhibit a reddish tinge, evidence of abundant red pigments within the plant tissue. Due to the shortened growing season plants flower and fruit earlier, condensing the reproductive cycle from months into weeks. Other years, certain plants may not flower or fruit at all. All of these adaptations may be considered either morphological (having to do with the plant's form), or reproductive.

Alpine plants grow as one of six morphological growth forms including cushions, mats, rosettes, grass-like forms, prostrate shrubs, and lichens. Cushions are hemispherical and tight-growing, with low, streamlined profiles. This growth form enables them to have maximum surface area exposed for photosynthesis while having a minimum amount of vertical material exposed to the wind. Cushion plants also protect and insulate themselves, and the interior of the cushion is often warmer than the exterior, with little or no wind within the plant. They typically have long singular rootstalks called taproots, necessary for obtaining water on the dry ridges and slopes that cushion plants usually occupy. Common cushion species in the Alpine Sierra include the drabas and rock-cresses of the mustard family and many of the eriogonums of the buckwheat family.

Mats are similar to cushions in that they are also low and have streamlined profiles. Mats, however, are spreading rather than tight-growing, and are thus less compact. Rather than a central taproot, mats have multiple rootstalks, and will root wherever and whenever their branches contact viable soil. They may root so often and so tightly that their original growth form becomes indiscernible. Mats, unlike most other alpine growth forms, are not specific to either wet or dry growing conditions, and range across moisture gradients. Some common mat species of the Alpine Sierra include red mountain heather, arctic willow, and matted phlox.

Rosettes are radially symmetrical, often succulent, confined whorls of leaves growing close to the ground, radiating outward from the center of the plant like a fanned skirt. Unlike cushions and mats, they are unable to extend outward. They are typically flatter to the ground and so have even less wind exposure than cushions or mats. Their radial symmetry insures that light, moisture, and nutrients can come from all directions. Succulent rosettes, such as those of the sedum family, are able to retain water in their leaves due to an abundance of interior cells filled with a mucous-like sap. This adaptation is especially advantageous during summer drought conditions because succulent plants are able to store water when it becomes less readily available. Rosettes, like cushions, are most commonly found in dry sites, such as slopes and ridges. Sierra and alpine saxifrages, pussypaws, and dwarf lewisia are good examples of rosettes in the Alpine Sierra.

Grass-like forms, called graminoids, have a different strategy from that of cushions, mats, and rosettes. Rather than lying flat on the ground, they dare to stand vertical, their slender leaves too small and flexible to be torn by the wind. Their flowers are reduced to their male and/or female parts, lacking the showy colors and fragrances of many of their alpine neighbors. As is the case with many alpine plants, they are pollinated by the plentiful alpine wind rather than animals. They often have root systems that enable them to send up new shoots from extensive networks beneath the ground. Graminoids, which include grasses, sedges, and rushes, are notoriously difficult to distinguish from one another, especially since over thirty-five species inhabit the Alpine Sierra. Generally, true grasses have hollow stems with sections separated by swollen nodes. Their leaves are alternate, usually in pairs of two. Their flowers are usually bisexual, meaning that they have both male and female parts in the same flower. Sedges, on the other hand, have edged or angular stems, which you can feel if you roll the stems between your fingers. Their leaves are usually in groups of three. Their flowers are unisexual, meaning that they have only male or female parts on a single flower, though both male and female flowers may be found on the same plant. Different than both grasses and sedges, rushes have round stems, leaves originating from the base of the plant, and bisexual flowers. While true grasses may be found in dry sites, graminoids in general are more typical of wet sites such as snowbanks, meadows, and streamsides.

Prostrate shrubs, including willows, currants, and alpine laurel, are the most vertical of the alpine vegetation. Even so, they rarely exceed a few feet in height even in protected sites, and remain entirely covered by snowpack throughout the winter. Shrubs range across moisture gradients, with willows and Labrador tea preferring wet streamsides and bogs, and currants growing on dry slopes and ridges. As a group, they have a wide variety of root schemes depending on the environmental conditions in which they grow.

Lichens are perhaps the most well adapted species to the most extreme alpine conditions, capable of growing in places where nothing else lives. They can continue to produce food below the freezing point, which no green plant can do. The presence of lichens and the absence of vascular plant life is indicative of nival conditions. Although they are commonly referred to as such, lichens are not true plants. Symbiotic relationships between fungi and either green or blue-green algae (cyanobacteria), or different combinations between these two types of organisms result in the varieties of lichens with which we are familiar. The fungi provide moist, sheltered microhabitats within which algae can grow, while the algae photosynthesize, producing food for both types of organisms. While this relationship has been considered mutually beneficial to both organisms, in some cases the fungi actually slowly parasitize the algae, which eventually die off, leaving the fungi starving for more food. Lichens typically grow in one of three growth forms. The crust-like lichens that pioneer rocks are called crustose, the toughest, tightest form. Leaf-like lichens may also pioneer bare rock surfaces. These are called foliose, different from the crustose in that they have a flaky, somewhat vertical arrangement. Loose, moss-like lichen, such as the widely known old man's beard, are called fruiticose, and typically occur on organic substrates.

Leaves are another aspect of alpine plant morphology that exhibit convergent adaptations with one another, and with plants of desert regions. Like desert plants, alpine plants in dry sites must cope with drought, having adaptations which prevent moisture loss due to the dry alpine air, lack of precipitation during the growing season, and desiccating winds. Plants of wetter sites, such as willows, grasses, sedges, and rushes, have no use for such adaptations, as they have access to water year-round. Succulent plants can actually retain moisture in their leaves, but most leaf adaptations actually work by controlling evaporation. In the alpine zone this is done by leaf size, thickness, coatings, and colorings.

Leaves are typically small, thick and leathery, dark or dusty, and evergreen, with either hairs or waxy or powdery coatings. Small size exposes less surface area to insolation and winds. Thick leaves have multiple cellular layers, which reduce the amount of exposed surface area relative to the number of photosynthetic cells within the leaf. Small, thick, leathery leaves, called sclerophyllous, are typically evergreen, as they photosynthesize slower and steadier due to cells blocking each other from direct sunlight. Small size and thickness work in combination with leaf hairs and coatings, all of which help prevent moisture loss. Hairs break up the surface area of the leaf and diffuse strong insolation. They may also have an insulating effect, trapping heat at the leaf surface. Both powdery and waxy coatings help seal in moisture and prevent its loss through the leaf's stomata, the tiny pores through which moisture vapor escapes. Leaves with powdery coatings are typically lighter in

Oval-leafed eriogonum *(Eriogonum ovalifolium)*. Photo: Martha McCord

color, gray-green to almost bluish, reducing the amount of insolation they absorb, thus helping to prevent moisture loss. Leaves with waxy coatings are usually darker in color and often shiny, increasing the amount of insolation they absorb, necessary for photosynthesis to occur through their thick cuticles. Unlike desert plants, alpine plants do not have the additional option of orienting their leaves vertically to prevent prolonged exposure to direct sunlight. In the alpine zone, such orientation would overly expose leaves to the desiccating winds.

The reproductive adaptations of alpine plants are a direct reflection of the short, relatively cold growing season. Most plants are perennial because the alpine growing season is simply too short for annuals to complete their entire life cycle in one season. The Sierra Nevada, however, does have a higher percentage of annuals than other North American alpine areas

due to its warmer summer temperatures and high levels of insolation. Most of these annuals are probably ephemeral invaders
from the lowlands, dependent on specific environmental conditions for their survival in the alpine zone. Perennials have
the advantage of being able to pick up where they left off the
previous year, thus continuously adding to what is already
established. They may live for ten to fifteen years before ever
flowering, depending on stable root systems to see them through
the winters, until finally their energy balance is positive enough
to produce reproductive parts. Even then, many alpine plants
put out buds one year and actually flower the next, spreading
the efforts of reproduction over two growing seasons.

Alpine perennials have the additional advantage of being
able to jumpstart themselves for the next season by storing food.
Among perennial herbs, this food is stored underground, as
carbohydrates in the plant's root system. Among prostrate
shrubs and cushions, food is stored above ground as lipids. In
all cases, such food reserves are not depleted during the winter
months, when plants enter dormancy. Winter dormancy is
broken by either the average temperature exceeding the freezing
point, or extended photoperiod, Soil temperature is actually
more important in this case than air temperature. Upon breaking
dormancy, the plant immediately taps into its food reserves,
and begins activity at around thirty-three degrees Fahrenheit.
Lowland plants, in comparison, typically require forty to fifty
degree temperature averages to begin activity. Such an early
start among alpine plants causes them to use up far more energy
than they can produce at the time, which is why food storage
the previous year is so necessary.

Growth continues at an accelerated pace throughout the
growing season. Daily productivity is exceptionally high during
this period of weeks, though annual productivity is remarkably

low. Alpine plants are able to achieve optimal photosynthesis at lower temperatures than their lowland relatives, as much a reflection of their genetic makeup as their environmental conditions. Among some plants, respiration occurs almost entirely at night, in the dark, allowing the plants to undergo maximum photosynthesis throughout the day. Alpine plants essentially hyperventilate their way through the growing season, to such a degree that when they have been transplanted into a non-competitive environment in the lowlands, they burn out and die off long before the extended growing season comes to an end.

Flowering occurs relatively early in the growing season, assisted by the development of buds the year (or years) before. Flowering is synchronous; all the flowers of a given species in a given microclimate will bloom at once. The development of flowers is not warmth dependent, but seed ripening is. It is advantageous for a plant to get its flowers out as soon as possible to reserve the warmth of summer for the ripening of seeds. Alpine flowers often seem oversized, as the rest of the plant is dwarfed while the flower itself retains the same size as its lowland relatives, a necessary trait if the plant is to successfully attract pollinators. Showy, colorful flower parts, stripes and patterns, fragrances, and sweet nectar are all adaptations among flowering plants for attracting various animal pollinators. Each particular color, pattern, and fragrance attracts specific animals to the flower. Bees, for example, do not see reds, and so are most attracted to white and yellow flowers. While open flowers such as daisies provide a platform for flightless insects to walk upon, flowers such as penstemons are tubular, leaning sideways, requiring flyers such as hummingbirds and butterflies to pollinate them.

Pollinators in the alpine are primarily insects, including bees, butterflies, ants, and a variety of flies. Bees, butterflies, and ants become immobile when temperatures drop below fifty degrees, so their activity is limited to summer days. Flies can remain active at colder temperatures, and thus assume more importance as pollinators at higher elevations and during times of both the day and the season when temperatures are lower than fifty degrees. Wind is also an important pollinating agent. Grasses, sedges, and rushes are all specially adapted to wind pollination. Their flowers have none of the colors, stripes, and fragrances of the cushions, mats, rosettes, and shrubs. They are typically tiny, white or green, and inconspicuous.

Once a flower is pollinated, the plant begins its next task of seed production, ripening, and dispersal. The high variability of the alpine growing season results in significant differences in both seed production and seedling establishment from year to year. Opportunistic plants, including most annuals and biennials, as well as some perennials, tend to produce high amounts of viable seed with high seed mobility. Among perennials, this incorporates the reproductive vigor typical of annuals with perennial longevity. These plants tend to have low rates of flower predation, are capable of self-pollination, and dedicate a relatively high percentage of their structure to reproductive parts. Although they have a low survival rate, these small seeds are so abundant that enough of them germinate for the species to persist. Less opportunistic species, typically perennials, produce less viable seed with less mobility. Such seeds, however, are larger, with more significant nutrient packages to aid in establishment, and so have a higher survival rate than those of the opportunistic plants. These plants tend to have higher rates of flower predation, do not self pollinate, and dedicate a relatively lower percentage of their total structure to reproductive parts.

Ripening depends upon ample warm temperatures, and

dispersal occurs only when ripening is complete. Many alpine plants, including willows and many of the graminoids, depend on wind for seed dispersal. Their seeds are small and light-weight, often with fluffy or wing-like appendages to aid in dispersal. Other plants, such as currants and other berries, are dispersed by animals. These seeds are encased in fleshy sweet fruit, an attractive food source for animals. When the outer fruit is digested, the seed is distributed through the animal's defe-cation. Still other plants depend on animals for dispersal by having sticky or hooked seeds, which attach themselves to animals passing by and move with the animal to another loca-tion. Water is another important dispersal agent, transporting countless seeds downstream and depositing them on the shore.

Once a seed is dispersed, its fate depends upon the ecolog-ical conditions of the site where it ends up. In general, seedling establishment in the alpine zone is both rare and slow. Seeds must survive dormancy, often for several years before condi-tions are right for germination to occur. Dormant seeds become trapped between soil particles, especially in disturbed sites, forming seed banks. Successful entrapment occurs when the soil particle size and seed size match. The soil particles must be large enough for the seeds to settle among them, but small enough to prevent seeds from sinking too far below the surface. If a seed reaches a site where the conditions of temperature, moisture availability, insolation, and soil are all favorable at the same time, germination will begin. Once germination begins, it does not insure success. Favorable conditions must persist for long enough for the seedling to establish itself sufficiently to survive the coming winter. Such conditions are an excep-tion in the alpine zone, where extremes are the rule.

In addition to sexual reproduction via flowers and seeds, many alpine plants are capable of reproducing asexually, through vegetative means. Though vegetative reproduction does not allow for the exchange of genetic material, it does help to insure reproduction in an environment where sexual reproduction is both slow and chancy. Vegetative reproduction becomes more important as environmental stress increases. Some plants, such as mats and willows, may root upon contact with favorable soil, beginning vegetative reproduction aboveground and working their way down. Other plants, such as the graminoids, have extensive root networks, bulbs, and corms, which allow their spreading roots to send up new shoots, beginning vegetative reproduction underground and working their way up. In this way, an entire field of sedges may actually be one organism united beneath the ground, but seemingly separate from above.

Successful reproduction, whether through sexual or asexual processes, means that a new plant is ready to join the ranks of the alpine vegetation. The cycle begins anew, as plants lie patiently awaiting their first flowering, crushed and caressed by wind and snow, warmed and dehydrated by the alpine sun. The alpine zone is their home, and in most cases, their one and only home. Every aspect of their life, from their overall shape and size, leaf structure, and root systems to their food production, storage, and reproductive strategies, bespeaks their alpine heritage. This is a life of extremes, and for these plants, there is no other.

To   Run   or   Hide?

Alpine Animal Adaptations

In late August, the yellow-bellied marmots of the Alpine Sierra Nevada lie like fattened sumo wrestlers basking in the sun of the boulder fields. Flocks of juvenile American Pipits are joined by the adults, flitting over the tundra in search of insects. They find a trove of them stranded on a lingering snowbank, paralyzed by the cold. The pipits seem to revel while the insects watch it all happen, unable to escape their fate. Pikas set plants out to cure in the sun like maids putting laundry out to dry. Pocket gophers tunnel beneath meadows, chewing on the tender root crop of the growing season. A rare lone harrier glides across the turf, low to the ground, in search of unwary meadow voles straying too far from their tiny burrows. Rock falls from a bony ridge as a group of bighorn sheep scramble up slope, away from view. The animals of the high country are at their best, living the good life off the fat of summer.

In a matter of weeks the whole scene changes dramatically. The snows are back with vigor, blanketing the alpine zone in cold white. The last of the green turns to brown, wilts, dries up, and goes under. The bighorn tiptoe downslope in search of food. The harrier retreats as the meadow voles go back into their burrows. As the ground freezes repeatedly, the pocket gophers make new tunnels in the snow. Pikas draw their hay back into their hideouts. Pipits take wing for the valleys. Insects

Yellow-bellied marmot *(Marmota flaviventris)*. Photo: David Gilligan

go dormant. The marmot, barely able to walk beneath its seemingly obscene weight, bumbles into its den, puts its hands over its eyes, and enters into eight months of deep sleep. The temperature drops, the wind roars, and the snow keeps coming. A few feet away, the ptarmigan is heard clucking as it picks willow twigs from beneath the snow. Camouflaged because it's all white, the bird seems as if it were made for such a life. Freezing cold, you look around one last time before heading for lower elevation, and wonder how anything could emerge from such a winter alive.

Animals of the alpine zone, like plants, exhibit specialized adaptations that are key to their success in the alpine environment. Extremes of cold, wind, snow, soils, and insolation, in combination with a relatively restricted food supply, all contribute to the development of morphological, behavioral, and physiological adaptations among alpine animals. Though the overall diversity of animal species decreases as latitude increases, representative species from every major group of vertebrates, as well as insects and other invertebrates, can be found in the alpine zone during some part of the year. Endotherms, including birds and mammals, are able to control their body temperature giving them an advantage over ectotherms, such as reptiles and amphibians, which cannot. A handful of amphibians and reptiles do maintain a tenacious foothold in the Sierran alpine zone. While many animals come and go from here, others remain year-round. These residents are frequently strictly alpine, and are found nowhere else in the world but above the trees.

Alpine animals share similarities with alpine plants in that both are subject to the same set of environmental conditions of cold, wind, snow, soils, and insolation. Two key factors, however, differentiate between the two. First, animals are heterotrophic, meaning they cannot produce their own food, and so are dependent on plants and/or other animals as a food source. This puts an additional stress on alpine animals that is not a factor among plants, and limits the distribution of alpine animals according to the distribution and abundance of available food sources. The stress of the shortened growing season of the alpine zone is passed on through the food chain from plants to animals. The second factor is that alpine animals are mobile. This enables them to both find food and move amongst different environments if conditions become too adverse where they are, thus avoiding many environmental stresses that must be endured by alpine plants.

Animals may be classified by how they respond to cold conditions. Those animals that avoid cold conditions at all costs, such as opossums, ocelots, and Black Vultures, are called chiono-phobes, meaning "snow fearers." Those animals that can cope with snow, but lack specialized adaptations for living in snowy conditions are called chioneuphores, meaning "snow tolera-tors". Those animals with specialized adaptations for living in the snow are called chionophiles, meaning "snow lovers." Chionophobes obviously do not occur in alpine conditions, so we turn our attention to those animals that do: the chione-uphores and chionophiles.

One of the most obvious ways an animal deals with an alpine lifestyle is through its morphology, or physical form. The fore-most morphological adaptation associated with alpine animals is specialized insulation. Insulation is of greatest importance among resident animals, as they must endure rather than avoid the rigors of winter. Thickness of fur and feathers is controlled by seasonal molts. Equally important to thickness is the orien-tation of fur and feathers to maximize dead air space between layers of insulation. Animals do this by muscular control of fur and feather position, called "fluffing." Among birds, the white-tailed ptarmigan is known for its shaggy legs and feet, addi-tional feathers put on for both warmth and flotation in the snows of the alpine winter. Ptarmigans also change from their dusky gray-brown and white summer plumage to pure white in winter, as protection from predators in the snowy winter environment.

Other morphological adaptations reflect the rocky condi-tions of the alpine zone. Large grazing mammals, such as bighorn sheep, have enlarged front feet with flexible-soled hooves. Pikas have specialized furry pads on their feet which enable them to move silently over rock surfaces.

The overall sizes and shapes of alpine animals also reflects their environmental conditions. Having a high volume relative to surface area is advantageous among birds and mammals, meaning relatively less surface area through which heat loss can occur. Alpine mammals and birds tend to have large, rounded bodies and reduced extremities. The short, rounded ears of pikas relative to their lowland rabbit cousins exemplifies this well. Among birds, the large size and small wings of White-tailed Ptarmigan relative to lowland birds is another good example. For opposite reasons, high surface area relative to volume is advantageous among ectotherms. Increased surface area means that ectotherms are able to take in more external heat. Ectotherms therefore tend to have smaller, slender bodies relative to larger, longer extremities.

Behavioral adaptations are another way animals cope with alpine environmental conditions. Among behavioral adaptations, mobility is the most important among alpine animals. The majority of animals of the alpine zone do not live there year-round, but rather migrate to and from the high country at various intervals. Migrations can occur on a seasonal, daily, or even hourly basis, depending on the animal. The distribution and abundance of food, as governed by climatic conditions, are the determining factors in migratory behavior.

Among Sierran birds, few remain in the alpine zone as permanent residents. White-tailed Ptarmigan, introduced in the 1970's, and native Gray-crowned Rosy Finches both brave the alpine winters, though both of these species are known to retreat to subalpine elevations during the most severe winter storms, and remain at such elevations for extended periods. In addition to ptarmigan and Rosy Finches, several other species breed in the alpine zone, spending their summers in the high country and departing for lower land when the weather turns foul and food sources become scarce. These "split-decision" birds include American Pipits, Horned Larks, Peregrine Falcons, and White-crowned Sparrows. Still more species visit the alpine zone, either on a daily basis or as a seasonal feeding ground. Daily visitors include Clark's Nutcrackers, Steller's Jays, Dark-eyed Juncos, Ruby-crowned Kinglets, Wilson's Warblers, Yellow-rumped Warblers, and ravens. Seasonal visitors include Northern Harriers, Sharp-shinned Hawks, Prairie Falcons, and kestrels. Among mammals, only the smaller species who are able to make use of shelter beneath the snow overwinter, including yellow-bellied marmots, pikas, meadow voles, Sierra pocket gophers, several species of mice, and weasels. Grazing mammals and most predators are seasonal migrants. Among these, mule deer, coyotes, and mountain lions, descend to lower elevations in early autumn, while bighorn sheep descend in later autumn.

Mobility is also important on a smaller scale. Both bodily orientation and use of microclimates allow animals to avoid environmental stresses of the alpine zone. Ectotherms are perhaps the most dependent on such techniques, as their body temperatures fluctuate with that of the environment. Thus the few reptiles of the alpine zone are often seen sunning on rocks throughout the day, absorbing insolation from above and absorbed heat from the rock below. Among insects, butterflies orient their wings to absorb more or less insolation according to their needs. Many insects take advantage of the protection that nooks and crannies have to offer, sheltering themselves from alpine winds that would otherwise waft them away. Those that are blown by the wind are often deposited on snow-fields, paralyzed by the cold snow surface temperature, and eaten by foraging birds. Overwintering mammals also utilize microclimates in their use of burrows and snowcover for protection from the elements.

Among resident alpine animals, securing food for the long winter is another factor requiring specialized behavioral adaptations. Some mammals, such as pikas, store food in dens, spending much of the summer finding and preparing their winter caches. Pikas harvest large quantities of grasses, sedges, flowers, and stems, which they set out on rocks to dry before stashing them in their hideaways. Once the snow falls they are unable to gain access to meadows and herbfields, and are completely dependent on their stored food until the following spring. Other mammals, such as the yellow-bellied marmot, eat incessantly through the summer months, accumulating thick layers of fat that will see them through the winter in their sleepy dens. Weasels that remain in the high country rely on constant hunting, making frequent raids on the otherwise quiet dens of their furry neighbors. White-tailed Ptarmigans scrounge through the snow for whatever buds, twigs, leaves, and seeds they can find, preferring those of the arctic willow whenever they are available.

In addition to morphological and behavioral adaptations, physiological adaptations are essential for success among many alpine animals. Physiological adaptations are typically in response to cold temperatures and/or short growing seasons. These include hibernation, increased metabolic rate, circulatory adaptations, shortened breeding cycles, or rapid and delayed maturity.

Winter hibernation, or dormancy, is a necessity among all alpine ectotherms and many mammals as well. It serves animals in two ways. First, their metabolic rates are slowed down by as much as two-thirds, greatly reducing the amount of energy necessary to sustain basic biological functions. Second, their body temperatures are lowered, reducing the difference between body and air temperature and reducing heat loss from the body, thus further reducing the amount of energy required to sustain life. Marmots are deep hibernators, as opposed to other mammals such as bears, that enter a relatively shallow state of hibernation through the winter. Marmots may spend to eight months in their dens before emerging in late spring, often less than half the weight they were at the end of the previous summer.

Non-hibernating animals may cope with cold temperatures by increasing their metabolic rates. This adaptive strategy, quite opposite from hibernation, requires additional energy intake by the animal and results in increased heat production. It is therefore limited to animals that store food for the winter, such as pikas, mice, and meadow voles, or that depend on hunting, such as weasels. Two methods of controlling heat through increased muscular activity are increased behavioral activity and shivering. In addition, all mammals respond to cold physiologically by breaking chemical bonds and rebuilding them as glucose, or simple sugar. This process allows mammals to generate heat without actual muscular activity. A more chronic mechanism for maintaining warmth is increased cellular mitochondria, which consume fats, which keep the inner fires burning, but conserve carbohydrates.

Circulatory adaptations involve the control of circulation by vascular heat exchange, as well as constriction and dilation of blood vessels. In the case of vascular heat exchange, the warmer outgoing blood of the arteries is shunted to the veins as they course blood through the core organs, thereby increasing the temperature of the core relative to the extremities. While the core is protected, the temperature difference between the extremities and the outside environment is lowered; thus heat loss is reduced. Dilation and constriction of blood vessels are additional insurance against damage from the cold, allowing an animal to bring more or less blood to a given part of its body according to its needs.

The shortened growing season of the alpine zone necessitates compressed breeding cycles and rapid maturity among some animals and delayed maturity among others. This is especially evident among breeding bird species, which do not have the advantage of beginning many breeding activities prior to the growing season as resident birds and mammals do. Horned Larks, for example, lay only one clutch per season in the alpine zone, while populations of the lowlands typically lay two clutches. Young must be fledged and able to forage for themselves by summer's end, when flocks begin to form and move to lower ground. American Pipits also lay only one clutch per season, juveniles forming flocks by mid-August. Among mammals, pika young mature rapidly, are weaned and able to live on plant material by the time they are a third grown. Other animals, such as marmots, use the opposite strategy of delayed maturity and extended parental care, and may take years before reaching adulthood.

The ecological conditions of the alpine zone require specialized adaptations of animals that utilize the high country. Alpine adaptations among animals are varied according to the ecological criteria of individual species. These include its place of residence, feeding habits, method of regulating body temperature, and breeding ecology. Morphological, behavioral, and physiological adaptations work singly or in concert with one another to insure the success of alpine animals. With their array of adaptations, life in the high country is no more a struggle for alpine animals than for those animals specifically adapted to lowland conditions. Not only do alpine animals survive the cold, wind, and short growing season of the alpine zone, but they do so in comfort, living the good life of the high mountains with a character all their own.

Migrations

Floristic Origins and Biogeographic Perspectives

"...a 'place' has a kind of fluidity to it; it passes through space and time...a place will have been grasslands, then conifers, then beech and elm. It will have been half-riverbed, it will have been scratched and plowed by ice. And then it will be cultivated, paved, sprayed, dammed, graded, built up. But each is only for a while, and that will be just another set of lines on the palimpsest. The whole earth is a great tablet holding the multiple overlaid new and ancient traces of the swirl of forces. Each place is its own place, forever (eventually) wild."

Gary Snyder

A   R a n g e   A p a r t

The Alpine
Sierra Nevada Flora

The Alpine Sierra Nevada hosts a unique alpine plant assemblage, or "flora," hailed by scientists as the largest and richest of any alpine area in North America. All alpine floras of the northern hemisphere contain a portion of circumpolar species, as well as a portion of strictly alpine species, a percentage of which is typically "endemic," or found nowhere else in the world. The Alpine Sierra has the lowest percentage of circumpolar species, and correspondingly the highest percentages strictly alpine species of any North American alpine zone. As endemic proportions of alpine floras increases the further a range is from the poles, the Alpine Sierra also have a high percentage of endemics relative to other North American alpine regions.

The present composition of the Sierran alpine flora may be attributed to four major factors. First, recent uplift of the range dictates that the flora is young. Second, isolation of the range from pre-existing alpine seed sources indicates that introductions of species to the region were slow, and that many could not make the long migratory journey. Third, both glaciers and post-Pleistocene climatic shifts placed further restrictions on migration. Fourth, mixing and telescoping of Sierran alpine and Great Basin desert floras during Pleistocene migrations contributed significantly to the number of species unique to the Alpine Sierra. These and other factors all contribute to the geographic distribution of the species which compose the present day alpine flora. Understanding these factors enables us to decipher the variety of plant associations, ranging from lush subtropical forests to arid scrub, which have inhabited the Sierran region throughout its history. Understanding this history is essential to understanding the origins and ecology of the present-day Sierran alpine flora, through which we may gain insight into the origins and ecology of alpine floras across the continent.

In Early Tertiary times the Ancestral Sierran range had eroded away to rolling highlands. The climate at this time was warm and humid. The Sierra Nevada region was populated by a plant association of broad-leaved evergreens referred to by ecologists as the Neotropical-Tertiary geoflora. This floristic group was of tropical origins, and migrated northward during the warm, wet period spanning the Late Cretaceous to the Mid-Tertiary times. Lands to the north and at higher elevations were dominated by a temperate mixed deciduous and coniferous group with primarily holarctic origins, called the Arcto-Tertiary geoflora. Within and between these groups, as determined by local climatic conditions, was the Madro-Tertiary geoflora, originating in the more arid regions of the American Southwest and Mexico. This group included sclerophyllous taxa adapted to arid conditions. The coexistence of these three floras in the same region was dependent on the topographic and climatic conditions of the Tertiary times. The warm-wet climate regime, in combination with the long period of passivity along the North American plate margin, allowed for an extended period during which Tertiary floras could develop into distinct communities. Resumed uplift during the Late Tertiary, in combination with the onset of the ice-age, brought an end to this period of development.

Top left: Lemmon's paintbrush *(Castilleja lemmonii)*; top right: alpine gentian *(Gentiana newberryi)*. Bottom left: Sierra penstemon *(Penstemon heterodoxus)*. Bottom right: red mountain heather *(Phyllodoce breweri)*. Photos: Martha McCord

Pliocene times brought increasing aridity, augmented by the rising of the Sierra Nevada and the resulting rain shadow to the east of the range. Pliocene climatic changes restricted the Neotropical-Tertiary species to the more moist regions of the coast. Few representatives of this floristic group exist in the Sierra today. Coniferous woodland and forest, including such Arcto-Tertiary members such as mountain hemlock and giant Sequoia, became restricted to moist upland sites, moving with the rising lands to higher elevations. Species such as coast redwoods, which were dependent on year-round precipitation, were restricted to the coast. Madro-Tertiary species spread to become the live-oak woodlands, chaparral, and deserts of today. Although desert habitats and associated flora have been present in North America since Pliocene times or earlier, the present deserts of the Sierran region are relatively new features, their biota being "ecosystem recombinations." The Great Basin deserts developed simultaneously with the rising Sierra Nevada, due to the rain shadow resulting from uplift.

The present day Sierra Nevada alpine flora is composed of nearly two hundred species of vascular plants recognized as being unique to the Sierran alpine zone. Of these species, some were later found to extend into lower elevation plant communities. Other sources have recognized as many as six hundred plant species in the Sierran alpine flora, but most of these species are not limited to alpine conditions.

The Sierran alpine flora may be divided into elements, or groups, according to the origins of species. Three main elements are recognized, including Boreal, Arctic-Alpine, and Alpine. All three of these floristic divisions presumably have origins in the Arcto-Tertiary geoflora, excluding some endemic species within the Alpine element. Boreal species, with origins in the boreal forest regions of the north, account for 3.8 percent of the Sierran alpine flora. Arctic-Alpine species, which are circumpolar, have origins in the arctic tundra and polar deserts. These account for 14.2 percent of the Sierran alpine flora, a smaller percentage than in any other alpine region in the North America. Alpine species, with origins in both high and mid-latitude alpine regions, account for eighty-two percent of the Sierran alpine flora. This percentage of alpine species, which includes endemics, is higher than that of any other alpine region in the continent. Nearly half the Sierran alpine flora finds its origins in mid-latitude alpine regions of the North American Cordillera. Thirty-eight percent of the flora finds its origins in the Sierra Nevada, Cascade, and Coast Ranges of the Pacific Cordillera. Seventeen percent of the Sierran alpine species are endemics, found nowhere else in the world but the Alpine Sierra.

Getting   Around

Migration Pathways

With such an extraordinary assemblage of alpine plants, one cannot help but ask where did they come from? Migration pathways to and from the Sierra Nevada were diverse. The southward-moving circumpolar species of the Boreal and Arctic-Alpine flora, as well as those of the Cordillera, both originated from regions which predate the Sierra Nevada. These taxa found their major inroads along the axis of the Sierra, Cascade, and Coast Ranges, establishing themselves in suitable habitats as they were available en route. This is indicated by the decrease in boreal species southward, corresponding to an increase in alpine areas to the south. Some species may have come to the Sierra by alternative migrational paths such as permafrost bogs across the Great Basin during glacial times. These bogs may have served as stepping stones between the Rockies and the Sierra Nevada. However, there is a marked decrease in Rocky Mountain species as one moves southward in the Sierra Nevada. A similar decrease in Rocky Mountain flora occurs as one moves west across the Great Basin. This, in combination with the fact that endemism in the Sierra Nevada increases southward, seems to indicate a north-south migratory route. Species may have also moved in from the Klamath region of the Coast Ranges, also along the larger Pacific Cordilleran migratory path.

Because the Sierran alpine environment did not exist prior to the Late Pliocene, taxa of Arctic-Alpine or Cordilleran origin could not have migrated to the region until after that time. Quaternary times brought climatic fluctuations resulting in three million years of glacial and interglacial periods. Glacial ice repeatedly scoured away vegetation from the still-rising Sierra Nevada, causing the extinction of many species. Alpine plants found refugia on high peaks and plateaus that rose above the ice. Intensive selection took place on these isolated nunataks due to limited space and low diversity of habitat. Such refugia were critical to the reestablishment of alpine taxa following the retreat of the ice. Of equal or greater importance were interglacial refugia. Rising treelines during warmer interglacial periods effectively squeezed many alpine species to extinction, shading them out or out-competing the specialized alpine species due to increased temperatures and longer growing seasons. Warm, dry periods eliminated many species that may have briefly colonized the Sierra Nevada during the Pleistocene.

The high percentage of endemism in the Sierran alpine flora relative to other mid-latitude alpine floras is a result of several important factors. Its southern position in relation to sources of pre-adapted circumpolar flora meant a long journey for taxa of such origins to make. This migratory journey was further complicated by the lack of a contiguous north-south migration pathway, especially during interglacial periods, due to the sporadic crest of the Cascades. Late Cenozoic uplift and Pleistocene glaciation resulted in a young, high, recently exposed landscape for alpine flora to colonize. Many of the endemic's morphological distinctions from lowland relatives, however, suggest an early origin of no later than Pleistocene times, as such distinctions take time to develop.

Species of lowland origin did not have to make such a long journey. Endemic elements of the Sierran alpine flora with origins in the Madro-Tertiary geoflora of both the Great Basin region to the east and the western Californian region rose with the uplift of the Sierra Nevada. Rare members of the Neotropical-Tertiary geoflora may have found their way into the Sierran alpine flora in this way, though it is less likely for taxa of such origins to have been pre-adapted to alpine conditions. Their occurrence in the Sierra Nevada is thought to be ephemeral, depending on specific favorable climatic conditions for germination. Eastern taxa from the Great Basin region were more successful in influencing the Sierran alpine flora than taxa of the west for several reasons. The close proximity of the alpine zone and the basin deserts due to the short, steep eastern escarpment meant that species from the Great Basin had only a short distance to migrate. Early studies recognized a close relationship between Sierran alpine endemics and taxa of the deserts to the east. The longer west slope hosted vast woodland and forest habitats through which western plants had to ascend. Where such communities did not exist, glaciers covered the west-slope, inhibiting establishment of plants. Of perhaps greatest importance, many of the desert taxa were pre-adapted for success in Sierran alpine systems.

Pre-adaptation for success in the Sierran alpine environment was dependent on specific plant characteristics. Winter annuals and perennials, already evolved to undergo metabolic processes in low temperatures, were pre-adapted both physiologically and morphologically to alpine conditions. Species with dispersal strategies which allowed them to migrate upward during favorable climatic periods to new but similar environments also had an advantage. Species able to degrade starches at low temperatures and translocate sugars at night were pre-adapted for winter carbohydrate storage. This was a definite advantage for getting an early start in the brief alpine growing season. The metabolic ability to acclimate rapidly was yet another advantage for success. Finally, taxa had to be able to flower and seed-set in short, dry, cool growing seasons.

Circumpolar species of both Arctic-Alpine and Boreal floristic elements underwent evolutionary changes as they moved southward into alpine regions. Thus alpine representatives of circumpolar plants are almost always morphologically and/or physiologically different. This is because of both differences between arctic and alpine environments and isolation and evolution during the Pleistocene glaciations. Compared to their arctic relatives, alpine plants are larger, have larger leaves, greater leaf area per plant, and produce flowers and seeds while days are shorter. These factors reflect the fact that alpine plants must photosynthesize more in a shorter period of time, while their arctic counterparts may photosynthesize nearly a full twenty-four hours of sunlight per day at mid-summer. Lower chlorophyll content, peak photosynthesis at higher temperatures, and higher heat intensity for photosynthetic saturation reflect the intense nature of insolation in mid-latitude alpine regions, as compared to the arctic. Alpine varieties tend to have no vegetatively reproductive root networks, perhaps related to the close proximity of mesotopographic gradients, as well as denser inflorescences.

Origins of Sierran alpine flora may also be traced to the forest communities below. Davidson's penstemon speciated from the lower elevation mountain pride, while Coville's columbine speciated from crimson columbine. Both of these pairs still commonly hybridize with one another, indicating recent divergence. Once a plant is adapted to low temperatures, high light intensities are required for basic metabolic needs to be met. As a result, there is very little back-migration of these plants to the forest, where light is limiting and alpine plants cannot compete with shade-tolerant species.

Geographic boundaries can be defined across the Great Basin which divide alpine floristic groups. The Rocky Mountain and Great Basin floras are separated along a line running from the Ruby Mountains of northeastern Nevada, southward between the Spring Mountains of southern Nevada and the San Francisco Peaks in north-central Arizona. A second boundary separates the Great Basin from the Sierra Nevada types. This line runs between the Carson and Pinenut Mountains of the Tahoe region, southward between the Sierran crest and the White-Inyo ranges. This second boundary is less defined, with many representatives straddling both sides of the line. The Sierran alpine flora in particular is represented by Davidson's penstemon, matted phlox, club-moss ivesia, Lemmon's draba, sandwort, alpine sedge, Drummond's cinquefoil, and several eriogonums, all at common alpine elevations, as well as sky pilot and alpine gold at the highest elevations.

D r a w i n g   C o n c l u s i o n s

Island Biogeography and the Alpine Sierra

The Alpine Sierra Nevada hosts the largest and richest alpine flora on the continent. Such a truly alpine flora with so small a constituency of arctic-alpine species does not occur in any other North American mountain system. These assertions are further supported by the theory of island biogeography and its applications to the Sierran alpine region.

The theory of island biogeography asserts that the number of species found on a given island is dependent on the relationship between two key factors: 1) the nearness of the island to the source(s) of its colonists, and 2) the size of the island. The sources are most often mainlands, but may also include other islands. The less isolated an island is from sources, the higher its rate of species introductions will be, as colonizing species have a shorter distance to cross in order to reach the island habitat(s). More isolated islands require colonizers to have specialized long-distance dispersal adaptations in order to reach such far-away lands, and so there is a negative correlation between distance and colonization rates. The larger an island is, the lower its extinction rate will be, as its larger area typically means greater diversity of habitat and more niches to be filled. Smaller islands have lower diversity of habitats, fewer niches, and higher extinction rates.

The relationship between the colonization rate of new species and the extinction rate of established species is called turnover.

Accordingly, an island which is both small and close to mainland sources will have both high introduction rates and high
extinction rates, and thus a high turnover. And, of course, a large
island far from mainland will experience precisely the opposite.
The species diversity of an island is not determined by the above-
stated factors alone, but also by the dynamic equilibrium between
the rate of colonization of new species and the rate of extinction of established species. The achievement of such equilibrium
is dependent on stable conditions over time. The equilibrium
point itself depends on the rates of colonization and of extinction. In the case of the hypothetical island bubbling out of the
oceanic brine, colonization rates start high and taper off. Conversely,
extinction rates start low and rise. Where these two gradients
meet, equilibrium is found.

The mountains of western North America create islands
of alpine habitat surrounded by a sea of lowlands. While the
Basin Ranges are considered "sky islands," the vast mountain systems of the Sierra in the west and the Rockies in the east
are mainlands, or "sky continents." As with oceanic islands,
these mainlands are sources from which the islands are inhabited. As a range vast in size, but its state of equilibrium questionable, the Sierra Nevada may be considered both as a large
island and a mainland.

As a rising mountain range, the Sierra Nevada could be
equated to a large island rising from the sea. Its mainland sources
were the vast arctic and boreal regions to the north and Rocky
Mountains to the west. Both of these sources predate the Sierra
Nevada by at least fifty million years. Not one of the mainland
sources was in close proximity to the Sierra Nevada, and this
isolation resulted in slow colonization rates. Extinction rates
were low, however, due to the immense size of the Sierra Nevada.
Consequently, the species turnover rate was low. Those species
that made it to the range were theoretically destined for success,

Conness Lake. Photo: Wynne Benti

assuming habitat requirements could be met. The onset of the ice ages during the late Pleistocene, however, broke the theoretical pattern. As continental ice caps covered the northern mainland source of the arctic and boreal regions, species shifted south in response to climatic changes. Many of these species were squeezed into extinction by both advancing ice during glacial periods and rising treelines during warmer interglacial periods. Upon the repeated retreat of the ice, the newly exposed northern lands were colonized by species which had sought refuge in the south. The northern lands which once served as mainland sources for the southern islands now themselves became dependent for recolonization on the refugia to the south. In Europe, arctic species were squeezed between the continental ice sheets and the vast mountain glaciers of the Alps. With no refugia where they could wait out the ice, such taxa were pushed into extinction. This resulted in lower levels of diversity throughout the European continent. North America, in comparison, had the necessary refugia to the south to maintain diversity across the continent.

Species of the Sierran region, nevertheless, still had the rigors of three million years of telescoping habitat to deal with. While the glaciers and treelines advanced and retreated, mountain refugia offered some critical relief. However, many species that may have briefly inhabited the Sierra were pushed to extinction. This was offset by the high rates of speciation that occurred throughout this time, partially responsible for today's high percentage of endemism in the Sierra Nevada. The repeated advance and retreat of glacial ice caused the island of Sierran alpine habitat to contract and expand. During periods of maximum glacial ice, the Sierran alpine zone became a series of small, almost completely isolated islands, thereby exhibiting the characteristic high rates of speciation that take place on such islands. During interglacial periods, the Sierran alpine zone became once again a large, isolated island, with a characteristic low turnover rate.

Sky islands are unique in their ability to draw colonizing species from lowland terrestrial sources. Obviously oceanic islands cannot do this. This is a major distinction that must be considered when drawing parallels between oceanic and continental island dynamics. The Sierra Nevada, then, was not limited to its mainland sources of the arctic, boreal, and Rocky Mountain regions, but also drew from the adjacent "ocean" of lowland floras to the east and the west.

Not until the close of the Pleistocene could the Sierra Nevada be considered a viable mainland source for adjacent sky islands, and even at present it exhibits more characteristics of a large island than of a continent. It is characteristic of mainlands to have well-developed and stable floras. Accordingly, the Sierra Nevada must achieve equilibrium as an island if it is to be regarded as a mainland. The application of equilibrium theory to real land has been the subject of some scrutiny. While doubt remains as to the possibility of equilibrium, it is certain that the Sierran alpine flora was still in its embryonic stages of development as long as the ice continued to advance and retreat. Our perception of the range as a mainland source for other islands should be directly related to our perceptions of how far along the Sierran Alpine flora is to equilibrium. The present composition of the flora reflects a tumultuous past followed by only 10,000 years of relatively stable conditions. The youth of the flora indicates that species uniquely Sierran have not played a major role in colonizing other alpine islands, many of which formed earlier than or simultaneously with the Sierra. If we are to consider the Sierra Nevada as a mainland source, then what does it mean for the island to precede the continent?

The simple question of size is another factor to consider. While the Sierra Nevada may be large relative to the alpine islands of the Basin Ranges, it is small relative to the alpine regions of the Rockies, and dwarfed by the arctic and boreal mainland to the north. The question remains: a sky island, a sky continent, or both?

Several important points support the idea of the Sierra Nevada as an important mainland source for neighboring sky islands. Unlike the Rockies, which are actually a series of broken ranges without a contiguous crest, the Sierran alpine zone extends unbroken for 150 miles, reaching nearly 250 miles in total length. This vast tract of alpine habitat, rich in meso-topographic gradients and associated microhabitats, is essential for the development of species diversity, genetic diversity, and species health and integrity. Additionally, the Sierran alpine system serves as an essential corridor along the north-south migratory route of the greater Pacific Cordillera. Thus, the maturation of the Sierran alpine flora and resulting biodiversity have important implications for the future of alpine floras throughout the continent.

The Alpine Sierra Nevada supports an ecosystem like none other on earth. Changes in topography due to geologic activity, climatic fluctuations, and the evolution of species have all contributed to a rich assemblage of alpine habitats, plant associations, and related fauna. This diverse assemblage of life reflects the special conditions of the Sierran alpine zone, bringing flesh and blood, root and leaf to the stone bones of the mountains. The Alpine Sierra, as a massive island in the sky surrounded by a diverse sea of lowlands, shares its heritage with that of all other alpine regions across the continent, and even the globe. As this relationship continues, the maintained health and integrity of the alpine Sierra is essential not only for its own sake, but for the ecological health of high mountain systems across the land.

E p i l o g u e

Seeing the Light

It was early June, and I was camped in the Alabama Hills near Lone Pine in the southern Owens Valley. The day was bending into the evening hours. The mountains on either side of the valley had been obscured by fantastic thunderclouds throughout the day. They were the remnants of an evanescent, late-season storm. Lightning had pranced across the sky to the rolls and cracks of thunder that seemed intent on renting the earth. By that afternoon the clouds broke. They opened to reveal brilliant fresh snow powdering the mountain crests. The valley seemed particularly enveloped by mountains that day, as if cradled in the massive arms of the earth.

Once again I found myself saying good-bye to the Sierra Nevada for awhile, thinking about the significance of this place in my life. Gazing over the two parallel crests, I asked myself why the Sierra Nevada were so significant, so world-renowned, while the White-Inyo Range remained in relative obscurity. What was so special about the Sierra? Why was it really so important to me?

To the east rose the long back of the Inyo Range, approaching the Sierra in height, spanning far to the south, and even farther to the north. A Basin Range, it rose like a whale's back over the desert floor. Sparsely watered, it was dotted widely with junipers and pinyons to near 10,000 feet, then perhaps bristlecones thousands of years old. Here was a large range, a hundred miles in length when taken with the Whites to the north, nearly three times as long as the magnificent Tetons of Wyoming, and longer than nearly every one of the Basin Ranges to the east. This was a huge island in the sky, surrounded by a sea of desert. Truly this was a range of extraordinary possibilities, left relatively alone by humankind.

To the west rose the Sierra Nevada, sharp, stark gray, almost forbidding. Staring up at the eastern escarpment, I remembered the rich heritage of the range. The ancient movements of the earth, shrouded in the mystique of millions of years of time, revealed themselves here before my very eyes. Looking at the rampart of granite, I thought of the diving sea-floor and upheaval of the Ancestral Sierra, the vast reservoir of magma beneath the surface slowly cooling, lying in wait, the warm rain wearing the mountains away to the sea, the birth of the San Andreas fault system, and sinking of the Owens Valley along with the abrupt rise of this awesome wall of rock. I thought of gigantic mountain glaciers thousands of feet thick scraping their way over the mountains, squeezed into valleys, picking the mountains apart and depositing the pieces in valleys below. I envisioned green plants rising like a tide as the glaciers melted off, engulfing the mountains in an ocean of trees for thousands of years, only to fall as the air turned cold once again, continuing the cycle of three million years as the mountains continue to rise.

The ice left its mark on these steel-gray mountains. Unlike the mellow contours of the valleys of the Inyos, those of the Sierra were gouged, sculpted, fluted, wide-bottomed and steep-walled. If the Inyos were a whale back, the crest of the Sierra was the spine of a dragon. It was not sleeping, but laying in wait, as if at any moment it would rise, rip itself from the crust of the earth, scrape open the sky above, and fly off into the heavens. Over four times as long as the Whites and Inyos combined, the Sierra Nevada was more like a sky continent, with unique plant and animal assemblages specially adapted to the ecological conditions of the Sierran alpine zone. This was a world of its own, vast enough for anything to occur up there.

On and on I went in my attempt to discern the one thing that distinguished between Alpine Sierra Nevada from so many other amazing places, yet was unable to put my finger on just what it was that made me love this place. I was first drawn to it for aesthetic reasons. Then it became the feeling in my stomach when I was in the mountains. That was what initially led me to explore the scientific aspects of the Alpine Sierra Nevada, the natural history of the range. Yet after years of such exploration, thousands of pages of scientific literature and naturalist's writings, and hundreds of nights out in the alpine air, the truth became apparent that none of these things alone were what really made this place inspire awe in me. What it really came down to were the happenings, the real-life exchange of experience with the land, permitted by time, enhanced by study, and illuminated by true mountain light.

Sunset. The last vestiges of clouds rose up and off the snowy Sierran crest, exposing every last point and drop in its jagged profile. The sun's rays were broken, scattered, backlighting the dragon's spine and flooding through the passes in glory beams, illuminating the edges of the mountains, the valley floor, and my face. Utterly transfixed, I watched as this ephemeral wonder of the world came to pass. I did not dare look away, nor was there any need to. All sustenance, physical, psychological, spiritual, could be derived from this moment. Looking up at the meeting of earth and sky before me, there could be no more doubt in my mind. "That's why the Sierra Nevada is the Sierra Nevada," I thought, "that's why it's the Range of Light."

Appendices

Appendix A: Vascular Plants of the Alpine Sierra Nevada

From Weeden 1996, Hickman 1993, and personal observations. Taxonomy from Weeden 1996, except graminoids and draba spp., from Hickman 1993. This species list is not comprehensive of all species within the Sierran alpine flora.

PTERIODOPHYTES (ferns and related genera)

Alpine lady fern	*Athyrium alpestre,* moist habitat; 6,000-11,000'; Sierra Nevada SN(all).
Little grape fern	*Botrychium simplex,* moist, open places; 5,000-11,200'; SN(all).
American parsley fern	*Cryptogamma achrostichoides,* rocky ledges and crevices; 6,000-11,000'; SN(all).
Cascade rock brake	*Cryptogamma cascadensis,* talus slopes and crevices; 6,000-11,000'; SN(all).
Brittle fern	*Cystopteris fragilis,* cool, moist places below 12,000'; SN(all).
Brewer's cliff-brake	*Pallaea breweri,* rocky places; 7,000-11,000'; Tulare County n.
Bridge's cliff-brake	*Pallaea bridgesii,* dry, rocky places; 5,000-11,000'; Tulare County n.
Alpine selaginella	*Selaginella watsoni,* rocky places; 7,500-13,000'; Nevada County s.

SPERMATOPHYTES
GYMNOSPERMS
Cupressaceae (cypress family)

Common juniper	*Juniperus communis var. saxatilis,* rocky or wooded slopes; 6,400-11,000'; Mono Pass n.
Western Juniper	*Juniperus occidentalis,* dry, rocky places; 3,000-10,500'; SN (All)

Pinaceae (pine family)

Whitebark pine	*Pinus albicaulis,* rocky places near treeline; 7,000-12,000'; Tulare County n.
Foxtail pine	*Pinus. balfouriana ssp. austrina,* rocky slopes; 9,000-11,500'; Onion Valley, Inyo County s. to Siretta Peak, Tulare County
Limber pine	*Pinus flexilis,* dry slopes; 8,000-12,000'; Mono Pass s., e. SN.
Mountain hemlock	*Tsuga mertensiana,* moist, often n. facing slopes; 6,000-11,000'; Fresno Co. n.

ANGIOSPERMS
DICOTYLEDONS
Apiaceae (carrot-parsley family)

Gray's cymopteris	*Cymopteris cinerarius,* white; dry, open slopes 8,000-11,000'; Jun-Jul.
Sierra podistera	*Podistera nevadensis,* yellow; rocky areas 10,000-13,000'; Mono & Tuolomne to Placer County; Jul-Sep.

Asteraceae (aster family) formerly compositae

Anderson's alpine aster	*Aster alpigenus ssp. andersoni,* blue/purple; moist, boggy meadows; 400-11,500'; SN(all); Jul-Sep.
Alpine goldenrod	*Solidago multiradiata,* yellow; open rocky or grassy places; 8,000-12,500'; SN(all); Jun-Sep.
Dwarf daisy	*Erigeron pygmaeus,* lavendar/purple/white; rocky slopes and flats; 10,000- 12,000'; SN(all)
Cutleaf daisy	*Erigeron compositos,* (yellow) ray fls inconspicuous; above 8,000'; SN(all)
Alpine daisy	*Erigeron vagus,* purple; scree and crevices; 11,000-14,100'; Tulare to Mono & Tuolumne County.

Greenleaf raillardella   *Raillardella scaposa*, orange-yellow, purple phyllaries; dry, rocky places and edges; 6,500-11,000'; SN(all); Jul-Aug.
Silver raillardella   *Raillardella* argentia, yellow; dry, rocky places; 9,000-12,000'; SN(all); Jul-Aug.
Alpine everlasting (pussytoes) *Antennaria media*, phyllaries dark; above 6,000'
Pussytoes   *Antennaria umbrinella*, phyllaries light to rose; Plumas County
Alpine gold   *Hulsea algida*, yellow/purple; rocky places; 9,500-14,000'; Tahoe s.; Jun-Aug.
Golden-aster   *Haplopappus apargioides*, yellow; open, rocky places and meadows; 7,500-12,000'; Tulare to Plumas County: Jul-Sep.
Goldenbush   *Haplopappus macronema,* yellow; rocky slopes and talus; 9000-12,000'; Tulare to Nevada County; Jul-Sep.
Yarrow   *Achillea lanulosa ssp. alpicola*, white; meadows and moist places; 9000-13,000'; SN(all); Jun-Aug.
Mountain groundsel   *Senecio fremontii*,   yellow; rocky places; 8500-12,400'; SN(all)
Alpine groundsel   *Senecio werneriifolios*, yellow; dry, rocky places; 10,400-13,000'; Tulare & Inyo to Fresno & Mono County
Alpine pincushion   *Chaenactis alpigena*, cream; sandy or gravelly soils; 8000-12,500'; Tulare to Eldorado County; Jul-Aug.
Shaggy hawkweed   *Hieracium horridum*, yellow; dry, rocky places; 5000-11,000'; SN(all); Jul-Aug.
Boraginaceae (borage family)
Sierra cryptantha   *Cryptantha nubigena*
Brascaceae (mustard family) formerly Cruciferae
Phoenicaulis   *Anelsonia eurycarpa*, yellow; open slopes and flats; 10,500-14,000'; Tuolumne County s.; Jul-Aug.
Lyall's rockcress   *Arabis lyalli var. pilosellus*, white-purple; rocky places; 8000-12,000'; SN(all); Jul-Aug.
Broad-seeded rockcress   *Arabis platysperma var. howellii*, pink-white; dry benches and slopes; 5500-12,750'; SN(all); Jun-Aug.
Draba sp.   *Draba brewerii*, white; above 8500'; SN(all).
Draba sp.   *Draba crassifolia*, yellow; damp, shaded places; 7000-12,000'; SN(all).
Draba sp.   *Draba cruciata var. integrifolia*, yellow; above 9000'; Tulare County & Lake Tahoe region.
Draba sp.   *Draba densifolia*, yellow; 8500-13,000'; Fresno County n.
Draba sp.   *Draba lemmonii*, yellow; rocky places; 8500-14,200'; Eldorado County s.
Draba sp.   *Draba nivalis,* white; above 10,000'
Draba sp.   *Draba oligosperma*, yellow; 8700-14,200'; Inyo to Eldorado County
Draba sp.   *Draba praealta*, white; above 10,000'; Dana Plateau s.
Draba sp.   *Draba sierrae*, yellow; 11,000-12,500'; Inyo County
Sierra wallflower   *Erysimum capitatum*, yellow; dry slopes below 12,000'; SN(all); May-Aug.
Mountain jewelflower   *Streptanthus tortuosis var.orbiculatus*, purple-white; dry slopes; 7000-11,500'; SN(all); Jun-Sep.
Caprifoliaceae (honeysuckle family)
Parish's snowberry   *Symphoricarpos parshii*
Caryophyllaceae (pink family)
King's sandwort   *Arenaria kingii var. glabrescens*, white-rose; dry, rocky slopes; 6000-11,000'; Inyo to Nevada County; June-Aug.
Sargent's campion   *Silene sargentii*, white-rose-purple; rocks and talus; 6500-12,000'; Plumas Co. s.; Jul-Aug.
Crassulaceae (sedum family)
Rosy stonecrop   *Sedum rosea ssp. integrifolia*, purple; moist, rocky places; 7500-12,500'; Tulare to Eldorado County; May-Jul.

Narrow-petaled stonecrop *S. lanceolatum,* rocky places; 6000-12,000'; Tulare to Alpine County; Jun-Aug.

Ericaceae (heath family)

White mountain heather *Casipope mertensiana,* white; rocky ledges and crevices; 7000-12,000'; Fresno County n.; Jul-Aug.

Bog kalmia *Kalmia polifolia var. microphylla,* rose-purple; boggy places and wet meadows; 7000-12,000; SN(all); Jun-Aug.

Dwarf bilberry *Vaccinum caespitosum,* white-pink; wet meadows and near snow banks; 6700-12,000'; SN(all); May-Jul.

Western blueberry *Vaccinum uliginosum ssp. occidentale,* white-pink; wet meadows; 5000-11,000'; SN(all); Jun-Jul.

Red mountain heather *Phyllodoce breweri,* pink; rocky, often moist places; 6,000-12,000'; SN(all); Jul-Aug.

Labrador tea *Ledum glandulosum,* white; boggy and wet places; 4,000-12,000'; SN(all); Jun-Aug.

Fabaceae (pea family)

Alpine spiny rattleweed *Astragalus kentrophyta,* white/purple; alpine summits on metamorphic bedrock; 11,000-12,000'; Mono County e.; Fresno County; Jul-Sep.

Mottled rattleweed *Astragalus lentiginosus,* rocky slopes; up to 12,000'; mainly e. SN; May-Oct.

Raven's locoweed *Astragalus. ravenii,* open, rocky places on metamorphic strata; 11,250'; n. of Sawmill Pass; Jul-Aug.

Whitney's locoweed *Astragalus whitneyi,* dry, gravelly crests and slopes; 6,800-12,000'; Inyo to Alpine County; May-Sep.

Brewer's lupine *Lupinus brewerii,* violet/white-yellow; dry slopes and flats; 4,000-12,000'; SN(all); Jun-Aug.

Alpine lupine (dwarf, Lyell) *Lupinus lepidus var. lyelli,* violet; dry ridges and summits; 8,000-11,000'; SN(all); Jul-Sep.

Gentianaceae (gentian family)

Tufted gentian *Gentianopsis holopetala,* blue-violet; wet meadows; 6,000-11,000'; Tulare to Tuolumne, Co.; Jul-Sep.

Alpine gentian *Gentiana newberryi,* white w/green spots or pale blue-purple; moist meadows and banks; 7,000-12,000'; SN(all); Jul-Sep.

Explorer's gentian *Gentiana calycosa,* blue-violet; moist places; 4,000-10,500'; SN(all); Jul-Sep.

Dane's gentian *Gentianella tenella,* whitish or green-bluish; meadows; 8,000-12,200'; Rock Creek Lake basin and Whitney Meadows; Jul-Aug.

Grossulariaceae (gooseberry family)

Alpine prickly currant *Ribes montigenum,* dry, rocky places; SN(all); Jun-Aug.

Whitesquaw *Ribes cereum,* green-white to reddish; dry, rocky places; 5,000-12,600'; SN(all); Jun-Jul.

Hydrophyllaceae (waterleaf family)

Silverleaf phacelia *Phacelia hastata var. compacta,* lavendar-white; gravelly, rocky places; 7,000-13,000'; SN(all); Jul-Sep.

Lamiaceae (mint family) formerly Labiatae

Mountain mint *Monardella odoritissima,* purple; dry slopes; 3,000-11,400'; SN(all); Jun-Sep.

Linaceae (flax family)

Western blue flax *Linum lewisii,* blue; dry slopes and ridges; 4,000-11,000'; SN(all); May-Sep.

Onagraceae (evening primrose family)

Rock fringe *Epilobium odcordatum,* pink; rock crannies; 7,000-13,000'; SN(all); Jul-Sep.

Polemoniaceae (phlox family)

Showy polemonium *Polemonium pulcherrimum,* blue-purple; dry,rocky, often volcanic slopes; 8,000-11,000'; Mono & Mariposa Counties. n.; Jul-Aug.

Sky pilot *Polemonium eximium,* blue-purple; dry, rocky ridges and crannies; 10,000-14,200'; Tuolumne to Tulare & Inyo Counties; Jul-Aug.

Granite gilia   *Leptodactylon pungens*, white-purple; dry, rocky and sandy places; 5,000-12,000'; SN(all); May-Aug.

Spreading phlox   *Phlox diffusa*, white-lilac-pink; dry slopes and flats; 3,300-13,300'; SN(all); May-Aug.

Matted phlox   *Phlox dispersa*, white; dry, sandy or gravelly granitic flats; 11,000-12,500'; Tulare & Inyo Counties.; Jul-Aug.

Clustered phlox   *Phlox pulvinata*, white-pink; dry, rocky places; 10,000-13,000; Inyo & Fresno to Mono & Tuolumne Counties; Jul-Aug.

Polygonaceae (buckwheat family)

Leafy dwarf knotweed   *Polygonum minimum*, green-white; moist meadows and banks; 5,000-11,200'; SN(all); Jul-Sep

Shasta knotweed   *Polygonum shastense*, white-rose; rocky or gravelly slopes; 7,000-11,000'; SN(all); Jul-Sep.

Knotweed sp.   *Polygonum polygaloides*, green/white; moist, silty or gravelly places; 4,500-11,500'; SN(all); Jun-Sep.

Oval-leafed eriogonum   *Eriogonum ovalifolium*, white-rose; dry, rocky places; 7,000-12,000'

Lobb's eriogonum   *Eriogonum lobbii*, white-rose; dry, rocky places; Inyo & Mariposa Counties n.

Eriogonum sp.   *Eriogonum rosense*, yellow; dry, rocky places; 7,000-12,000'

Frosty eriogonum   *Eriogonum incanum*, yellow; dry, rocky places 7,000-12,000'; Alpine County s.

Mountain sorrel   *Oxyria digyna*, red; rocky places; 7,000-13,000'; SN(all), Jul-Sep.

Portulaceae (purslane family)

Pussypaws   *Calyptridium umbellatum*, pink-white; sandy and gravelly places; 2,500-12,000'; SN(all); May-Aug.

Dwarf lewisia   *Lewisia pygmaea*, pink; moist gravel; 9,000-12,750'; SN(all); Jul-Aug.

Nevada lewisia   *Lewisia nevadensis*, white; moist to wet places; 4,500-12,000'; SN(all); May-Jul.

Three-leaved lewisia   *Lewisia triphylla*, white-pink; moist gravel; 5,000-11,200'; SN(all); Jun-Aug.

Sierra claytonia   *Claytonia nevadensis*, white-pink; wet gravel; 5,000-12,000'; Alpine County s.; Jul-Aug.

Primulaceae (primrose family)

Alpine shooting star   *Dodecatheon alpinum*, purple/yellow; boggy meadows; 6,400-12,000'; SN(all); Jul-Aug.

Mountaineer's shooting star   *Dodecatheon redolens*, purple/yellow; moist places; 8,000-11,500; Fresno Co. s.; Jul-Aug.

Sierra shooting star   *Dodecatheon subalpinum*, purple/yellow; moist, shaded places; Tulare to Tuolumne County; May-Jul.

Sierra primrose   *Primula suffrutescens*, magenta/yellow; rock crannies and cliffs; 8,000-13,500'; SN(all); Jul-Aug.

Ranunculaceae (buttercup family)

Crimson columbine   *Aquilegia formosa*, crimson red; moist woods and meadows; 3,000-10,000'; SN (all); May-Aug.

Colville's columbine   *Aquilegia pubescens*, cream-yellow; rock crannies and talus; 9,000-12,000'; Tulare to Tuolumne County; Jul-Aug.

Alpine buttercup   *Ranunculus eschscholtzii*, yellow; moist meadows and rocks; 8,000-13,300'; SN(all); Jul-Aug.

Water plantain buttercup   *Ranunculus alismaefolius*, yellow; wet meadows to 12,000'; SN(all); May-Jul.

Rosaceae (rose family)

Sibbaldia   *Sibbaldia procumbens*, cold, soggy, acidic soils (late snowbank sites), also dry, rocky places; 6,000-12,000'; SN(all); Jun-Aug.

Drummond's cinquefoil   *Potentilla drummondii*, yellow; moist places; 4,500-13,000'; SN(all); Jun-Sep.

Diverse-leaved cinquefoil   *Potentilla diversifolia*, yellow; moist, rocky places; 8,000-11,600'; SN(all); Jun-Sep.

Mt. Rainier cinquefoil   *Potentilla flabellifolia*, yellow; moist places; 5,800-12,000'; SN(all); Jun-Sep.

Bush cinquefoil	*Potentilla fruticosa,* yellow; moist places and slopes; 6,400-12,000'; SN(all); Jun-Sep.
Sticky cinquefolia	*Potentilla glandulosa,* yellow; dry to moist places; below 12,400'; SN(all); Jun-Sep.
Pennsylvnia cinquefoil	*Potentilla pennsylvanica var. strigosa,* yellow; moist places; 9,000-12,000'; Inyo County; Jun-Sep.
Strigose cinquefoil	*Potentilla pseudosericea,* yellow; dry, rocky places; Inyo & Tuolumno Counties n.; Jun-Sep.
Wheeler's cinquefoil	*Potentilla wheeleri,* yellow; meadow edges; 6,500-11,500'; Tulare County; Jun-Sep.
Club-moss ivesia	*Ivesia lycopodoides,* yellow; moist places; 7,500-12,500'; Eldorado County s.; Jul-Aug.
Dwarf ivesia	*Ivesia pygmaea,* yellow; rocky slopes; 9,500-13,000'; Inyo & Tulare Counties; Jul-Aug.
Gordon's ivesia	*Ivesia gordonii,* yellow; dry, rocky places; 7,500-13,000'; Tuolumne & Mono Co. n.; Jul-Aug.
Muir's ivesia	*Ivesia muirii,* yellow; gravelly slopes; 9,500-12,000'; Fresno to Tuolumne & Mono Counties; Jul-Aug.
Mouse-tail ivesia	*Ivesia santolinoides,* white; dry, gravelly flats and ridges; 5,000-12,000'; Eldorado Counties s.; Jul-Aug.
Shockley's ivesia	*Ivesia shockleyi,* yellow (pale); gravelly and rocky places; 9,000-13,000'; Inyo to Placer County; Jul-Aug.
Creambush	*Holodiscus microphyllus,* white-pink; dry, rocky places; 5,500-11,000'; Plumas County s.; Jun-Aug.
Mountain spiraea	*Spiraea densiflora,* pink; moist, rocky places; 5,000-11,000'; SN(all); Jul-Aug.

Salicaceae (willow family)

Alpine willow	*Salix arctica,* moist places; 8,500-12,000'; Lassen County s.; Jul-Aug.
Snow willow	*Salix reticulata var. nivalis,* moist places; 10,000-12,000'; Mono County; Jul-Aug.
Mono willow	*Salix planifolia var. monica,* moist places; 8,000-12,500'; Tuolumne County s.; Jun-Aug.
Sierra willow	*Salix orestra,* moist places; 7,400-12,000'; SN(all); Jun-Jul.

Saxifragiaceae (saxifrage family)

Sierra saxifrage	*Saxifraga aprica,* white; moist, gravelly and rocky places; 5,500-12,000'; SN(all); May-Aug.
Alpine saxifrage	*Saxifraga tolmei,* white; moist, rocky places; 8,500-11,800'; SN(all); Jul-Aug.

Scrophulariaceae (figwort family)

Little elephant's head	*Pedicularis attolens,* lavendar-pink; meadows; 5,000-12,000'; SN(all); Jun-Sep.
Greater elephant's head	*Pedicularis groenlandica,* red-purple; meadows; 6,000-11,200'; SN(all); Jun-Aug.
Alpine paintbrush	*Castilleja nana,* gray white or pinkish; rocky places; 6,400-12,000'; Jul-Aug.
Lemmon's paintbrush	*Castilleja lemmonii,* magenta; meadows; 7,000-11,500; SN(all); Jul-Aug.
Sierra penstemon	*Penstemon heterodoxus,* purple; rocky slopes and meadows; 8,000-12,000'; Plumas County s.; Jul-Aug.
Davidson's penstemon	*Penstemon davidsonii,* purple-violet; rocky places; 9,000-12,300'; SN(all); Jul-Aug.
Mountain pride	*Penstemon newberryi,* rose-red to purple; rocky and gravelly places; 5,000-11,000'; SN(all); Jun-Aug.
Alpine monkeyflower	*Mimulus primuloides,* yellow; meadows; 4,000-11,200'; SN(all); Jun-Aug.
Suksdorf's monkeyflower	*Mimulus suksdorfii,* yellow; moist, sandy places; 5,000-13,000'; SN(all); May-Aug.
Larger mountain monkeyflower	*Mimulus tilingii,* yellow; wet banks; 6,400-12,000'; SN(all); Jul-Sep.

MONOCOTELYDONS
Cyperaceae (sedge family)

Brewer's sedge	*Carex breweri,* dry, sandy to gravelly open places; 7,600-12,200'; SN(all).
Sedge sp.	*Carex haydeniana,* rocky slopes and flats, moist soils; 8,000-13,800'; s. & c. SN.
Sedge sp.	*Carex helleri,* dry, rocky or gravelly slopes; 8,000-13,500'; SN(all).

Sedge sp.   *Carex incurviformes var. danaensis*, dry, open rocky to gravelly slopes; 12,200-
                              13,200'; s. & c.SN.
Sedge sp.   *Carex phaeocephala*, rocky soils; 8,800-12,800'; SN(all).
Sedge sp.   *Carex pseudoscirpoidea*
Alpine sedge   *Carex subnigricans*, meadows and dry, rocky slopes; 8,500-12,500'; SN(all).
Clement's bulrush   *Scirpus clementis*, meadows; 8,000-12,000'; Jul-Aug.
Iridaceae (iris family)
Western blue-flag iris   *Iris missouriensis*, violet-blue;   meadows and moist places; 3,000-11,000; May-Jun.
Juncaceae (rush family)
Rush sp.   *Juncus drummondii*, green-brown to purplish; moist places; 6,000-12,000'; SN(all).
Rush sp.   *Juncus parryi*, green-brown to purplish; moist places; 6,000-12,000'; SN(all).
Mountain wood rush   *Luzula orestera*, moist places; 9,000-11,500'; Tuolumne & Mono Counties s.; Jul-Aug.
Spiked wood rush   *Luzula spicata*, moist places; 8,000-12,500'; SN(all); Jul-Aug.
Donner wood rush   *Luzula subcongesta*, moist places; 7,000-11,200'; SN(all); Jul-Aug.
Juncaginaceae (arrow-weed family)
Marsh arrow grass   *Triglochin palustris*, mud flats and springs; 7,500-11,500'; Tulare & Inyo Co; Jul-Aug.
Lilaceae (lily family)
Red Sierra onion   *Allium obtusum*, sandy or gravelly slopes and benches; 7,000-12,000'; Plumas
                              County s.; May-Jul.
Poaceae (grass family)
Needlegrass sp.   *Achnatherum nelsonii*, open places below 11,500'; SN(all).
Western needlegrass   *Achnatherum occidentalis*, dry, open places below 12,000'; SN(all)
Pine stipa   *Achnatherum pinetorum*, rocky places; 7,000-12,500'; e. SN; Eldorado County s.
Idaho bentgrass   *Agrostis idahoensis*, meadows; 5,000-11,500'; SN(all); Jul-Aug.
Variable bentgrass   *Agrostis variabilis*, 5,000-12,000; SN(all); Jul-Aug.
Short-awned foxtail   *Alopecurus aequalis*, moist-wet places to 11,500'; SN(all).
Brewer's reedgrass   *Calamagrostis breweri*, meadows; 6,200-12,200'; SN(all); Jul-Sep.
Blue-joint   *Calamagrostis canadensis*, moist places; 5,000-12,000'; SN(all); Jun-Sep.
Purple reedgrass   *Calamagrostis purpurascens*, rocky places; 9,500-13,000'; SN(all); Jul-Sep.
Squirreltail   *Elymus elymoides*, dry, open places below 13,000'; SN(all).
Spiked hesperachloa   *Festuca kingii*, dry slopes; 7,000-12,000'; s, SN; Jun-Aug.
Needle and thread   *Hesperostipa comata*, e. slope SN to 11,300.
Nodding melic   *Melica stricta*, rocky places; 4,000-11,600'; SN(all).
Alpine timothy   *Phleum alpinum*, moist to wet places; 5,000-11,500'; SN(all); Jul-Aug.
King's ricegrass   *Ptilagrostis kingii*, moist places; 9,300-11,500'; Tuolumne and Mono Counties
Bluegrass sp. *Poa cusickii*, 5,000-12,000'; Nevada County s.
Bluegrass sp. *Poa secunda*, 6,000-12,000'; Butte County s.
Bluegrass sp. *Poa wheeleri*, 4,500-12,500; Nevada County s.
Spike trisetum   *Trisetum spicatum*, montane places; 7,200-13,000; SN(all); Jul-Aug.
Typhaceae (cattail family)
Narrow-leafed bur-reed   *Sparganium angustifolium*, in water 10" deep; 4,000-12,000'; SN(all).

Appendix B: Birds of the Alpine Sierra Nevada

From Gaines 1988, Beedy and Granholm 1985, Peterson 1990, and personal observations. Taxonomy from Peterson 1990. This list includes species found at and above treeline (above 10,000' in the Yosemite Region).

CICONIIFORMES
Ardeidae

Great Blue Heron	*Ardea herodias*, rare summer visitor
Black-crowned Night Heron	*Nycticorax nicticorax*, extremely rare transient

ANSERIFORMES
Anatinae

Mallard	*Anas platyrhnchos*, uncommon summer breeder
Northern Pintail	*Anas acuta*, extremely rare transient

FALCONIFORMES
Cathartidae

Turkey Vulture	*Cathartes aura*, extremely rare transient

Accipitridae

Osprey	*Pandion haliaetus*, rare transient
Northern Harrier	*Circus cyaneus*, rare transient
Sharp-shinned Hawk	*Accipiter striatus*, uncommon transient
Cooper's Hawk	*Accipiter cooperi*, uncommon transient
Northern Goshawk	*Accipiter gentilis*, rare summer visitor
Red-shouldered Hawk	*Buteo lineatus*, extremely rare transient
Swainson's Hawk	*Buteo swainsoni*, irregular transient
Red-tailed Hawk	*Buteo jamaicensis*, fairly common summer visitor
Golden Eagle	*Aquila chrysaetos*, uncommon summer breeder

Falconidae

American Kestrel	*Falco spaverius*, uncommon summer visitor
Merlin	*Falco columbarius*, rare transient
Peregrine Falcon	*Falco peregrinus*, rare transient
Prairie Falcon	*Falco mexicanus*, uncommon summer visitor

GALLIFORMES
Phasianidae

Blue Grouse	*Dendragapus canadensis*, rare summer visitor
White-tailed Ptarmigan	*Lagopus leucurus*, uncommon resident breeder
Mountain Quail	*Oreortyx pictus*, rare summer visitor

GRUIFORMES
Rallidae

American Coot	*Fulica americana*, extremely rare transient

CHARADRIIFORMES
Scolopacidae

Spotted Sandpiper	*Actitis macularia*, uncommon summer breeder
Red-necked Phalarope	*Phalaropus lobatus*, extremely rare transient

Laridae

California Gull	*Larus californicus*, fairly common summer visitor
Caspian Tern	*Sterna caspia*, extremely rare transient

COLUMBIFORMES
Columbidae

Band-tailed Pigeon	*Columba fasciata*, rare summer visitor
Mourning Dove	*Zenaida macroura*, rare transient

STRIGIFORMES
Strigidae
Western Screech Owl | *Otus kennicottii*, extremely rare transient
Great Horned Owl | *Bubo virginianus*, uncommon resident breeder
Long-eared Owl | *Asio otus*, rare transient
CAPRIMULGIFORMES
Caprimulgidae
Common Poor-will | *Phalaenoptilus nuttallii*, rare transient
APODIFORMES
Apodidae
Black Swift | *Cypseloides niger*, rare summer visitor
Vaux's Swift | *Chaetura vauxi*, extremely rare transient
White-throated Swift | *Aeronautes saxatalis*, rare summer visitor
Trochilidae
Black-chinned Hummingbird | *Archlochus alexandri*, extremely rare transient
Anna's Hummingbird | *Calypte anna*, rare transient
Calliope Hummingbird | *Stellula calliope*, rare summer breeder
Rufous Hummingbird | *Selasphorus rufus*, common transient
CORACIIFORMES
Alcedinidae
Belted Kingfisher | *Ceryle alcyon*, rare transient
Picidae
Lewis' Woodpecker | *Melanerpes lewis*, irregular transient
Acorn Woodpecker | *Melanerpes formicivorus*, extremely rare transient
Red-breasted Sapsucker | *Sphyrapicus ruber*, uncommon summer breeder
Williamson's Sapsucker | *Sphyrapicus thyroideus*, rare summer visitor
Hairy Woodpecker | *Picoides villosus*, uncommon resident breeder
White-headed Woodpecker | *Picoides albolarvatus*, extremely rare transient
Black-backed Woodpecker | *Picoides arcticus*, extremely rare winter visitor
Northern Flicker (red-shafted) | *Colaptes auratus*, fairly common summer breeder
Northern Flicker (yellow-shafted) | *Colaptes auratus*, extremely rare vagrant
PASSERIFORMES
Tyrannidae
Olive-sided Flycatcher | *Contopus borealis*, rare summer breeder
Western Wood Pewee | *Contopus sordidulus*, rare summer visitor
Willow Flycatcher | *Empidonax traillii*, extremely rare transient
Hammond's Flycatcher | *Empidonax hammondii*, rare transient
Dusky Flycatcher | *Empidonax oberholseri*, common summer breeder
Gray Flycatcher | *Empidonax wrightii*, extremely rare transient
Pacific-slope Flycatcher | *Empidonax difficilis*, rare transient
Cordilleran Flycatcher | *Empidonax occidentalis*, rare transient
Black Phoebe | *Sayornis nigricans*, extremely rare transient
Say's Phoebe | *Sayornis saya*, extremely rare transient
Alaudidae
Horned Lark | *Eremophila alpestris*, fairly common summer breeder
Hirundinidae
Tree Swallow | *Tachycineta bicolor*, extremely rare transient
Violet-green Swallow | *Tachycineta thalasinna*, rare summer visitor
Northern Rough-winged Swallow | *Stelgidopteryx serripennis*, extremely rare transient
Cliff Swallow | *Hirundo pyrrhonota*, extremely rare transient

Corvidae
Steller's Jay   *Cyanocitta stelleri*, uncommon summer breeder
Scrub Jay   *Aphelocoma coerulescens*, rare summer visitor
Pinyon Jay   *Gymnorhinus cyanocephalus*, irregular transient
Clark's Nutcracker   *Nucifraga columbiana*, common summer breeder; irregular fairly
                           common winter visitor
Common Raven   *Corvus corax*, rare summer visitor
Paridae
Mountain Chickadee   *Parus gambeli*, common resident breeder
Aegithalidae
Bushtit   *Psaltriparus minimus*, rare summer visitor
Sittidae
Red-breasted Nuthatch   *Sitta canadensis*, irregular common transient
White-breasted Nuthatch *Sitta carolinensis*, unusual resident breeder
Pygmy Nuthatch   *Sitta pygmaea*, extremely rare transient
Certhiidae
Brown Creeper   *Certhia americana*, irregular uncommon winter visitor
Troglodytidae
Rock Wren   *Salpinctes obsoletus*, unusual summer breeder
Canyon Wren   *Catherpes mexicanus*, unusual resident breeder
House Wren   *Troglodytes aedon*, fairly common transient
Winter Wren   *Troglodytes troglodytes*, extremely rare transient
Cinclidae
American Cipper   *Cinclus mexicanus*, uncommon summer breeder; irregular fairly
                           common winter visitor

Muscicapidae
Golden-crowned Kinglet *Regulus satrapa*, rare summer breeder
Ruby-crowned Kinglet   *Regulus calendula*, rare summer breeder; uncommon transient
Mountain Bluebird   *Sialia currucoides*, uncommon summer breeder
Townsend's Solitaire   *Myadestes townsendi*, irregular uncommon summer breeder
Hermit Thrush   *Catharus guttatus*, fairly common summer breeder
American Robin   *Turdus migratorius*, common summer breeder
Varied Thrush   *Ixoreus naevius*, extremely rare transient
Mimidae
Northern Mockingbird   *Mimus polyglottos*, extremely rare transient
Montacillidae
American Pipit   *Anthus rubescens*, uncommon summer breeder
Bombycillidae
Cedar Waxwing   *Bombycilla garrulus*, extremely rare transient
Laniidae
Northern Shrike   *Lanius excubitor*, extremely rare tramsient
Loggerhead Shrike   *Lanius ludovicianus*, extremely rare transient
Vireonidae
Solitary Vireo (Cassin's) *Vireo solitarius*, rare transient
Warbling Vireo   *Vireo gilvus*, rare transient
Emberizidae
(Parulinae)
Orange-crowned Warbler *Vermivora celata*, common summer visitor
Nashville Warbler   *Vermivora ruficapilla*, uncommon transient
Virginia Warbler   *Vermivora virginiae*, extremely rare transient
Yellow Warbler   *Dendroica petechia*, extremely rare transient

Yellow-rumped Warbler (Audubon) *Dendroica coronata*, common summer breeder
Black-throated Gray Warbler *Dendroica nigrescens*, rare transient
Townsend's Warbler *Dendroica townsendi*, uncommon transient
Hermit Warbler *Dendroica occidentalis*, rare transient
Prairie Warbler *Dendroica discolor*, extremely rare transient
Palm Warbler *Dendroica palmarum*, extremely rare vagrant
American Redstart *Setophaga ruticilla*, extremely rare transient
MacGillivray's Warbler *Oporornis tolmiei*, irregular common transient
Common Yellowthroat *Geothlypis trichas*, extremely rare summer visitor
Wilson's Warbler *Wilsonia pusilla*, uncommon summer breeder; fairly common transient
(Thraupinae)
Western Tanager *Piranga ludoviciana*, rare transient
(Cardinalidae)
Black-headed Grosbeak *Pheucticus melanocephalus*, **rare transient**
Lazuli Bunting *Passerina amoena*, uncommon transient
(Emberizinae)
California Towhee *Pipilo crissalis*, rare transient
Rufous-sided Towhee *Pipilo erythrophthalmus*, rare transient
Chipping Sparrow *Spizella passerina*, irregular fairly common summer breeder
Brewer's Sparrow *Spizella breweri*, rare transient
Lark Sparrow *Chondestes grammacus*, rare transient
Vesper Sparrow *Pooecetes gramineus*, extremely rare transient
Black-throated Sparrow *Amphispiza bilineata*, extremely rare transient
Sage Sparrow *Amphispiza belli*, extremely rare transient
Savannah Sparrow *Passerculus sandwichensis*, rare transient
Fox Sparrow *Passerella iliaca*, rare transient
Song Sparrow *Melospiza meloidia*, rare summer visitor
Lincoln's Sparrow *Melospiza lincolnii*, uncommon transient
Golden-crowned Sparrow *Zonothrichia atricapilla*, rare transient
White-crowned Sparrow (mountain) *Zonothrichia leucophrys*, common summer breeder
White-crowned Sparrow (Gambel's) *Zonothrichia*, fairly common transient
Harris' Sparrow *Zonothrichia querula*, extremely rare transient
Dark-eyed Junco (Oregon) *Junco hyemalis oreganus*, common summer breeder
Dark-eyed Junco (slate-colored) *Junco hyemalis hyemalus*, extremely rare transient
(Icterinae)
Red-winged Blackbird *Agelaius phoeniceus*, extremely rare transient
Western Meadowlark *Sturnella neglecta*, rare transient
Brewer's Blackbird *Euphagus cyanocephalus*, irregular frequent summer visitor
Brown-headed Cowbird *Molothrus aeneus*, uncommon summer breeder
Northern Oriole (Bullock's) *Icterus galbula bullockii*, extremely rare transient
Fringillidae
Rosy Finch (gray-crowned) *Leocosticte arctoa*, fairly common summer breeder; irregular rare
winter visitor
Pine Grosbeak *Pinicola enucleator*, irregular uncommon resident breeder
Purple Finch *Carpodacus purpureus*, extremely rare transient
Cassin's Finch *Carpodacus cassinii*, common summer breeder
House Finch *Carpodacus mexicanus*, extremely rare transient
Red Crossbill *Loxia curvirostra*, irregular fairly common resident breeder
Pine Siskin *Carduelis pinus*, irregular uncommon summer breeder
Lesser Goldfinch *Carduelis psaltria*, irregular uncommon summer visitor
Evening Grosbeak *Coccothraustes vespertina*, extremely rare summer visitor

Appendix C: Mammals of the Alpine Sierra Nevada

From Grater 1978 and Burt and Grossenheider 1952. Taxonomy from Burt and Grossenheider 1952.

INSECTIVORA
Soricidae
Dusky shrew   *Sorex obscurus*, common resident
Mt. Lyell shrew   *Sorex lyelli*, rare local resident
Northern water shrew   *Sorex palustris*, rare resident
Vagrant shrew   *Sorex vagrans*, rare resident
CARNIVORA
Ursidae
Black bear   *Ursus americanus*, uncommon visitor
Mustelidae
Marten   *Martes americana*, uncommon visitor
Fisher   *Mertes pennanti*, rare visitor
Longtail weasel   *Mustela frenata*, uncommon resident
Shorttail weasel   *Mustela erminea*, uncommon resident
Wolverine   *Gulo gulo*, rare resident
Canidae
Coyote   *Canis latrans*, common visitor
Red fox   *Vulpes fulva*, rare visitor
Felidae
Bobcat   *Lynx rufus*, rare visitor
RODENTIA
Sciuridae
Yellow-bellied marmot   *Marmota flaviventris*, common resident
Belding ground squirrel   *Spermophilus beldingi*, common resident
Golden-mantled ground squirrel   *Spermophilus lateralis*, common resident to treeline
Chickaree   *Tamiasciurus douglasii*, common resident to treeline
Geomyidae
Sierra pocket gopher   *Thomomys monticola*, common resident
Cricetidae
Deer mouse   *Peromyscus maniculatus*, common resident
Bushytail woodrat   *Neotoma cinerea*, common resident to treeline
Longtail meadow mouse   *Microtus longicaudus*, common resident
Heather vole   *Phenacomys intermedius*, uncommon resident
Zapodidae
Western jumping mouse   *Zapus princeps*, uncommon resident
LAGOMORPHA
Ochotonidae
Pika   *Ochotona princeps*, common resident
ARTIODACTYLA
Cervidae
Mule deer   *Odocoileus hemionus*, common summer visitor
Bovidae
Bighorn sheep   *Ovis canadensis*, rare summer visitor

References

Ahrens, C. Donald. 1991. Meteorology Today. West: St. Paul.

Alt, David D. And Donald W. Hyndman. 1975. *Roadside Geology of California*. Mountain: Missoula.

Andersen, Douglas C., Robert S. Hoffman, and Kenneth B. Armitage. 1979. Aboveground productivity and floristic structure of a high subalpine herbaceous meadow. *Arctic and Alpine Research* 11: 467-476.

Anderson, R. Scott. 1990. Holocene forest development and paleoclimates within the Central Sierra Nevada, California. *Journal of Ecology* 78: 470-489.

Armitage, Kenneth B. 1991. Social and population dynamics of yellow-bellied marmots: results of long-term research. *Annual Review of Ecology and Systematics* 22: 379-407.

Arno, Stephen. 1973. *Discovering Sierra Trees*. Yosemite Association, Sequoia Natural History Association: National Park Service, U. S. Department of the Interior.

----------. 1984. *Timberline: Arctic and Alpine Forest Frontiers*. The Mountaineers: Seattle.

Austin, Jane. 1903. *The Land of Little Rain*. Houghton-Mifflin: Cambridge.

Axelrod, Daniel I. 1940. Late Tertiary floras of the Great Basin and border areas. *Bulletin of Torrey Botanical Club* 67: 477-487.

----------. 1957. Late Tertiary floras and the Sierra Nevadan uplift. *Bulletin of the Geological Society of America* 68: 19-46.

----------. 1958. Evolution of the Madro-Tertiary geofloras. *Botanical Review* 24: 433-509.

----------. 1962. A Pliocene Sequoiadendron forest from western Nevada. *University of California Publications* 39: 195-268.

Barbour, Michael G. and William Dwight Billings (eds.). 1988. *North American Terrestrial Vegetation*. Cambridge University Press: Cambridge.

Barbour, Machael G. and Jack Major (eds.). 1990. *Terrestrial Vegetation of California*. California Native Plant Society: Sacramento.

Barmuta, Leon A., Scott D. Cooper, and Stephen K. Hamilton. 1990. Response of zooplankton and zoobenthos to experimental acidification in a high elevation lake (Sierra Nevada, California, U. S. A.). *Freshwater Biology* 23: 571-586.

Barry, Roger G. and Jack D. Ives. Introduction. Pp. 1-11. In Ives, J. D. And R. G. Barry (eds.). *Arctic and Alpine Environments*. Methuen: London.

Bates, Marston. 1950. *The Nature of Natural History*. Princeton University Press: Princeton.

Beedy, Edward C. and Stephen L. Granholm. 1985. *Discovering Sierra Birds*. Yosemite Natural History Association, Sequoia Natural History Association: National Park Service, U.S Department of the Interior.

Berg, Neil, Randall Osterhuber, and James Bergman. 1991. Rain-induced outflow from deep snowpacks in the Central Sierra Nevada, California. *Hydrological Sciences Journal* 36: 611-629.

Berman, Morris. 1984. *The Reenchantment of the World*. Bantam: Toronto.

Bettinger, Robert L. 1991. Aboriginal occupation at altitude: alpine villages in the White Mountains of Eastern California. C. A. Hall, Jr., V. Doyle-Jones, and B. Widawski (eds.). *Natural History of Eastern California and High Altitude Research* vol. 3. University of California: Los Angeles.

Billings, W. D. and L. C. Bliss. 1959. An alpine snowbank environment and its effects on vegetation, plant development, and productivity. *Ecology* 40: 388-397.

Billings, W. D. and H. A. Mooney. 1968. The ecology of arctic and alpine plants. *Biological Review* 43: 481-529.

Billings, W. D. 1973. Arctic and alpine vegetation-similarities, differences, and susceptibility to disturbance. *Bioscience* 23: 697-704.

----------. 1974a. Arctic and alpine vegetation: plant adaptations to cold summer climates. Pp 404-437. In Ives, J. D. and R. G. Barry (eds.). *Arctic and Alpine Environments*. Methuen: London.

----------. 1974b. Adaptations and origins of alpine plants. *Arctic and Alpine Research* 6(2): 129-142.

----------. 1978. Alpine phytogeography across the Great Basin. *Great Basin Naturalist Memoirs* 2: 105-117.

----------. 1988. Alpine vegetation. In Barbour, M. G. and W. D. Billings. *North American Terrestrial Vegetation*. Cambridge University Press: Cambridge.

Bliss, L. C. 1971. Arctic and alpine plant life cycles. *Annual Review of Ecology and Systematics* 2: 404-438.

Bradford, David F. 1989. Allotopic distribution of native frogs and introduced fishes in high Sierra Nevada lakes of California: importance of the negative effects of fish introductions. *Copeia* 3: 775-778.

Brumbaugh, Robert S. 1981. *The Philosophers of Greece*. State University of New York Press: Albany.

Bunting, B. T. 1965. *The Geography of Soil*. Aldine: Chicago.

Burt, William Henry, and Richard Phillip Grossenheider. 1952. *A Field Guide to the Mammals*. Houghton Mifflin: Boston.

Byron, Earl R., Richard P. Axler, and Charles R. Goldman. 1991. Increased precipitation activity in the Central Sierra Nevada. *Atmospheric Environment* 25: 271-275.

Callicott, J. Baird. 1989. *In Defense of the Land Ethic: Essays in Environmental Philosophy*. State University of New York Press: Albany.

Callicott, J. Baird and Roger T. Ames (eds.). 1989. *Nature in Asian Traditions of Thought: Essays in Environmental Philosophy*. State University of New York Press: Albany.

Callicott, J, Baird. 1994. *Earth's Insights: A Multicultural Survey of Environmental Ethics from the Mediterranean Basin to the Australian Outback.* State University of New York Press: Albany.
Canaday, B. B. and R. W. Fonda. 1974. The influence of subalpine snowbanks on vegetation pattern, production, and phenology. *Bulletin of the Torrey Botanical Club* 101(6): 340- 350.
Chabot, Brian F. and W. D. Billings. 1972. Origins and ecology of the Sierran alpine flora and vegetation. *Ecological Monographs* 42: 163-199.
Chambers, Jeanne C., James A. MacMahon, and James H. Haefner. 1991. Seed entrapment in alpine ecosystems: effects of soil particle size and diaspore morphology. *Ecology* 72: 1668-1677.
Chambers, Jeanne C. 1995a. Relationships between seed fates and seedling establishment in an alpine ecosystem. *Ecology* 76: 2124-2133.
----------. 1995b. Distribution, life history strategies, and seed fates in alpine Herbfields communities. *American Journal of Botany* 82: 421-433.
Chase, Clement G. And Terry C. Wallace. 1986. Uplift of the Sierra Nevada of California. *Geology* 14: 730-733.
Christianson, M. N. 1966. Late Cenozoic crustal movements in the Sierra Nevada of California. *Geological Society of America Bulletin* 77: 163-182.
Clark, Douglas H., Malcolm M. Clark, and Alan R. Gillespie. 1994. Debris-covered glaciers in the Sierra Nevada, California, and their implications for snowline reconstructions. *Quaternary Research* 42: 139-153.
Clark, Douglas H. and Malcolm M. Clark. 1995. New evidence of Late-Wisconsin deglaciation in the Sierra Nevada, California, refutes the Hilgard glaciation. *Geological Society of American Abstracts with Programs, Cordilleran Section* 27: 10.
Clark, Jennifer. 1992. The influence of spring snow depth on white-tailed ptarmigan breeding success in the Sierra Nevada. *Condor* 94: 622-627.
Clark, Malcolm M. 1976. Evidence for rapid destruction of latest Pleistocene glaciers of the Sierra Nevada, California. *Geological Society of America Abstracts with Programs, Cordilleran Section* p. 361-362.
----------. 1994. Reply to comment by M. Jakob on debris-covered glaciers in the Sierra Nevada, California, and their implications for snowline reconstructions. *Quaternary Research* 42: 359-362.
Clyde, Norman and Wynne Benti (ed.). 1997. *Close Ups of the High Sierra.* Spotted Dog Press: Bishop.
Collingwood, R. G. 1972. *The Idea of Nature.* Oxford University Press: Oxford.
Coonen, Lester P. 1977. Aristotle's biology. *Bioscience* 27: 733-738.
Cory, L. 1963. Effects of introduced trout on the evolution of native frogs in the high Sierra Nevada mountains. Page 172 in J. A. Moore (ed.). *Proceedings of the XVI International Congress of Zoology:* 20-27 August 1963, Washington, D. C.
Crough, S. Thomas and George A. Thompson. 1977. Upper mantle origin of Sierra Nevada uplift. *Geology* 5: 396-399.
Daubenmire, Rexford F. 1941. Some ecological features of the subterranean organs of alpine plants. *Ecology* 22: 370-378.
Demoz, Belay B., Renyi Zhang, and Richard L. Pitter. 1993. An analysis of Sierra Nevada winter orographic storms: ground-based ice-crystal observations. *Journal of Applied Meteorology* 32: 1826-1836.
Dott, Robert H. Jr. and Donald H. Prothero. 1994. *Evolution of the Earth.* McGraw-Hill: New York.
Drost, Charles A. And Gary M. Fellers. 1996. Collapse of a regional frog fauna in the Yosemite area of the California Sierra Nevada, U. S. A. *Conservation Biology* 10: 414-425.
Easterbrook, Don J. 1969. *Principles of Geomorphology.* McGraw-Hill: New York.
Edwards, Paul (ed.) 1967. *The Encyclopedia of Philosophy.* MacMillan: New York.
Eicher, Don L. and A. Lee McAlester. 1980. *History of the Earth.* Prentice-Hall: Englewood Cliffs, NJ.
Evans, Howard Ensign. 1993. *Pioneer Naturalists: The Discovery and Naming of North American Plants and Animals.* Henry Holt: New York.
Evans, Stephen G. And John J. Clague. 1994. Recent climatic change and catastrophic geomorphic processes in mountain environments. *Geomorphology* 10: 107-128.
Farquhar, Francis P. 1965. *History of the Sierra Nevada.* University of California Press: Berkeley.
Fiero, Bill. 1986. *Geology of the Great Basin.* University of Nevada Press: Reno.
Fliedner, Moritz M. and Stanley Ruppert. 1996. Three-dimensional crustal structure of the Southern Sierra Nevada from seismic fan profiles and gravity modeling. *Geology* 24: 367-370.
Fleischner, Thomas. (In Press). Revitalizing natural history. *Wild Earth.* Summer 1999.
Foth, Henry D. 1978. *Fundamentals of Soil Science.* John Wiley & Sons: New York.
Gaines, David. 1988. *Birds of Yosemite and the East Slope.* Artemisia: Lee Vining, CA.
Gerrard, A. J. 1990. *Mountain Environments.* M. I. T. Press: Cambridge.
Gilbert, F.S. 1980. The equilibrium theory of island biogeography: fact or fiction? *Journal of Biogeography* 7: 209-235.
Gillespie, Alan R. 1991a. Quaternary subsidence of Owens Valley, California. In C. A. Hall, Jr., V. Doyle-Jones, and B. Widawski (eds.). *Natural History of Eastern California and High Altitude Research* vol. 3. University of California: Los Angeles.
Gillespie, Alan R. 1991b. Testing a new climatic interpretation for the Tahoe glaciation. In C. A. Hall, Jr., V. Doyle-Jones, and B. Widawski (eds.). *Natural History of Eastern California and High Altitude Research* vol. 3. University of California: Los Angeles.
Grater, Russel K. 1978. *Discovering Sierra Mammals.* Yosemite Association, Sequoia Natural History Association: National Park Service, U. S. Department of the Interior.

Graumlich, Lisa J. 1993. A 1000-year record of temperature and precipitation in the Sierra Nevada. *Quaternary Research* 39: 249-255.

Hale, Mason E. and Mariette Cole. 1988. *Lichens of California.* University of California Press: Berkeley.

Halfpenny, James C. and Roy Douglas Ozanne. 1989. *Winter: An Ecological Handbook.* Johnson: Boulder.

Hall, Clarence A. Jr. (ed.). 1991. *Natural History of the White-Inyo Range, Eastern California.* University of California Press: Berkeley.

Hamblin, W. Kenneth. 1989. *The Earth's Dynamic Systems.* MacMillan: New York.

Hambrey, Michael and Jurg Alean. 1992. *Glaciers.* Cambridge University Press: Cambridge.

Heizer, Robert F. 1980. *The Natural World of the California Indians.* University of California Press: Berkeley.

Hickman, James C. (ed.). 1993. *The Jepson Manual: Higher Plants of California.* University of California Press: Berkeley.

Hill, Mary. 1975. *Geology of the Sierra Nevada.* University of California Press: Berkeley.

Hoffman, R. S. 1974. Terrestrial vertebrates. Pp. 484-507. In J. D. Ives and R. G. Barry (eds.) *Arctic and Alpine Environments.* Methuen, London.

Hughes, Donald J. 1975. *Ecology in Ancient Civilizations.* University of New Mexico Press: Albuquerque.

Jakob, M. 1994. Comments on debris-covered glaciers in the Sierra Nevada, California, and their implications for snowline reconstructions, by Douglas H. Clark, Malcolm M. Clark, and Alan R. Gillespie. *Quaternary Research* 42: 356-358.

Johnston, Verna R. 1994. *California Forests and Woodlands: A Natural History.* University of California Press: Berkeley.

Kennelly, Patrick J. And Clement G. Chase. 1989. Flexure and isostatic residual gravity of the Sierra Nevada. *Journal of Geophysical Research* 94: 1759-1764.

Klikoff, Lionel G. 1965. Microenvironmental influence on vegetational pattern near timberline in the central Sierra Nevada. *Ecological Monographs* 35: 187-211.

Lanner, Ronald M. 1996. *Made for Each Other: A Symbiosis of Birds and Pines.* Oxford University Press: Oxford.

LeChapelle, Edward R. 1969. *Field Guide to Snow Crystals.* University of Washington Press: Seattle.

Leopold, Aldo. 1966. *A Sand County Almanac with Essays on Conservation From Round River.* Oxford University Press: Oxford.

MacArthur, Robert H. and E.O. Wilson. 1963. An equilibrium theory of insular zoogeography. Evolution 17: 373-387.

----------. 1967. *The Theory of Island Biogeography.* Princeton University Press: Princeton.

MacMahon, James A. and Douglas C. Andersen. 1982. Subalpine forests: a world perspective with emphasis on western North America. *Progress in Physical Geography* 6: 368-425.

Major, J. and S. A. Bramberg. 1967a. Comparison of some North American and Eurasian alpine ecosystems. Pp. 89-118. In H. E. Wright and W. H. Osburn (eds.). Arctic and Alpine Environments. Indiana University Press: Bloomington.

Major, J. and S. A. Bramberg. 1967b. Some cordilleran plants disjunct in the Sierra Nevada of California and their bearing on Pleistocene ecological conditions. Pp. 171-188. In H. E. Wright and W. H. Osburn (eds.). *Arctic and Alpine Environments.* Indiana University Press: Bloomington.

Major, J. and D. W. Taylor. 1977. Alpine. Pp. 601-675. In M. G. Barbour and J. Major (eds.) *Terrestrial Vegetation of California.* Wiley: New York.

Marchand, Peter J. and Deborah A. Roach. 1980. Reproductive strategies of pioneering species: seed production, dispersal, and germination. *Arctic and Alpine Research* 12(2): 137-146.

Marks, Danny, and Jeff Dozier. 1992. Climate and energy exchange at the snow surface in the alpine region of the Sierra Nevada 2: snow cover energy balance. *Water Resources Research* 28: 3043-3054.

Martel, Stephen J., T. Mark Harrison, and Alan R. Gillespie. 1987. Late Quaternary vertical displacement rate across the Fish Springs fault, Owens Valley fault zone, California. *Quaternary Research* 27: 113-129.

Matthes, Francois. 1950. *The Incomparable Valley.* University of California Press: Berkeley.

Mayr, Ernst. 1982. *The Growth of Biological Thought.* Harvard University Press: Cambridge.

McPhee, John. 1981. *Basin and Range.* Farrar, Straus, and Giroux: New York.

Miller, Jon H. and Michael T. Green. 1987. Distribution, status, and origin of water pipits breeding in California. *Condor* 89: 788-797.

Molnar, Peter and Phillip England. 1990. Late Cenozoic uplift of mountain ranges and global climate change: chicken or egg? *Nature* 346: 29-34.

Monasterski, R. 1993. Here comes the sun-climate connection. *Science News* 143: 148.

Muir, John. 1894. *The Mountains of California.* Century: New York.

Munz, Philip A. and David D. Keck. 1949. California plant communities. *Aliso* 2: 87-105.

----------. 1949. California plant communities supplement. *Aliso* 2:199-202.

----------. 1959. *A California Flora.* University of California Press: Berkeley.

Nash, Roderick. 1982. *Wilderness and the American Mind.* Yale University Press: New Haven.

Norvell, John R. and Phillip D. Creighton. 1990. Foraging of horned larks and water pipits in alpine communities. *Journal of Field Ornithology* 61(4): 434-440.

Noss, Reed. 1996. The naturalists are dying off. *Conservation Biology* 10: 1-3.

----------. 1998. Does conservation biology need natural history? *Wild Earth Fall* 1998.

Oelschlager, Max. 1991. *The Idea of Wilderness: from Prehistory to the Age of Ecology.* Yale University Press: New Haven.
Pattie, D. L. and N. A. M. Verbeek. 1966. *Alpine birds of the Beartooth Mountains.* The Condor 68: 167-176.
Peterson, Roger Tory. 1990. Western Birds. Houghton Mifflin: Boston.
Price, Larry. 1981. *Mountains and Man.* University of California Press: Berkeley.
Putnam, Jeff and Genny Smith ed. 1995. *Deepest Valley: A Guide to Owens Valley, its Roadsides and Mountain Trails.* Genny Smith: Mammoth Lakes.
Schaffer, Jeffrey P. 1997. *The Geomorphic Evolution of the Yosemite Valley and Sierra Nevada Landscapes.* Wilderness: Berkeley.
Scuderi, Louis A. 1993. A 2000-year tree ring record of annual temperatures in the Sierra Nevada mountains. *Science* 259: 1433-1436.
Secor, R. J. 1992. *The High Sierra: Peaks, Passes and Trails.* The Mountaineers: Seattle.
Sharp, Robert P. 1972. Pleistocene glaciation, Bridgeport Basin, California. *Geological Society of America Bulletin* 83: 2233-2260.
Sharp, Robert and Allen F. Glazner. 1997. *Geology Underfoot in Death Valley and Owens Valley.* Mountain: Missoula.
Sharsmith, C. W. 1940. *A Contribution to the History of the Alpine Flora of the Sierra Nevada.* Ph.D. dissertation, University of California Berkeley.
Shoenherr, Alan A. 1992. *A Natural History of California.* University of California Press: Berkeley.
Simberloff, D. S. 1983. When is an island community in equilibrium? *Science* 220: 1275-1277.
Skinner, Brian J. and Stephen C. Porter. 1987. *Physical Geology.* Wiley: New York.
Small, Eric E. And Robert S. Anderson. 1995. Geomorphically driven Late Cenozoic rock uplift in the Sierra Nevada, California. *Science* 270: 277-280.
Snyder, Gary. 1992. *The Practice of the Wild.* North Point: San Francisco.
Spira, Timothy P. And Oren D. Pollak. 1986. Comparative reproductive biology of alpine biennial and perennial gentians (Gentiana: Gentianaceae) in California. *American Journal of Botany* 73: 39-47.
Stanton, Kent. 1983. Gnomes of the wind: krummholz islands. *American Forests* 89: 42-43.
Stebbins, G. Ledyard and Jack Major. 1965. Endemism and speciation in the California flora. *Ecological Monographs* 1: 1-35.
Stevens, George C. and John F. Fox. 1991. The causes of treeline. *Annual Review of Ecology and Systematics* 22: 177-191.
Storer, Tracey I. And Robert L. Usinger. 1963. *Sierra Nevada Natural History.* University of California Press: Berkeley.
Swan, L. W. 1967. Alpine and aeolian regions of the world. Pp. 29-54. In H. E. Wright and W. H. Osburn (eds.). *Arctic and Alpine Environments.* Indiana University Press: Bloomington.
Tierney, Tim. 1997. *Geology of the Mono Basin.* Kutsavi: Lee Vining.
Troll, Carl. 1973. The upper timberline in different climatic zones. *Arctic and Alpine Research* 5: A3-A18.
Unruh, J. R. 1991. The uplift of the Sierra Nevada and implications for Late Cenozoic epeirogeny in the Western Cordillera. *Geological Society of America Bulletin* 103: 1395-1404.
Van Ooy, Daphne J. and John J. Carrol. 1994. The spatial variation of ozone climatology on the west slope of the Sierra Nevada. *Atmospheric Environment* 29: 1319-1330.
Verbeek, Nicolaas A. M. 1967. Breeding biology and ecology of the horned lark in alpine tundra. *Wilson Bulletin* 79: 208-218.
----------. 1970. Breeding ecology of the water pipit. *Auk* 87: 425-451.
Ward, J. V. 1994. Ecology of alpine streams. *Freshwater Biology* 32: 277-294.
Wardle, Peter. 1974. Alpine timberlines. Pp. 371-400. In Ives, J. D. and R. G. Barry (eds.) *Arctic and Alpine Environments.* Methuen, London.
Weeden, Norman. 1996. *A Sierra Nevada Flora.* Wilderness: Berkeley.
Went, F. W. 1948. Some parallels between desert and alpine flora in California. *Madrono* 9:241-249.
Whitney, Stephen 1979. *A Sierra Club Naturalist's Guide to the Sierra Nevada.* Sierra Club Books: San Francisco.
Worster, Donald. 1977. *Nature's Economy: A History of Ecological Ideas.* Cambridge University Press: Cambridge.
Zwinger, Ann, and Beatrice E. Willard. 1996. *Land Above the Trees: A Guide to American Alpine Tundra.* Johnson: Boulder.

Index

About the Author

Photo: Martha McCord

David Gilligan has made the natural history of the Alpine Sierra Nevada his life's study. A graduate of Prescott College in natural history and ecology, where he now lectures, David has worked with several organizations as teacher and naturalist, focusing on programs and curriculum in forest, stream and intertidal ecology, environmental awareness, nature philosophy, and natural history. He has traveled extensively through the Sierra Nevada backcountry on trips of a hundred days in length by foot, ski, and snowshoe. Integrating his skills as an observer with his education as a scientist, he has studied and practiced primitive and pioneer skills such as fire making, shelter building, edible and medicinal uses of wild plants and animals. When David is not teaching natural history, ecology, and landscape geography, he is in the field studying the alpine zone of the Sierra Nevada.

Other books from Spotted Dog Press you may enjoy reading:

Close Ups of the High Sierra
By Norman Clyde.
California's greatest mountaineer, Norman Clyde, made more first ascents in the Sierra Nevada than anyone. This new edition contains previously unpublished manuscripts and photographs.

Climbing Mt. Whitney
By Walt Wheelock & Wynne Benti.
More than 100,000 copies sold of this comprehensive guide to climbing the tallest peak in the contiguous U.S., by numerous routes, trail and technical. Includes a step-by-step description of the classic Mt. Whitney Trail.

Death Valley to Yosemite: Frontier Mining Camps & Ghost Towns
By L. Burr Belden & Mary DeDecker
Historic travel guide to ghost towns, mining camps, and graves; a detailed account of California's early mining history from the wild boomtowns of Death Valley to the high camps of the eastern Sierra Nevada.

Desert Summits: A Climbing & Hiking Guide
Describes hiking routes up more than 300 desert peaks in California and Nevada by Northern Arizona University graduate, and professional geologist Andy Zdon.